Information Technology and Organizations

Information Technology and Organizations

Strategies, Networks, and Integration

Edited by
BRIAN P. BLOOMFIELD, ROD COOMBS, DAVID KNIGHTS, AND
DALE LITTLER

OXFORD
UNIVERSITY PRESS

OXFORD
UNIVERSITY PRESS

Great Clarendon Street, Oxford OX2 6DP

Oxford University Press is a department of the University of Oxford.
It furthers the University's objective of excellence in research, scholarship,
and education by publishing worldwide in

Oxford New York

Athens Auckland Bangkok Bogotá Buenos Aires Calcutta
Cape Town Chennai Dar es Salaam Delhi Florence Hong Kong Istanbul
Karachi Kuala Lumpur Madrid Melbourne Mexico City Mumbai
Nairobi Paris São Paulo Singapore Taipei Tokyo Toronto Warsaw

and associated companies in Berlin Ibadan

Oxford is a registered trade mark of Oxford University Press
in the UK and in certain other countries

Published in the United States
by Oxford University Press Inc., New York

© the various contributors 1997
First published 1997
First published in paperback 2000

British Library Cataloguing in Publication Data

Data available

Library of Congress Cataloging-in-Publication Data
Information technology and organizations : strategies, networks, and
integration / edited by Brian P. Bloomfield . . . [et al.].
Includes bibliographical references (p.   ).
1. Information technology.   I. Bloomfield, Brian P.
T58.5.I5375 1997 658.4′038′011—dc20 96–46458

ISBN 0–19–828939–1 (hbk.)
ISBN 0–19–829611–8 (pbk.)

1 3 5 7 9 10 8 6 4 2

Typeset by Graphicraft Ltd., Hong Kong
Printed in Great Britain by
Biddles Ltd., Guildford & King's Lynn

Contents

Contents

PART 3: NETWORKS

Preface

In the mid-1980s, the ESRC created a research programme designed to explore the role of information technology in the future development of the UK economic and social system. The programme was called PICT: Programme on Information and Communication Technology. By 1987, six university research centres had been given funds through the PICT programme, and set up as an interlocking network of researchers charged with studying all aspects of the role of IT—from changes in the geography of business, through the reorganization of broadcasting, to the changing nature of work and leisure.[1]

In UMIST, at the Manchester School of Management, one of these centres was formed by a group of academic staff drawn from various disciplinary backgrounds, including organization theory, marketing, accounting, and innovation studies. During the period 1987 to 1995 this group, as part of the Centre for Research on Organizations, Management and Technical Change (CROMTEC), took responsibility for that part of the PICT programme which focused on the management issues surrounding the development and use of information technology within organizations. The group carried out a variety of specific projects during this time, ranging from large-scale survey work on the utilization of IT in specific business applications, through to detailed longitudinal case studies of system development in individual companies. More than twenty people were involved in the research over the eight years, and over 150 publications were produced. The team evolved both in membership and in its theoretical perspectives, and long-term relationships developed with many of the organizations whose information systems we studied.

Throughout the PICT programme's life the UMIST centre also benefited from interactions with the other five PICT centres at Sussex, Newcastle, Westminster, Edinburgh, and Brunel. Conferences, workshops, and joint research created a turbulent but stimulating environment of intellectual exchange. Sometimes this resulted in the production of more research questions than answers, but this can be regarded as a testament to the value of an ambitious programme such as PICT.

Our own work evolved in a direction which primarily reflected the spirit of critical social science which informed the PICT programme's origins, rather than the relatively practical orientation to information systems which characterizes

---

[1] Details of the six centres and their work can be found in a variety of documents produced by the PICT central office and by ESRC. In particular see *PICT: A Profile of Research and Publications* (1995) (Swindon: Economics and Social Research Council).

much writing on this topic coming from business and management schools. Our concerns were as much with the significance of IT for our understanding of organizations as with the effective use of IT. This emphasis is reflected in this volume, which is an inevitably selective account of some of the primary themes which have emerged from our work. It is presented here not as the last word on UMIST PICT's work, but as a sort of extended abstract of the topics covered in our larger body of work.

We would like to record our gratitude to the many academics and managers who contributed in so many ways to our work. They are too numerous to mention by name, but the PICT Committee chaired by David Stout, the three successive directors of the PICT programme, and the directors and members of the six centres all played a vital role in enabling our work. Our own advisory panel chaired by John Turnbull was unfailingly supportive. Finally, we are of course grateful to ESRC for funding the work, and for persevering with a Programme which often posed them new organizational challenges.

As editors of this volume we are very grateful to our colleagues who have struggled to distil their ideas. In addition to the contributors who are cited in the chapters, we would mention also Richard Hull, Fiona Leverick, Ardha Danieli, Andrea Haworth, Kieran Cullingan, David Rea, Stephen Parsons, David Cooper, Malcolm Cunningham, and Alison Smith. All of these colleagues played roles just as important as those whose names happen to appear as authors of the chapters in this volume, and we acknowledge their contributions.

Three of the authors associated with this book have now moved on to other positions. Fergus Murray lives in Cornwall where he is training as a psychotherapist with a special interest in organizational behaviour; Jenny Owen lectures in applied research and quality evaluation in the Department of Sociological Studies at the University of Sheffield; and Paul Taylor lectures in the sociology of technology at the University of Salford.

Brian Bloomfield
Rod Coombs
David Knights
Dale Littler

1

Introduction: The Problematic of Information Technology and Organization

BRIAN P. BLOOMFIELD, ROD COOMBS, DAVID KNIGHTS, AND DALE LITTLER

It is said that we are living through an era in which organizations within industrialized societies are experiencing a prolific growth in the development and deployment of information and communications technologies. Across all sectors of the economy, both public and private, within and between organizational boundaries, computer-based information systems appear to be pervasive. Concomitantly, many observers and commentators have proclaimed the dawning of a new age—known variously as the information society, the information economy, or post-industrial society, and so on—in which society itself is on the verge of transformation through the use of information technology (IT).[1] However the claims surrounding the IT revolution—ranging from visions of technological utopia to dystopia—are evaluated, it is clear that this area merits critical attention.[2] The aim of this short introduction is to set out the starting-point for our PICT research on IT and organizations, and thus provide some of the background to the lines of argument developed in the later chapters.

In contrast to the surfeit of prophesies in the area, comparatively little effort has been expended in trying to understand how the discourse on organizations and IT operates. Yet all the attempts at analysis and prediction deploy tacit models and concepts of 'technology' and 'organization'. Thus, an important assumption underpinning this book is that the critical study of the development and use of IT in organizations has to start with an examination of these background assumptions and theories which govern how the relationship between technology and organizations is construed. It has to consider, for example, how technology and organization are brought together theoretically while remaining distinct objects of analysis.

While we do indeed set out to study the role of IT in changes within complex organizations, we also try to understand the very terms within which debates about organizations and technology take place. Seeking a critical stance on management, organizations, and IT, and united by a broad emphasis on the constitutive role of social relations in the development of technology, we aim to explore the concepts and issues which underpin the projected benefits and problems associated with IT; to define the various overlapping problematics which govern the questions we pose about it. As with many scientific and technological advances, developments in the area of IT and organization serve to provide a focus for debate in which a familiar stock of issues tend to be rehearsed (Bloomfield and Vurdubakis 1995). Thus questions regarding the proper place of technology in relation to society and social relationships, social order, control versus freedom, responsibility, and autonomy, and so on, are to be found in programmatic statements for, as well as reactions to, IT. Moreover it is interesting to note that despite the opposing stances of technological optimists and pessimists, they both tend to reproduce a technologically determinist problematic in which a limited set of alternatives are on offer: empowerment or managerial control; liberation through technology (e.g. the personal computer, the Internet), or domination by technology; competitiveness secured through technology or economic oblivion brought about by the failure to exploit technology. Either way then, whether for good or ill, IT is seen to be powerful, to have a transformative capacity, changing organizations and their members, societies, and communities. As a complement to this, organizations (as social entities) bear the burden of plasticity. In other words, organizations must adjust to the imperatives of technology.

The existence of this common ground beneath otherwise divergent views of IT underscores the need to examine closely the specific discursive resources through which its role in relation to organization, or society more generally, is articulated. For instance, claims about IT tend to emphasize either discontinuity—it will revolutionize everything (Kranzberg 1989)—or continuity—things will continue as before (Winner 1989). Thus, in contrast to the putative transformative character of IT, it may be pointed out that from an information perspective, one could regard a simple card index file as a form of information system; indeed one could go back through history and stress the importance of the development of writing, lists, and other inscription devices,[3] and in particular their role in the exercise of power. Appeals to history—whether they stress continuity or discontinuity—reinforce particular representations and understandings of technology and its place in the world. They thereby constitute appropriate objects of enquiry: in the effort to understand how questions in the area are posed and answered (see Tribe 1981); and how, for instance, the claims within the discourse on IT and organization are indexed and sustained.

The glare associated with advanced computing and communications technologies lures us like moths to a light. The ubiquitous microchip and its ever-diminishing dimensions, coupled with increasing processing power and concomitant computational speeds, rapidly expanding storage devices, and all the other attendant gadgetry, are all too frequently the predominant foci of attention. Images of utopia or dystopia thereby loom large as we seek to make sense of this apparently awesome potential, and we lose sight of the crucial task of trying to ask the right research questions (Roszak 1988).

While much effort has been expended by geographers, policy analysts, economists, and others, in efforts to map and measure the emerging information economy, in our own research we have been interested in how it is that such approaches can be deemed as the way to study IT. Though useful for other purposes, mapping and measuring cannot assist us in a critical approach to information technology because in a sense they are simply further expressions of it. Indeed, mapping and measuring are not neutral or passive instruments which merely reflect the objects they are deployed to reveal: they are constitutive of them; they inscribe the world in a particular way. Thus it is at least as important to consider other aspects of IT, such as the question of what counts as information—and how this intersubjective agreement is achieved in practice in specific organizational settings—rather than just how much of *it* is in circulation.

Given the points raised above it is clear that the study of the development and role of information systems in organizations leads the researcher into encounters with some very difficult problems. Questions of epistemology, expertise, knowledge and power, of language and meaning, information and representation, objectivity/subjectivity and the philosophy of science and technology, the putative division between the technical and the social, to name but some, are deeply implicated in any serious study of how information systems are developed, marketed, and used in organizations. However this would not necessarily be apparent from a reading of the mainstream journals and texts which deal with the area of organizations and IT.[4] In part this may be explained by the fact that as an academic field of investigation, information systems is a comparatively new area of endeavour reflecting a variety of influences and ideas. Amongst these one finds systems theory and cybernetics which share common roots in the very onset of the computer era; ideas on organizational design which are much influenced by socio-technical and contingency approaches to organizations; theories of decision-making; the study of accounting systems for enforcing responsibility and managerial control; and the plethora of systems development methodologies.

Though there is valuable critical work in the area (e.g. Kling 1996), in the main critical ideas have not entered the foreground of debate and remain effectively relegated to the margins of the subject—there is, for instance, no first rank critical journal in the area (unlike, for example, *Accounting, Organizations and Society* in the discipline of accounting).[5] Often critical perspectives tend to be treated as sources of interesting ideas and insights but almost by definition are not seen as directly relevant to the practicalities of getting on with the building of *better* information systems in the here and now. In fact this state of affairs represents something of a paradox. The pragmatic approach to 'getting on with using IT' can be seen to be at odds with the revolutionary claims made on its behalf. For if the technology is really revolutionary then surely there is a need to step back from the fray a little and attempt to take a broader view of the field, to be more circumspect towards the question of how the technology should be developed and used. Indeed, this is not just an academic or philosophical point for there is ample evidence that frequently the development and implementation of information systems can be extremely costly, at times going disastrously wrong (Dutton *et al.* 1995).

While the existing literature or approaches to IT and organizations formed part of the starting-point for our analysis, we also regard them as an integral part of the *wider* problematic of understanding information systems in organizations. In addition we also take into consideration changes within organization theory and social theorising more generally. For example, debates about power (Knights and Willmott 1985), post-modernism (Cooper and Burrell 1988), representation (Cooper 1992), textuality and grammatocentrism (Hoskin and Macve 1986), the social construction of technology (Bijker, Hughes, and Pinch 1987), and the actor-network (Latour 1987) approach in particular, are deemed pertinent to the research questions we seek to formulate—even if their precise relevance is not always readily apparent. Indeed, those debates and the different ontological, epistemological, methodological, and political commitments they bring to the surface, not to mention the disciplinary divisions, were re-enacted on numerous occasions in our own research centre during the conduct of the work reported here, as we struggled to bring a coherence to our various research activities and outputs.

Our aim in this volume is to avoid reducing the analytical focus to that associated with studies of the *impact* of technology on organizations.[6] Technology for us is not a variable to be factored into the accounts of organizational change; rather the social content of any particular technological system has to be examined. Indeed, returning for a moment to the example of the print revolution it is useful to note the argument that the large-scale printing and dissemination of books not only presupposed a literate public but, more subtly, subjects who would read the texts in private (as opposed to out loud in public). This example in the history of technology is matched by developments currently under way in modern organizations—as we argue in later chapters of this volume, the provision of information systems presupposes users with information needs. Therefore the conceptual and social changes which construct users who have these information needs should be seen as a condition rather than a consequence of the use of IT. Expressed in the more conventional terms of technological innovation studies, the technological push of IT is matched by the demand pull arising from the momentum associated with the message of the IT revolution—whether this be to grasp a competitive advantage, seek to reduce uncertainty, or simply reproduce a desire to appear modern, up to date, or at the leading edge of technology. In this regard it is evident that the assorted gurus, consultants, and academic prophets of the IT revolution help to shape the substance, as well as the perception, of the changes they claim to report.

It is important to acknowledge the evolution which resulted in the perspectives identified above. At the outset, the PICT work within CROMTEC also embodied a particular interest in three interrelated concepts which have been much in vogue in management theory and practice during the 1980s and 1990s—namely, culture, control, and competition (Coombs *et al.* 1992). Each of these had a theoretical as well as an empirical dimension in our research. More specifically, while these concepts provided a basis for theorizing about the changing inter-and intra-organizational relationships that were enabled, mediated, and reinforced by IT, they also formed increasingly compelling reference points within the recipes for, and accounts of, change articulated by management gurus and, increasingly, practitioners within organizations. For example, our interest in culture was tied to the necessity of appreciating the role of meaning and interpretation within organizational change. At the same time it was evident that what counts as 'culture' was continually being redefined within management/consultancy discourse such that it had become a key *factor* in change and regarded as something that could be subjected to management control and manipulation (Willmott 1993). In some of the chapters here it is clear that this conception of culture is viewed with some scepticism. Similarly, with control and competition we were interested in how these concepts were being redefined through the development of IT in and between organizations, and how they figured in the exercise of power and the reproduction of managerial identity.

This book presents some of the major themes which have been developed during our PICT research on the National Health Service, financial services, intermediary practices in the field of IT development and implementation, and new product development in the area of IT and mobile communications. As the output of a research centre which includes a variety of interests and academic disciplines, it inevitably contains a range of perspectives—in some places overlapping or perhaps even in contention in others. It is therefore not intended as a work of theoretical synthesis, nor does it attempt to summarize or represent all of the work carried out in our research centre under the auspices of PICT. However, there is an important connecting thread running through the book. All the chapters can be read as different approaches or answers to one central question—namely, the nature of the relationship between technology and organization. That is, each chapter represents a perspective on how the statement 'technology and organization' operates or may be construed. In ensemble then, the chapters make up a polyphony of arguments covering a range of problematics which have tended to dominate debate in social science, management, and organization theory on the role of IT in and between organizations. The book is organized into three parts according to the following concepts or themes: strategy and markets (Chapters 2–4); integrating technology and organization (Chapters 5–6); and networks (Chapters 7–8).

1.1 STRATEGIES AND MARKETS

Chapter 2 by David Knights, Faith Noble, and Hugh Willmott, presents a review of the academic literature on IT strategy. Conventionally, questions of IT strategy centre on the issue of how the appropriate *fit* between organizations and IT can be achieved. In other words, it reflects a concern with the establishment of proper order between the two. This approach is critiqued in terms of its rationalist assumptions, and is contrasted with alternative political and critical approaches to the understanding of strategy which are then illustrated in the case of a financial services company. The chapter considers how as part of a discourse, the notion of an IT strategy can be understood as a resource which mediates the self-discipline of managers in their search for control and the security of identity.

Chapter 3 by David Knights and Fergus Murray also locates the organizational development of IT within a problematic of power and identity and the formulation of strategy. It explores the issue of expertise and the deployment of material and symbolic resources in the context of the managerial labour process in another financial services company. In this case however, the connection between technology and organization is examined in relation to the operation of the specific power/knowledge relationships constitutive of the associations between markets, organizational change, and technology, and which managers reproduce in the pursuit of their careers.

In Chapter 4, Dominic Wilson, Dale Littler, and Margaret Bruce consider the development of marketing strategies in areas of uncertain markets and rapid technological innovation. The thrust of their argument derives from the problems associated with the predominantly rationalist conception of strategy to be found in the marketing literature. In its place an alternative perspective is set out by drawing on the notions of organizational and sector paradigms. These represent social, cultural, and cognitive frameworks which both provide specific recipes for action but also constitute sources of inertia. The argument is developed through the presentation and interpretation of two case studies from the computer industry.

Together then, Chapters 2, 3, and 4 address the concept of strategy and the question of how to understand its operation within managerial practice. In addition, Chapters 3 and 4 consider the notion of markets and its specific relationship to strategy. Though informed by quite different theoretical perspectives both regard management's view of markets as being socially produced. Chapter 3 argues that markets are a rhetorical resource within managerial discourse— providing both a need for strategic thinking and a legitimation (or alternatively a critique) of existing strategic moves within an organization, while Chapter 4 sees managers' perspectives on markets as being shaped and filtered by prevailing organizational and sector paradigms.

1.2 INTEGRATING TECHNOLOGY AND ORGANIZATION

Chapter 5 by Brian Bloomfield and Theo Vurdubakis, explores what is represented by the word *and* when we speak of 'technology and organization' in the same breath. A specific focus is on the form of *intermediation* which constitutes the shape and substance of the relationship between the *two* object domains. To this end the chapter uses a case study of a proposal produced by a firm of management consultants—in both authorizing and inaugurating a project to implement an information system at an NHS hospital as part of the national Resource Management Initiative. The argument considers how the specific discursive work carried out by the text—the inscribing/ordering/integrating on paper of technology and organization—paves the way for a particular configuration of technology and organization to be brought about, including the constitution of doctors and managers as users of IT with information needs.

Chapter 6 by Brian Bloomfield, Rod Coombs, Jenny Owen, and Paul Taylor retains the focus on resource management in the NHS. However in this instance the argument concerns the fate of this initiative—both in terms of IT systems and the emerging role of doctors in management—as a consequence of the introduction of the internal market in health care. The chapter considers the Resource Management Initiative and the setting up of a new organizational structure—clinical directorates—as two initially separate but increasingly overlapping and integrated networks. Moreover, it explores how the purpose of the IT systems and the understanding/organization of clinical directorates has effectively become translated owing to the machinations which are constitutive of the operation of the internal market. A particular focus is placed on business managers and the development of their role as, in effect, obligatory passage points between information/IT systems and practice within directorates.

The arguments in both Chapters 5 and 6 relate to the concept of integration between technology and organization. In the former, this issue is tackled in relation to the discursive integration of IT and organizational practice within the 'paper world' constructed by a consultancy report. In the latter, integration can be seen as a rhetorical device by which various groups in the NHS have understood, and sought to achieve, a practical connection between management and medical activity. In each case it would seem that integration was envisaged as something that would find its material expression in an information system which would enable a more efficient management of resources.

1.3 NETWORKS

Chapters 7 and 8 each consider the conditions, political issues, and rhetoric associated with the notion of networking. However, the first examines a particular instance of networking while the second investigates the articulation of the concept within recent developments in organization theory.

Chapter 7 by David Knights, Fergus Murray, and Hugh Willmott, presents a case study of a project to inaugurate an EDI system in the financial services industry. Here the actor-network approach is deployed to analyse the formation of this electronic network between a number of financial services companies, but this is tempered by a concern to ensure that in tackling the relationship between organization and technology the issue of power/knowledge remains firmly under the spotlight.

Finally, in Chapter 8, Fergus Murray and Hugh Willmott evaluate the role allocated to technology within current ideas on the development of new organizational forms—and in particular the notion of networked organizations. Critical of the hyperbole which has surrounded the notion of networking, and related initiatives such as business process re-engineering, the authors emphasize the importance of trust in the negotiation of working practices. They also stress that the problem of realizing the vision of networking is ultimately a political one, challenging the status quo which inheres in many present-day organizations.

NOTES

1. Rather than use the less common term ICT to refer to information and communication technology we will, in the main, use the prevalent term IT which is inclusive of communications technology.
2. For a useful overview of the range of perspectives from a now voluminous literature see, for example: Forester (1989). More detailed reviews of the literature are contained in the following chapters.
3. Of course though historical parallels can be informing they can also be misleading: the meaning of information now in the 1990s cannot necessarily be equated with the meaning of the things in the past which *we* might gather under the same heading.
4. Given our concern about what is included (and excluded) in mainstream accounts of IT and organization, it is appropriate to acknowledge some of the blind spots in our own work. For instance, the potential for IT to effect a compression of space and time as regards organizational operations, to enable the emergence of 'virtual' organizations, or the uses of virtual reality, and so on, do not form major foci of the arguments developed in this volume. Yet they are undoubtedly important in terms of the wider understanding of IT and organization. Indeed, some of these have been critically examined at the other PICT centres.
5. The critical journal *Accounting, Management and Information Technology* straddles the areas of accounting and information systems.
6. This is not, however, to deny that much useful work has been conducted under this label.

REFERENCES

Bijker, W., Hughes, T., and Pinch, T. (1987) *The Social Construction of Technological Systems* (Cambridge, Mass.: MIT Press).
Bloomfield, B. P., and Vurdubakis, T. (1995) 'Disrupted Boundaries: New Reproductive Technologies and the Language of Anxiety and Expectation', *Social Studies of Science*, 25(3): 533–51.

Coombs, R., Knights, D., and Willmott, H. (1992) 'Culture, Control and Competition; Towards a Conceptual Framework for the Study of Information Technology in Organizations', *Organization Studies*, Vol. 13(1): 51–72.

Cooper, R. (1992) 'Formal Organization as Representation: Remote Control, Displacement and Abbreviation', in M. Reed and M. Hughes (eds.), *Rethinking Organization: New Directions in Organization Theory and Analysis* (London: Sage), 254–72.

—— and Burrell, G. (1988) 'Modernism, Postmodernism and Organizational Analyses: An Introduction', *Organizational Studies*, 9(1): 91–112.

Dutton, W. H., MacKenzie, D., Shapiro, S., and Peltu, M. (1995) *Computer Power and Human Limits: Learning from IT and Telecommunication Disasters*, PICT Policy Research Paper No. 33.

Forester, T. (ed.) (1989) *Computers in the Human Context* (Oxford: Basil Blackwell).

Hoskin, K., and Macve, R. (1986) 'Accounting and the Examination: A Genealogy of Disciplinary Power', *Accounting, Organizations and Society*, 11(2): 105–36.

Kling, R. (ed.) (1996) *Computerization and Controversy*, 2nd edn. (London: Academic Press Limited).

Knights, D., and Willmott, H. (1985) 'The Theory and Practice of Power', *Sociological Review*, 33: 22–46.

Kranzberg, M. (1989) 'The Information Age', in T. Forester (ed.) *Computers in the Human Context* (Oxford: Basil Blackwell), 19–32.

Latour, B. (1987) *Science in Action* (Milton Keynes: Open University Press).

Roszak, T. (1988) *The Cult of Information* (London: Paladin Books).

Tribe, K. (1981) 'Industrialisation as a Historical Category', in *Genealogies of Capitalism* (London: Macmillan).

Willmott, H. (1993) 'Strength is Ignorance; Slavery is Freedom: Managing Culture in Modern Organizations', *Journal of Management Studies*, 30(4), 515–52.

Winner, L. (1989) 'Mythinformation in the High-tech Era', in T. Forester (ed.), *Computers in the Human Context* (Oxford: Basil Blackwell), 82–96.

PART 1
Strategies and Markets

2

'We Should be Total Slaves to the Business': Aligning Information Technology and Strategy—Issues and Evidence

DAVID KNIGHTS, FAITH NOBLE, AND HUGH WILLMOTT

2.1 A REVIEW OF INFORMATION TECHNOLOGY AND STRATEGY

The integration of Information Systems/Information Technology (IS/IT) planning and strategy with corporate strategy and the strategic use of information systems have been of topical interest to management practitioners and IT theorists for some time.[1] For example, from 1988–91, the issue of most concern to data-processing (DP) managers in the UK was that of integrating IT with corporate strategy (Price Waterhouse Information Technology Review 1989/90, 1990/1, 1991/2, 1992/3). In part this reflects a long-standing preoccupation with the problem of making IT fit business 'needs'. But what is understood to comprise these business 'needs' in relation to IT has not remained historically static or uniform. The discursive focus has shifted from improving administrative and productivity performance in the 1960s and 1970s to contributing to the development and implementation of business strategy in the 1980s and 1990s.

The shift of emphasis can be linked to improvements in connectivity and cost-performance ratios in technology. It can also be related to consequent changes in potential applications: from data processing (administrative, mainframe computing) and management information systems (MIS), to individual and office support on PCs and office systems, and then to electronic data interchange (EDI) and inter-organizational systems, organizational 'platforms', and networks (Ward et al. 1990). The merging of computer and communications technologies, and the more widespread use of databases, networks, and integrated systems requiring long-term planning perspectives, also stimulated IS managers' interest in IT planning (Boynton and Zmud 1987). The 'progressive' hype and 'follow-my-leader' ideologies were sufficient to sustain the dramatic growth of IT expenditure in

We would like to acknowledge the substantial contribution of Fergus Murray to this chapter.

the early days. More recently, the sheer size of the resource demand and the increasing dependence of organizational activity on IT have focused managerial attention on cost-benefit calculations and a more rationally planned approach to the use of IT.

The development of an IT-strategy discourse has thus been partly the result of technology developments. It also reflects however a more widespread concern with strategic planning in organizations (Hoskin 1990; Knights and Morgan 1991; Mintzberg 1994). A further stimulus to change was the increasing aware-ness that the strategic use of information technology could transform the com-petitive position of a company in a rapidly changing market-place. Each of these trends has pushed IS towards the centre stage of strategic development and planning of late. A recent manifestation is Strategic Information Systems Plan-ning (SISP).[2]

The supposed benefits of IT strategy formulation and SISP are better align-ment of IS with business needs, gaining top management support and involve-ment, better priority setting, improved budgeting and resourcing, and competitive advantage applications (Earl 1990; Ward *et al.* 1990). Conventionally, SISP is seen as a process in which inputs (business plans, organizational mission, IS mission) are converted into outputs (strategies, information architecture, and so on) (Premkumar and King 1991). The process itself is analytical, using tools and techniques such as Critical Success Factors, the value chain, and the Strategic Option Generator, and methodologies such as Business Systems Planning, Stra-tegic Systems Planning, and Information Engineering (for a comparison see Lederer and Sethi (1988)). Further, consultancies as well as many organizations claim to have their own approaches to the articulation of business strategy and IT/IS strategy (Premkumar and King 1991).

Although these techniques vary in detail, it is significant that the first step is invariably identification of the firm's business objectives and corporate strategy (O'Connor 1993). The entire exercise of SISP in other words is dependent on the existence of an explicit and stable business strategy. For example, a basic principle of Information Engineering is 'if the business objectives do not change then the data the organization needs to use and the functions it needs to carry out will not change . . . therefore we can model the enterprise' (Goldsmith 1991). If no strategy is apparent, SIS planners are advised to create one (Remenyi 1991; Ward *et al.* 1990).

As this brief overview of the IS/IT strategy and planning literature indicates, much of it shares an unproblematic rational approach to management, organiza-tion, and change, involving a set of rather mechanistic assumptions about how organizations function and managerial and non-managerial labour behaves. Organizations are seen to be no more than the planned outcome of rational decisions made by senior management. Employees are presumed to behave in accordance with the detailed demands made of them by their seniors as if they were simply the pieces of a jigsaw that form a coherent picture designed by the strategic planners. In this paper we contrast the rationalism of these assumptions in the IT literature and management thinking with organizational practices as observed through an intensive case study of IT in a major financial services company. Our objective is to demonstrate the misfit between theory and practice in this field which can be remedied, we suggest, by IT researchers broadening their theoretical horizons to encompass some of the more sophisticated developments on strategic management within organization studies.

In doing so, we note and explore how 'strategy' is a 'buzz-word' for purposes of projecting onto IT activities the laudatory associations of strategic thinking. This reflects the great prestige of 'strategic' management thinking generally, due to its associations with higher levels of thought and the most senior executive management. The concept of 'strategy' is often used not so much to reflect planning for competitive advantage as merely to attract the legitimacy of what is being done (Alvesson and Willmott 1995). The chapter is organized as follows. The first section provides a detailed yet critical review of the dominant, rationalist approach to IT and strategy. In the second section we present our case-study material to show how strategies tend to emerge as particular conditions and contexts stimulate managerial interventions to render existing practices more strategic. While contradicting the rational model, these developments can be readily interpreted as validating a conception of strategy as emergent and contingent (Mintzberg and Waters 1985; Mintzberg and McHugh 1985; Pettigrew 1988). Drawing upon this perspective, we offer some additional theoretical and empirical insights in the final concluding section that potentially take the study of IT and corporate strategy to a new level of analysis. This involves extending the analysis to incorporate a conception of power and identity that helps to understand how and why business and IT strategy are emergent and contingent.

2.1.1 *Strategic Approaches to Information Technology*

While there is considerable dispute in the literature as to the history or genealogy of strategic thinking and planning (Ansoff 1965; Hoskin 1990; Knights and Morgan 1991; 1995; Steiner 1963), its impact on IT has been relatively recent. The value of information as a resource and its intimate connection with strategy and structure were recognized in the 1970s (Mason 1984). At that time, however, few of the business strategy planning approaches took any account of IT, while traditional IS/IT planning was an exercise in resource allocation among the various 'shopping lists' generated from lower levels of the organization. That is to say, it was incremental and bottom up, and in no way linked to business strategy (Ward *et al.* 1990; Remenyi 1991).

The IT-strategy discourse was not launched in earnest until the 1980s, following Porter's (1980, 1985) analyses of industry competition. He and others used the forces of industry competition, generic strategies (Parsons 1983; McFarlan 1984; Cash and Konsynski 1985), the value chain, and industry variations in information intensity (Porter and Millar 1985) in order to indicate the connections between IT and business strategy. Also very influential was McFarlan's strategic grid, in which the implications for investment, management control and structure, attitude to risk, and corporate strategy were shown to vary according to the role that IS played in organizations (Gerstein 1987; Synnott 1987; Atkins 1994).

By the late 1980s, numerous companies were attempting to use information systems strategically, and analytical and prescriptive frameworks proliferated. Conveniently, Ward et al. (1990) reduced 150 empirical examples of strategic applications to four generic types:

- linking the organization via technology-based systems to its customers/ consumers and/or suppliers;
- improved integration of internal value-adding processes;
- enabling the organization 'to develop, produce, market and deliver new or enhanced products or services based on information';
- top management support, especially external databases (pp. 22–4)

Earl (1987), by contrast, organized the mushrooming literature into frameworks according to their function in the planning process. Awareness frameworks help senior executives assess the potential impact of IT on their business, opportunity frameworks assist in the identification of strategic applications, and positioning frameworks indicate how the IS function should be managed.

The proliferation and popularity of these heuristic devices indicate how much build-up there was for advice and information on IT strategy amongst corporations in the 1980s. The problem which was identified was a lack of understanding and awareness of the potential of IT on the part of senior executives. The solution was rational analysis of the potential impact of IT on firms and their industries, the provision of analytical tools and techniques, and exemplars of the strategic use of information systems. In this regard, the approach was consistent with the discourse on corporate strategy from which much of the impetus for an IT-strategy discourse emanated. The assumptions underlying such discourse are that problems can be analysed and broken down into their component parts, whereupon rational solutions are devised and imposed upon the organization through top-down executive decisions and imperatives.

Some of the more optimistic leading assumptions about the ease with which strategic gains could be secured from IT were challenged before the decade's end. The idea that there could be any sustainable competitive advantage from IT was subjected to increasing scrutiny (Clemons 1986; Finlay 1991; Scott Morton 1991). Just as the idea of the 'information weapon' was being popularized, it became increasingly apparent that most 'strategic' applications of IT could be quickly copied and even improved on by competitors. The strategic advantages of the celebrated Sabre reservation system were played down by its director (Hopper 1990). In most cases, it transpired that strategic applications had been 'discovered' by users and had emerged from mundane transaction processing systems, rather than being the result of top-down analysis and planning (Andreu *et al.* 1991; Cavaye and Cragg 1993; Ciborra 1991). There was also more discussion of the 'productivity paradox'—in spite of major investment in IT (by then at least 50 per cent of all capital investment in the USA, according to Keen (1991)), US white-collar productivity had actually declined (Franke 1989; Scott Morton 1991).

One result of these criticisms was to move the discourse into a more organizationally aware or contingent phase, as implementation and organizational issues began to supplement the overwhelmingly rationalistic approach to the IT-strategy link (McFarlan 1992; Scott Morton 1991; Walton 1989). Attention was drawn to the need to make organizational and structural changes in order to realize productivity gains (Thurow 1992). This extended to the strategic use of IT to transform organizations (Malone 1985; Rockart and Short 1989). Although not an entirely original theme (see Beer 1974; Checkland and Scholes 1990; Galbraith 1973; Huber 1990), the MIT90s research programme (Massachusetts Institute of Technology, Management in the 1990s) helped to popularize the idea that IT could be used to deliver the kind of flatter, leaner, empowered customer-orientated 'new organization' which fickle markets and global competition seemed to demand.[3] The 'new' strategic use of IT is to transform the organization, of which the striking interest in business process re-engineering (BPR) has been the most recent expression.[4]

IT-strategy thus edged towards and onto the ground of organization theory, but in a very partial and incomplete way, as the example of BPR shows; leading formulations of BPR are extremely rationalistic, linear, and hierarchical in their assumptions about organizational change (Coombs and Hull 1995; Grint 1994; Jones 1994; Willmott 1994). The more humanistic legacy of socio-technical systems and of 'informating' work has been subsumed in a concept of 'empowerment' which just seems to mean making fewer people work harder.

2.1.2 Experience/Practice

The ideas of IT-strategy alignment and SISP are now backed up by a discourse of at least fifteen years' standing. The evidence on practice, both with regard to the use of formal planning methods and the outcome of their use, is rather contradictory but on the whole disappointing. In the 1987 study by King *et al.* (1988), more than half of the UK organizations sampled reported that they had no regular or formal process for identifying strategic uses of IT or information. 'Some of the most widely-publicised methods and strategic planning for IT were not used by many companies, and strategic uses of IT to deal with the market-place or other aspects of the environment were not being found as a result of the information technology strategy formulation process.' While 75 per cent of British companies in Galliers's study (1991) said they undertook SISP or had an IS strategy (and most were satisfied with it), most said that their SISPs were weakly linked with business plans, and business planners were rarely involved in the process—a highly dubious interpretation of 'strategic'. In Wilson's (1989) survey of *The Times* 500 plus financial services companies, while 75 per cent had an information systems strategy, for less than half was it a formalized, documented part of business strategy. In another 42 per cent of cases the IS strategy was seen as related to particular aims, especially improving product or service performance and reducing costs. Other research showed that only 33 per cent of UK companies had even an IT strategy (Kobler Unit Report, *Computer Weekly*, 11 Oct. 1990).

In Lederer and Sethi's survey (1992) of 251 members of the Strategic Data Planning Institute, 80 had completed an SISP study in their organizations, 83 had not, and the rest did not reply. Among the firms which had carried out SISP, few of the projects recommended by the plan had been initiated more than two years after the end of the study, while many others, not in the plan, had been. Thus 'much of what SISPs propose is not developed or implemented'. Half of the firms used rigorous methodologies; more than half of the respondents were fairly satisfied with the methodology they had used, but only a third with its execution (Lederer and Sethi 1988). Finnegan and Fahy's survey (1993) of 300 top companies in Ireland in 1991 showed that the vast majority had engaged in IS planning for less than ten years. The degree of linkage between IS and business plans was very weak, and strategic plans were considered far less important than operational and tactical plans.

2.2.3   A Critical Analysis of SISP Problems

Studies of the difficulties companies have experienced in trying to carry out IT-strategy alignment and SISP have identified the following problems:

obtaining management commitment and involvement;
inadequate current capabilities, in terms of available skills and so on;
difficulty in measuring, reviewing, and assessing the benefits of SISP;
linking SISP with business planning (Galliers 1991);
resource constraints;
implementation;
lack of top management acceptance;
length of time involved;
poor user-IS relationships (Earl 1990);
lack of sophistication in business planning;
exclusion of the IS department from the highest levels of management and from the business planning process (Lederer and Sethi 1988).

Many of these issues are related; lack of top management acceptance and involvement are likely to be associated with resource constraints and failure to implement much of the plan. Lederer and Sethi (1992) found that the problems associated with SISP in their sample could be grouped into five factors and that organizational problems were associated with implementation problems, via cost (takes too long, too much detail, too many meetings). Premkumar and King (1991) found that the 'inputs' had the greatest impact on the effectiveness of the planning process, the most important inputs being the information derived from business plans, top management, and user involvement.

Two broad areas of difficulty which underlie many of these problems are a continuing lack of understanding and appreciation of the importance of IT at higher levels of management, and the nature of corporate objectives and the strategic planning process (Lederer and Sethi 1988; Earl 1990; Galliers 1991). According to the IT Directors Survey 1990 (Computer Weekly, 18 Oct. 1990), the largest problem facing IT directors was the culture and communication gap between IT specialists and other management functions. As SISP studies are usually led by an IS professional, not by a senior manager, this could help explain why they do not get more support from the business side (Galliers 1991; Earl 1994). The second largest problem for IT directors in 1990 was imprecise corporate objectives. Earl (1994) notes that formal ISP methodologies are usually applied 'against the odds' because there are no business plans or they are too abstract. Galliers (1991) also warns that in many organizations the strategy process is 'more informal and creative', or there is no formal strategy. Politics and disputes over unresolved corporate issues are also recognized as obstacles to SISP (Earl 1990).

These difficulties indicate how detached the IT-strategy discourse has been from the real world of managers and organizations. It has reproduced most of the characteristics and weaknesses of orthodox strategic planning, including excessive rationalism, a linear and hierarchical approach, the separation of planning from doing, of strategy from tactics. It has assumed that IT can be related to strategy by analytical means alone. If organizations do not have an explicit strategy, one can be created for the purpose. IT/IS is assumed to be highly malleable, subject to managerial control and direction. Strategic applications are believed to be discovered by means of a planning mechanism. This approach ignores the large body of criticism and evidence against the rational perspective which has developed, both in the field of business strategy and that of IS development and implementation.

We now present some detailed case-study material which illustrates why the rational perspective on IT and business strategy provides an idealized and misleading representation of everyday practices within an organization.

2.2 THE CASE STUDY

2.2.1 The Evolution of Strategy in Salesco

Salesco was established in 1967 by a major UK bank in order to sell unit trusts to its customers, as a response to inflation which was reducing the value of customers' savings. Insurance was added to the articles of incorporation as an afterthought, but eventually life insurance became the more important part of the business. The sale of unit-linked policies was seen as a way that customers could invest in unit trusts on a regular basis, with the advantage of tax relief. Also, unit-linked insurance reduced the barriers to entry to the insurance market, because the customer bore the risk of changing economic conditions, and therefore the company did not need to have large reserves.

After its launch in 1968, the company was immediately successful, but thereafter until 1971 a depressed stock market and the oil crisis resulted in reduced sales. Salesco was reliant on bank staff to sell unit trusts and insurance policies to its customers; there was no compulsion on them to do so, and bank managers could earn commission from selling competitors' products. Unit trusts and life insurance are not 'demand' products like chequing and savings accounts, and have to be sold; therefore a trained and specialized sales staff would be an advantage.

In 1972 a small sales force was appointed, specifically in order to sell unit-linked life insurance within bank branches. This was extremely successful; the salesmen were able to use leads from bank clerks and the bank brand name to make sales far higher than the industry average. Gradually Salesco gained access to all of the bank branch network and by 1978 the commission paid to the banks reached £1.25 million. However, there was still considerable conflict between Salesco and the bank managers and staff, who did not think the products were good value for money, and resented the methods and high rewards of the sales staff.

The company was well positioned to benefit from the boom and grew rapidly between the mid-1970s and 1988. It built lavish new headquarters, launched new products, and branched into offshore investment and general insurance. In 1985 it was selected as one of the twelve most innovative financial service organizations worldwide. Funds under management exceeded £1 billion by 1986, £2 billion by 1988.

This was not achieved through formalized strategic planning but through an implicit and emergent strategy, which was to focus on selling a narrow range of simple financial products to the bank's large customer base and to respond quickly to external events as they occurred. The company was described by managers as 'sales-driven' and 'short-term, reactive'. Lack of direction or too much discipline was seen as a virtue, as it allowed the company to be entrepreneurial. Strategic planning would have been difficult in any case because the Group to which it belonged did not as yet engage in formal planning. The strategy centred on the 'vision' of the managing director (MD), who had led the company since its inception, and which was apparently shared by the senior management. In retrospect, the MD identified an underlying trajectory, which was progression towards becoming a full-range insurance company and a major player in the industry. The shift of emphasis from unit trusts to life insurance, the appointment of the sales force, taking over its own administration, and branching into general insurance were seen as steps towards this goal. Apart from some corporate functions, the company was organized around the main product lines, which were very independent and competed for resources. One of the main difficulties for both corporate strategy and for IT strategy was how to establish corporate priorities over and above the sum of the product line priorities. The decision-making process was one of consensus-building and compromise; there was no clear way of resolving remaining differences without going to the MD. However, the culture was described as 'gentlemanly'. The executive directors had 'grown up with the company' and had always been involved in its day-to-day running. Their tendency was to go for the 'quiet life'. Keeping the company's strategy implicit therefore enabled it to be adaptive to the internal political situation as well as to external events.

There was not a great deal of concern over controlling administrative costs. From the point of view of outsiders and newcomers, the company was lavishly equipped with new buildings and computer equipment, which were financed out of retained profits. This also had implications for IT planning, as there was little to force the company to focus its spending on the most critical areas.

Later strategic developments were more additions to the product range, a major reorganization which established the main product lines as profit centres each with its own MD, and the appointment of an external sales force. At the same time, however, the other arm of the strategy was to continue to exploit the immense advantages the company derived from its connection with the bank to sell to the very large 'warm' customer base—a full-fledged bancassurance model. Although tensions arising from conflicts between the sales culture of the insurance company and the more conservative culture of the bank were well recognized, the senior management apparently saw no contradiction between the company's aspirations to autonomy and industry leadership and its dependence for success on the continued cooperation of the bank.

2.2.2 Information Technology Strategy and Planning

Administration and data processing were at first contracted out, but in the late 1970s the company acquired a mainframe and attempted to develop a life administration system in-house with the aid of consultants. This was an expensive disaster; the project was ultimately stopped because of time and cost overruns and because it looked as though it would never work. At the same time Salesco was overwhelmed by a rising volume of business, and the sales force had to be frozen until the mess was sorted out. Administrative and systems failure thus interfered with the company's policy of growth. This experience was later described as 'a nightmare', 'traumatic'. A life administration package was eventually installed, which successfully dealt with the high volume processing of simple products, and other systems were later added to support functions and new products.

Senior management did not see IT as a competitive factor; its role was to support the volumes of the business. The 'real' or effective strategy for IT is exemplified in the comments of an executive director, who said that his goals for IT were responsiveness and efficiency: '. . . being quick on our feet, taking short cuts and risks and if something goes wrong patch it and come back next month'. He likened the company's systems to 'a big sausage machine . . . using technology to standardize products . . . maximize efficiencies of the direct sales force'. The efforts of IT staff to promote innovative and strategic uses of IT were greeted thus: 'IT people whenever they come up with things that will do the business good the business tends to say: let's get the basics right, we've got too much money to make out of that, then come back if you've got some other bright ideas'.

The dominance of the product lines was reflected in the organization of IT: there were separate IT Steering Committees and Business Systems Managers with their own staff for each of the product lines within the IT Division. The individual business systems were structured in different ways, as the objective had been 'to equip ourselves to grow in individual businesses'. The IT division as a whole lacked an identity; it had 'a lot of subcultures, identifying with particular systems . . . different styles of project management, different approaches to projects, different technological environments'. These centrifugal tendencies were exaggerated by the reorganization, in which IT and marketing were devolved to the product divisions.

Likewise, IT planning consisted of the annual resource allocation among the different business areas in a bottom-up process; the divisions identified their requirements, Business Systems Managers developed independently the strategies for their areas, these were put together, and as total demand always exceeded resources the executive directors

would take decisions after an hour of thrashing about and that was it till next year, very simplistic.

Each system area (was) given a budget each year—represents a compromise between supply and demand—it has nothing to do with corporate priorities, absolutely zilch.

As there was no corporate plan there were no explicit criteria for setting priorities; 'obviously a bunfight between directors on how best to spend the IT effort—apples and pears—at the end of the day you've got to make a value judgement'.

This approach was characterized by IT staff as 'haphazard, short-term reactive to meet immediate business needs and then you find later on things don't come together'.

Thus, in the first twenty years at Salesco, business strategy was implicit, evolutionary, and reactive. IT planning was bottom up, unguided by any sense of corporate priorities, and only loosely related to business strategy. However, the company had become highly dependent on product-based operational systems which had been developed in isolation on incompatible hardware and software.

2.2.3   The Initiation of Strategic Planning

In the mid-1980s, there were many pressures on Salesco to engage in formalized strategic planning. These arose from the organization's own success and growth, increased competition, the Financial Services Act and other legislation, and developments within the Group. The company responded with an increased marketing and customer orientation, and new marketing strategies, including new products, markets, and distribution channels. These in turn had major implications for IT systems development and kept in the foreground the question of integration between business strategy and IT planning.

The Group became more interested in the profits which could be derived from Salesco. As a result, there was a major corporate planning review in 1986. Consultants were brought in to investigate opportunities for growth in the next ten years. The strategy they produced emphasized cross-selling to Group customers and developing products to sell them throughout the customer life cycle, from setting up home to retirement services. Although there was resistance towards developing new products (which might not be very profitable) in order to retain customer loyalty throughout the whole life cycle, the strategy of promoting cross-selling within the Group was generally accepted. A major implication for systems was the need to create a customer database which would cross the separate product lines within the company, at that time impossible with existing technology.

In 1987 the Group set Salesco ambitious targets for growth in profits, which led to the company's first strategic plan in its twenty-year history. The plan was reviewed in early 1988 because of changes within the Group, especially its acquisition of other insurance-related businesses, as well as major external events like the stock market crash and the Financial Services Act (FSA) regulations. The 1988 Strategic Framework Review put forward a marketing strategy which included: increasing the size of the direct sales force; developing business within the Group companies and selectively outside; and a stronger customer orientation involving customer relationship marketing and more market segmentation.

Not least of the pressures for strategic business planning derived from the need to plan IT development more effectively. More integration was beginning to be sought between systems, and between IT and the business. A single mainframe supplier policy was established, for example, and when new developments were initiated an important criterion for software selection was compatibility with existing systems. Internal IT staff were asking for clear business objectives. As one said:

[we are] one of the few areas of the company that plans in detail six months in advance —we tend to be the ones asking the questions—we have to be as much ahead as possible —we could be constraining the company getting something out—we're very end-date driven.

According to another:

we are constantly, that is regularly for the last ten years, saying we cannot maximize the effectiveness of the IT trends without some clear corporate visions and strategies. We have repeatedly been in a company driven by expedient and reactiveness looking for a technology strategy . . . the plea for better business planning so that we can get better IT value is coming from systems, partly due to lead times and culture.

A planner argued:

we will be victims . . . unless we can produce a coherent strategy based on a vision of the future—vision is what is missing. The great danger of an IT vision is that people will see it as IT people trying to create a world for themselves. What we desperately need is a business vision we can latch onto . . . (with) technology rapidly expanding, we can see a tremendous choice, we need some focus.

A project manager said:

the business plan doesn't take account of systems—if we had integration we could supply IT at the rate it's demanded. I think we've taken too much control for what we do, which I think is wrong. I think *we should be total slaves to the business*, they tell us exactly what to do, they decide, we'll do exactly as they tell us . . . I don't know why they don't. It baffles me actually, why they don't just turn around and insist upon it.

Further impetus to business and IT planning came from outside, as in 1985 consultants were brought in to sort out the second major in-house systems development disaster the organization had experienced in ten years. The resulting Strategic Technology Review pointed out a number of serious weaknesses not only in technology strategy and systems development but in product development and strategic business planning in general. Consultants criticized what they saw as the inadequacies of the current bottom-up approach to technology planning and noted the lack of integration between technology strategy and business strategy, which they saw as partly owing to the absence of either clear guidance from the Group or a sufficiently detailed planning horizon much beyond a year within the company. The consultants argued that the company needed to take a more strategic view of technology as a competitive weapon. To this end, it should formulate a strategic technology plan and a 'strong top-down approach to developing technology strategy'. The corporate strategic planning process itself should be improved by making more detailed business plans, trying to find out what the Group's intentions were, or failing that, agreeing a set of working assumptions with the Group.

Thus the terms of the IT-strategy discourse were introduced into the company from outside, although some internal IT staff held similar views. As well as recommending improvements in the strategic business planning process, the consultants provided a model of strategic IT management, involving a clear IT planning framework and integration with business strategy. The report implied that the company could achieve these goals by listening to advice and establishing better planning processes. There was no evidence of any attempt to analyse the obstacles to strategic planning in the organization.

2.2.4 The Experience of Strategic Information Technology Planning

Following the recommendations of the consultants in the Strategic Technology Review, Salesco undertook specific steps to integrate IT planning with business planning. The major ones were the establishment of a high-level IT Committee to oversee all IT projects, review and approve tactical plans, and establish priorities, and setting up a Planning and Development section of the Technology Services Division, whose responsibilities included developing strategic technology plans, tactical plans, technology research and experimentation, and coordination with Group technology plans. They were supplemented by a small team of IT specialists. There were also two revisions of the annual IT planning/resource allocation process in an attempt to make it reflect corporate business needs, but it was still basically bottom up.

The IT strategy group met regularly and produced a series of IT planning documents within a short period of time, including two Technology Strategic Frameworks and an IT Strategy Mission Statement, as well as the annual Technology Plans. The first Technology Strategic Framework was essentially a mission statement; the second was intended to feed into an IT Strategy statement. There was thus a proliferation of documents, but an examination of their contents reveals that they were either very general and abstract (the frameworks and mission statements), or very short term (the annual plans). This reflects the difficulty the group had in integrating IT with business strategy-making. The second IT Strategic Framework, for example, was supposed to be based on the Business Strategic Framework (as well as the Group IT Strategy, which as yet did not exist). However, the only reflection of the business strategy in this document was the objective of cross-selling within the Group. How this was to be supported by technology was not discussed. The ostensible purpose of the document was to provide IT managers with a framework to guide all future IT acquisition, development, and support, but as it is mainly a disquisition on information architecture it is hard to see how they could have used it. As much attention is paid to explaining IT strategy in very mechanistic terms the main purpose seems to have been to demonstrate and justify IT strategic planning activity to IT managers.

The manager of IT services, who was in charge of the IT strategy group, observed that there had been competition within it for the role of IT strategist:

[it] hasn't worked too well. It proved not easy to effectively run, because we all like to have those areas close to ourselves. A has seen himself as responsible for systems strategy, B is rather strategically inclined, there's quite a bit of tension between the two halves of IT in terms of who's responsible for it. I've tried to do it on a democratic basis. A, B, C meet regularly, B carves out his own niche. The group had a good dynamic, but it broke down recently.

The team was ultimately broken up when the company reorganized. IT strategy became a specialist function at the corporate level, while decisions about system development were made in the product divisions. This disjunction was just as unsuccessful, as the strategies developed at the top could not be enforced on the product divisions.

The difficulty of relating company-wide IT planning to business strategy in the context of inter-group competition is also illustrated by the history of the IT Committee. Its purpose was to 'ensure priorities are being set and projects are being managed [and] . . . ensure a best fit with the overall corporate objectives'. Its principal functions were to review and approve annual technology plans and all major systems projects, establish priorities, review the status of current projects, and review, approve, and monitor the IS Division budget and expenditures. Its high-level membership consisted of the MD, the Executive Directors of Sales, Marketing, and Finance, the Divisional Manager of the IS Division, and a representative of Corporate Planning. It was chaired by the Director of Customer Services and Technology, the individual at the highest level with overall responsibility for IT, and met quarterly.

From its first meeting in August 1985, the ITC discussed, as envisaged, the annual systems development plans and progress in the light of them. It reviewed improvements to existing systems, the development of new products and new systems projects, the strengths and weaknesses of existing applications systems, computer centre capacity, conversion to a single mainframe supplier, new technologies such as networking of PCs and electronic data handling, system development productivity, systems staff turnover and shortages, senior management computing, and corporate data policy.

In the first year of its existence, the Committee was presented with a number of significant papers, and it was kept well briefed on the progress of a major systems development project. Gradually, the number of papers declined, and the minutes became more terse. In its final year (1988) it was poorly attended or its meetings were cancelled. In June, the Committee complained that it had been circumvented in one of its main functions, setting priorities for systems projects. Then it ceased meeting at all.

Although the Committee members were at a high enough level both to know the business strategy and to make decisions, the ITC could not fulfil its strategic function because it was unwilling or unable to deal with the political conflicts between the different groups which were referred to it soon after its inception. The Committee's view was that its function was to deal with strategic issues, not to resolve mere tactical issues and 'petty problems and conflicts'. It could not avoid these issues, however, as there was nowhere else they could be dealt with. Participants blamed the infrequency with which the ITC met, the low level of its members' technical knowledge, and poor leadership for its failure, but the members' lack of awareness of a relationship between everyday conflicts over IT resources and long-term strategy seems equally at fault.

2.2.5 Outcomes

Despite three years of strenuous efforts on the part of consultants, internal think tanks, IT planning documents, and committees, at the time of the interviews in 1988 and 1989 the connection between business and IT strategy had not been made and IT was quite widely seen as being out of control, as evidenced by interviews with organization members and the reports of successive waves of consultants. The ITC gained a poor reputation, and strategic IT decisions were finally left to political contest, and to decisions made by IT staff. The competition for IT resources and lack of clear priorities led to long delivery times, wasted resources, poor quality systems, and possibly foregone business opportunities.

Although business plans were becoming more formalized, the company's explicit strategic objectives proved too vague and diffuse to use as a basis for IT planning, and were in any case very dependent on developments at Group level. Furthermore, the implicit strategy took precedence. Regardless of written plans, senior management maintained their freedom to react to events as they occurred. The discrepancy between the explicit and implicit strategies only led to confusion for IT planners. Problems in both strategy formulation and IT planning reflected the political competition in the organization and the inability of anyone but the MD to settle important issues:

Fishing in that pond is very very difficult, where were the company's priorities. What you had were the product line priorities. Very difficult, apart from at the very top, for anyone to take a corporate view of the thing. (Senior executive)

2.3 DISCUSSION

Despite following the textbook recommendations of consultants, Salesco's efforts to improve IT planning and align it with corporate strategy over the period in question were unsuccessful. Some now widely recognized 'pitfalls' or difficulties of aligning IT strategy or SISP were evident, such as the organization's lack of experience in business planning, and senior managers' failure to understand or appreciate the significance of technology. However, we would argue that other, more fundamental reasons for failure in this case arose from organizational politics and the nature of strategy—considerations that have a relevance beyond our case study.

Salesco's emergent and implicit strategy focused on selling and reactiveness and served it well for decades. Despite the pressures for formalized strategic planning, executive managers continued to follow the implicit strategy. The impetus for formalization of strategic planning developed at precisely the time when the environment for insurance companies was becoming more dynamic because of changing legislation and increased competition. The resulting discrepancy between the explicit or written strategy and the implicit one which was actually followed was almost worse than no plan at all, from the perspective of IT planners.

Strategy formulation at Salesco was essentially a political process involving consensus-building. This resulted in written strategy statements having several objectives, some of them contradictory in their implications, and above all not giving expression to the opportunistic implicit strategy. Internal political competition between functional departments and product lines also made imposing a corporate view of IT planning difficult. These conflicts were reproduced in system development and the various committees, including the ITC, which were unable to deal with prioritization issues which, however important to rational IT planning, went to the heart of the political struggles in the organization. *De facto* IT 'strategy' thus emerged from conflicts at tactical level, *ad hoc* senior management decisions, and accidents, rather than from the rational planning process.

In illustrating major shortcomings of the rational perspective, evidence from the case study supports a processual perspective on IT—strategy alignment. The processual approach, which is well established within the strategic management literature (Mintzberg 1994; Pettigrew 1988; Quinn 1980; Whittington 1993), stresses the internal complexity of organizations and the cognitive limits on rational action. In this approach, strategy in many organizations is conceived to be implicit and emergent, not explicit and planned. It evolves incrementally over time as the result of a series of decisions and actions taken by a number of different individuals and groups. Decision-makers proceed cautiously, testing the waters, building on their competences, adapting to their interpretations of the environment, while maintaining internal cohesion so far as possible. It may indeed be possible to perceive a strategy only retrospectively, as an underlying pattern that, with hindsight, is understood to have evolved from a 'strategic intent'. Although dominant coalitions will probably be involved, strategy can emerge from anywhere in the organization. Organizational goals are not unitary, may be conflicting, and are frequently left unstated or unclear for political reasons. Tactics may add up to a strategy, which is more a collective than an individual product, and is highly political. At best, strategic planning gives managers a sense of security and confidence to act; at worst it can seriously impede strategic action.

In Salesco, the discourses of strategic planning and of IT-strategy alignment were introduced as a result of pressures emanating from the Group, the analyses and recommendations of external consultants, and internal staff. Demands from IT for a more coherent framework for technology planning contributed to the formalization of business planning. The result was a series of rather ritualistic exercises which did little to promote the actual integration of technology and strategy.

One of the effects of the IT-strategy discourse was to legitimate the position of IT in organizations at a time when it appeared to be under attack, due to more sophisticated and demanding users, and rising costs. In the case-study organization, IT staff expressed insecurity as to their position; they were not at all sure they were appreciated by senior management, that they were not viewed as obstructive or a necessary evil. They were fearful of appearing to usurp senior management's decision-making functions. The IT-strategy discourse legitimated the role of IT and defined it as subordinate to the business. It also endorsed the desires of some members of the IT Division for more rationalized IT and business planning. It was also used to promote individual careers, by creating the formal role of IT strategist or planner. The competition for this role shows that some prestige and power were thought to be attached to it. Thus the banner of IT-strategy was associated with individuals' needs to secure their own identities and position in the organization. Others were critical of this activity, and emphasized their role as providers of IT necessities, not 'frills'. Thus IT-strategy alignment, like the strategic management discourse, 'develops in discontinuous, contested and contingent ways' (Knights and Morgan 1995).

2.4 CONCLUSION

In this chapter, we have reviewed the established body of knowledge on IT-strategy alignment and raised difficulties with its over-rationalist and idealized formulation. We have argued that this literature takes inadequate account of the politics of organization and the process of organizing, and, as a consequence, it advances prescriptions and remedies for problems that are destined to fail. An appreciation of how and why such formulations and prescriptions fall short of expectations was developed through an in-depth study of Salesco.

In our case study, we argued that attempts to align IT with corporate strategy are more adequately formulated as a political process (Knights and Murray 1994), in which IT-strategy discourse is involved in the constitution of what is meaningful, becomes part of the internal self-discipline of subjects, provides a sense of security and confidence, and demonstrates managerial competence internally and externally. However, as we also showed, the progress of the IT-strategy discourse within an organization is far from inevitable, it encounters resistance from competing discourses and those individuals who are attached to them.

In short, 'the problems of SISP' can best be understood in relation to the organizational context, especially the strategy process and the political context. The processual literature on strategy, coupled with a growing concern about the difficulties experienced in attempting to implement SISP in organizations, has begun to foster some awareness of the limitations of the rational model of IT-strategy alignment. As early as 1986, Turner argued that it is difficult to relate IT to strategy because the corporate strategy process may be 'diffuse, covert and obscure' rather than 'orderly or visible'. More recently, Galliers (1991) has observed that 'many companies do not formulate strategy according to this rational/analytical model, nor do they adequately plan their information systems, let along incorporate competitive considerations into their planning efforts'.

Evolutionary and learning models of IS-strategy development explicitly based
on the processual corporate strategy literature are beginning to appear (Ciborra
1991; Earl 1990; Galliers 1993; Walsham 1993b). Yetton *et al.* (1994) give an
example of incremental strategy development in an architect's office, where
strategic vision grew out of incremental investment, integration, and experimentation with IT. In this case, they argue, strategic advantage was discovered
through a process of organizational learning which was technology-led. In the
prescriptive IT-strategy literature, there is more emphasis on the analysis of
politics and culture (Walsham 1993a and b), the use of soft systems methodology (Galliers 1993), stakeholder analysis (Ruohonen 1991), workshops and
multidisciplinary teams (Earl 1990, 1994; Kovacevic and Majluf 1993). Most of
the literature however is still predominantly rationalist.

2.4.1   *Analysis from a Social Perspective*

From a social perspective, strategy is conceived as a contested terrain of discourse rather than a description of a rational process or a prescription for rational action. It is a set of ideas and practices which condition ways of acting
upon particular phenomena, which has effects on power and subjectivity (Knights
and Morgan 1991). The concept of strategy itself should be viewed as problematic; the meaning of strategy is constructed for managers (Knights and Morgan
1990; 1991; 1992; Morgan and Sturdy forthcoming). While agreeing with many
of the criticisms of the rational model found in the processual approach, which
tend to focus on the internal political context, we would argue it is necessary
also to consider social and institutional aspects of the external context (Alvesson
and Willmott 1995).

NOTES

1. It is also a distinct academic field, with its own large and growing literature, scholarly
   journal (*Journal of Strategic Information Systems*) and international annual conference (SISnet).
2. Two conceptually different and rather contradictory aspects are both covered by strategic information systems planning (SISP): aligning IT/IS planning with corporate
   strategy and planning, and the discovery and implementation of strategic applications
   (Lederer and Sethi 1988). A 'strategic information system' may be either an IT
   application which provides (or is designed to provide) sustainable comparative advantage (King *et al.* 1988; Reponen 1993), or more loosely any IS which supports an
   organization's competitive strategy (Cavaye and Cragg 1993). (A third strategic use
   of IT is to support strategic decision-making, but this tends to be subsumed under
   Decision Support or Executive Support and will not be discussed here.) Similarly, SISP
   may be 'intentional action to create a competitive edge and business transformation

through information systems' (Reponen 1993), or 'the process of deciding the objectives for organizational computing and identifying potential computer applications which the organization should implement' (Lederer and Sethi 1988), which is equivalent to IS planning with, at most, a notional link to business strategy (Earl 1990; Galliers 1991). Further, 'IS strategy' (which concerns the applications portfolio) and 'IT strategy' (which includes technology policies such as architecture and standards) may be in no way strategic in themselves, nor do they necessarily have any relationship to business strategy.

3. And it has been indeed in the first half of the 1990s that we have seen some of the long-standing predictions about the 'impact' of IT on organizations coming to be realized, with the redundancy of thousands of workers at a time, including whole layers of middle management, in industries such as computing and financial services which have had long experience with IT and built up a large investment in infrastructure, and which have found themselves exposed to much more difficult market conditions.

4. BPR through IT is now the biggest challenge facing IS managers, according to a survey conducted by Computer Sciences Corporation in 500 corporations (Computing Canada, 30 March 1994).

REFERENCES

Allen, T. J., and Scott Morton, M. (eds.) (1994) *Information Technology and the Corporation of the 1990s: Research Studies* (Oxford: Oxford University Press).

Alvesson, M., and Willmott, H. (1995) 'Strategic Management as Domination and Emancipation: From Planning and Process to Communication and Praxis', in *Advances in Strategic Management*, 11A: 85–112.

Andreu, R., Ricart, J. E., and Valor, J. (1991) 'The Strategic Dimension of Transactional Information Systems: Some Organizational Implications', *Journal of Information Systems*, 1: 223–32.

Ansoff, H. I. (1965) *Corporate Strategy* (New York: McGraw-Hill).

Atkins, M. H. (1994) 'Information Technology and Information Systems Perspectives on Business Strategies', *Journal of Strategic Information Systems*, 3(2): 123–35.

Beer, S. (1974) *Designing Freedom* (London: Wiley).

Boynton, A. C., and Zmud, R. W. (1987) 'Information Technology Planning in the 1990's: Directions for Practice and Research', *MIS Quarterly* 11(1): 58–71.

Broadbent, M., and Weill, P. (1993) 'Improving Business and Information Strategy Alignment: Learning from the Banking Industry', *IBM Systems Journal*, 2(1): 162–79.

Brynjolfsson, E., and Hitt, L. (1993) 'Is Information Systems Spending Productive? New Evidence and New Results', Proceedings of the 14th International Conference on Information Systems, Orlando, Fla., 47–64.

Cash, J. J., and Konsynski, B. R. (1985) 'IS Redraws Competitive Boundaries', *Harvard Business Review*, 85: 134–42.

Cavaye, A. L., and Cragg, P. B. (1993) 'Strategic Information Systems Research: A Review and Research Framework', *Journal of Strategic Information Systems*, 2(2): 125–37.

Chan, Y. E., and Huff, S. L. (1993) 'Investigating Information Systems Strategic Alignment', Proceedings of the 14th International Conference on Information Systems,
Orlando, Fla., 345–62.

Checkland, P., and Scholes, J. (1990) *Soft Systems Methodology in Action* (London:
Wiley).

Ciborra, C. (1991) 'From Thinking to Tinkering: The Grassroots of Strategic Information
Systems', Proceedings of the 12th ICIS, New York, 283–91.

—— and Jelassi, T. (eds.) (1994) *Strategic Information Systems: A European Perspective* (London: Wiley).

Clemons, E. K. (1986) 'Information Systems for Sustainable Competitive Advantage',
Information and Management, 11: 131–6.

Coombs, R., and Hull, R. (1995) 'BPR as "IT-enabled Organizational Change": An
Assessment', *New Technology, Work and Employment*, 10(2): 121–31.

Davenport, T., and Short, J. (1990) 'The New Industrial Engineering: Information Technology and Business Process Redesign', *Sloan Management Review*, 11: 11–27.

Earl, M. J. (1987) 'Information Systems Strategy Formulation', in R. J. Boland and
R. A. Hirschheim, (eds.), *Critical Issues in Information Systems Research* (London:
Wiley), 157–78.

—— (1988) *Information Management: The Strategic Dimension* (Oxford: Clarendon
Press).

—— (1989) *Management Strategies for Information Technology* (Hemel Hempstead:
Prentice Hall Business Information Technology Series).

—— (1990) 'Approaches to Strategic Information Systems Planning: Experience in
Twenty-one United Kingdom Companies', Proceedings of the 11th International Conference on Information Systems, Copenhagen, 271–7.

—— (1994) 'Putting Information Technology in Its Place: A Polemic for the Nine-
ties', in R. D. Galliers and B. S. H. Baker (eds.), *Strategic Information Management*
(Oxford: Butterworth–Heinemann), 76–90.

Finlay, P. (1991) 'Information Technology and Sustainable Advantage within the Competitive Arena', paper presented to British Academy of Management Conference, 22–4
Sept.

Finnegan, P., and Fahy, M. (1993) 'Planning for Information Systems Resources?' *Journal of Information Technology*, 8: 127–38.

Franke, R. (1989) 'Technological Revolution and Productivity Decline: The Case of U.S.
Banks', in T. Forester (ed.) *Computers in the Human Context* (Oxford: Blackwell),
281–90.

Galbraith, J. (1973) *Designing Complex Organizations* (Reading, Mass.: Addison-Wesley).

Galliers, R. D. (1987a) 'Information Systems Planning in the United Kingdom and
Australia—A Comparison of Current Practice', in *Oxford Surveys in Information Technology*, 4: 223–5.

—— (1987b) 'Information Technology for Comparative Advantage: Serendipity or Strategic Vision?' Keynote Address of the AUSCAM National Conference, Perth, Western
Australia, 23 Oct.

—— (1991) 'Strategic Information Systems Planning: Myths, Reality and Guidelines for
Successful Implementation', *European Journal of Information Systems*, 1(1): 55–64.

—— (1993) 'Towards a Flexible Information Architecture: Integrating Business Strategies, Information Systems Strategies and Business Process Redesign', *Journal of
Information Systems*, 3(3): 199–213.

Gerstein, M. (1987) *The Technology Connection: Strategy and Change in the Information Age* (Reading, Mass.: Addison-Wesley).

Goldsmith, N. (1991) 'Linking IT Planning to Business Strategy', *Long Range Planning*, 24(6): 67–77.

Grint, K. (1994) 'Re-engineering Utopia', paper presented to Management Challenges in Information Systems Conference, Cranfield, 12–13 July.

Gunton, T. (1989) *Infrastructure: Building a Framework for Corporate Information Handling* (Hemel Hempstead: Prentice Hall).

Hammer, M. (1990) 'Reengineering Work: Don't Automate, Obliterate', *Harvard Business Review*, 90 (July–Aug.): 104–12.

Henderson, J. C. and Venkatraman, N. (1989) *Strategic Alignment: A Process Model for Integrating Information Technology and Business Strategies*, MIT Sloan School of Management Center for Information Systems Research Working Paper No. 196.

Hopper, M. D. (1990) 'Rattling SABRE—New Ways to Compete on Information', Harvard Business Review, 90 (May–June): 118–25.

Hoskin, K. W. (1990) 'Using History to Understand Theory: A Reconsideration of the Historical Genesis of "Strategy"', paper delivered at the EIASM Workshop on Strategy, Accounting and Control, Venice, Oct.

Huber, G. P. (1990) 'A Theory of the Effects of Advanced Information Technologies on Organizational Design, Intelligence, and Decision making', *Academy of Management Review*, 15(1): 47–71.

Huysman, M., Fischer, S., and Heng, M. (1994) 'An Organizational Learning Perspective on Information Systems Planning', *Journal of Information Systems*, 3(3): 165–77.

IT Directors Survey 1990, *Computer Weekly*, 18 Oct. 1990.

Jones, M. (1994) 'The Contradictions of Business Re-engineering', paper presented to Management Challenges in Information Systems Conference, Cranfield, 12–13 July.

Keen, P. G. W. (1986) *Competing in Time: Using Telecommunications for Competitive Advantage* (Cambridge Mass.: Ballinger).

—— (1991) *Shaping the Future: Business Design through Information Technology* (Boston: Harvard Business School Press).

King, W., Hufnagel, E., and Grover, V. (1988) 'Using Information Technology for Competitive Advantage', in M. J. Earl (ed.) *Information Management: The Strategic Dimension* (Oxford: Clarendon Press).

Knights, D., and Morgan, G. (1990) 'The Concept of Strategy in Sociology', Sociology, 24(3): 475–83.

—— —— (1991) 'Corporate Strategy, Organizations and Subjectivity: A Critique', *Organization Studies*, 13(2): 211–28.

—— —— (1992) 'Leadership as Corporate Strategy: Towards a Critical Analysis', *Leadership Quarterly*, 3(2) (Summer).

—— —— (1995) 'Strategic Management, Financial Services and Information Technology', *Journal of Management Studies*.

—— and Murray, F. (1994) *Managers Divided: Organizational Politics and IT Management* (London: Wiley).

Kobler Unit Report (1990) *Computer Weekly*, 11 Oct.

Kovacevic, A., and Majluf, N. (1993) 'Six States of IT Strategic Management', *Sloan Management Review*, 77–87.

Lederer, A. L., and Sethi, V. (1988) 'The Implementation of Strategic Information Systems Planning Methodologies', *MIS Quarterly* 12(3): 444–61.

—— —— (1992) 'Root Causes of Strategic Information Systems Planning Implementation Problems', *Journal of Management Information Systems* 9(1): 25–45.

McFarlan, F. W. (1984) 'Information Technology Changes the Way You Compete', *Harvard Business Review*, 84: 98–103.

—— (1992) 'IT and Organization Transformation in the '90s: The Implementation Challenge', Keynote Address, Thirteenth International Conference on Information Systems, Dallas.

—— McKenney, J. L., and Pyburn, P. (1983) 'The Information Archipelago—Plotting a Course', *Harvard Business Review,* 83: 145–56.

Malone, T. (1985) *Organizational Structure and Information Technology: Elements of a Formal Theory*, MIT Sloan School of Management Center for Information Systems Research Working Paper No. 130, Aug.

Mason, R. (1984) 'IS Technology and Corporate Strategy—Current Research Issues', in F. W. McFarlan (ed.), *The Information Systems Research Challenge* (Boston: Harvard Business School Press).

Mintzberg, H. (1994*a*) *The Rise and Fall of Strategic Planning* (New York, London: Prentice Hall).

—— (1994*b*) 'Rethinking Strategic Planning Part I: Pitfalls and Fallacies', *Long Range Planning*, 27(3): 12–21.

—— and McHugh, A. (1985) 'Strategy Formation in an Adhocracy', *Administrative Science Quarterly*, 30: 160–97.

—— and Quinn, J. B. (1991) *The Strategy Process: Concepts, Contexts, Cases*, 2nd edn. (Englewood Cliffs, NJ: Prentice Hall).

—— and Waters, J. (1985) 'Of Strategies, Deliberate and Emergent', *Strategic Management Journal*, 26: 257–72.

Morgan, G., and Sturdy, A. (forthcoming) *The Dynamics of Organizational Change: Critical Studies in the Financial Services Industry* (London: Macmillan).

O'Connor, A. D. (1993) 'Successful Strategic Information Systems Planning', *Journal of Information Systems*, 3: 71–83.

Parsons, G. L. (1983) 'Information Technology: A New Competitive Weapon', *Sloan Management Review*, 3–14.

Peattie, K. (1993) 'Strategic Planning: Its Role in Organizational Politics', *Long Range Planning*, 26(3): 10–17.

Pettigrew, A. (ed.) (1988) *The Management of Strategic Change* (Oxford: Blackwell).

Porter, M. E. (1980) *Competitive Strategy: Techniques for Analyzing Industries and Competitors* (New York: The Free Press).

—— (1985) *Competitive Advantage* (New York: Free Press).

—— and Millar, V. E. (1985) 'How Information Gives You Competitive Advantage', *Harvard Business Review*, 85: 149–60.

Premkumar, G., and King, W. R. (1991) 'Assessing Strategic Information Systems Planning', *Long Range Planning*, 24(5): 41–58.

Price Waterhouse Information Technology Review (1989/90, 1990/1, 1991/2, 1992/3).

Quinn, J. B. (1980) *Strategies for Change: Logical Incrementalism* (Homewood, Ill.: Richard Irwin).

Remenyi, D. (1990) *Strategic Information Systems: Development, Implementation, Case Studies* (Manchester and Oxford: National Computing Centre/Blackwell).

—— (1991) *Introducing Strategic Information Systems Planning* (Manchester and Oxford: National Computing Centre/Blackwell).

Reponen, T. (1993) 'Strategic Information Systems: A Conceptual Analysis', *Journal of Strategic Information Systems*, 2(2): 100–4.

Rockart, J., and Short, J. (1989) 'IT and the Networked Organization: Towards More Effective Management of Interdependence', MIT Sloan School of Management Center for Information Systems Research Working Paper No. 200, Dec.

Ruohonen, M. (1991) 'Stakeholders of Strategic Information Systems Planning: Theoretical Concepts and Empirical Examples', *Journal of Strategic Information Systems*, 1(1): 15–28.

Scott Morton, M. S. (ed.) (1991) *The Corporation of the 1990s* (Oxford: Oxford University Press).

Senn, J. A. (1992) 'The Myths of Strategic Systems', *Information Systems Management* (Summer): 7–12.

Steiner, G. (1963) *Managerial Long-Range Planning* (New York: McGraw-Hill).

Synnott, W. R. (1987) *The Information Weapon: Winning Customers and Markets with Technology* (New York: Wiley).

Thurow, L. (1992) *Head to Head: The Coming Economic Battle Among Japan, Europe, and America* (New York: Warner Books).

Turner, J. (1986) 'End-User Computing: Impact on Education and Organizational Development', in M. Jarke (ed.) *Managers, Micros and Mainframes: Integrating Systems for End-Users* (Chichester: Wiley), 269–83.

Waema, T., and Walsham, G. (1990) 'Information Systems Strategy Formulation', Information and Management, 18(1): 29–39.

Walsham, G. (1993*a*) 'Reading the Organization: Metaphors and Information Management' *Journal of Information Systems*, 3(1): 33–46.

—— (1993*b*) *Interpreting Information Systems in Organizations* (Chichester: Wiley).

Walton, R. E. (1989) *Up and Running: Integrating IT and the Organization* (Boston: Harvard Business School Press).

Ward, J., Griffiths, P., and Whitmore, P. (1990) *Strategic Planning for Information Systems* (Chichester: Wiley).

Whittington, R. (1993) *What Is Strategy—And Does It Matter?* (London: Routledge).

Willmott, H. (1994) 'Will the Turkeys Vote for Christmas? The Reengineering of Human Resources', paper presented to 2nd European Academic Conference on BPR, Cranfield, 2–3 June.

Wilson, T. D. (1989) 'The Implementation of Information Systems Strategies in UK Companies: Aims and Barriers to Success', *International Journal of Information Management*, 9(4): 245–58.

Yetton, P., Johnston, K., and Craig, J. (1993) 'The Pencil-less Architect's Office: A "Deviant" Case Study of the Dynamics of Strategic Change and Information Technology', Proceedings of the 14th International Conference on Information Systems, 5–8 Dec., Orlando, Fla., 145–55.

3

Markets, Managers, and Messages: Managing Information Systems in Financial Services

DAVID KNIGHTS AND FERGUS MURRAY

The analytical focus of this chapter is upon relationships between markets, technology, organizational change, and their mediation by the exercise of managerial power and the production of specific 'expert' knowledge. Studies of technology[1] have a long tradition in industrial/organizational psychology and sociology (e.g. Woodward 1958; 1965; Sayles 1964; Trist *et al.* 1963; Blauner 1964; Miller and Rice 1967; Zuboff 1988; Child and Loveridge 1990; Scarborough and Corbett 1992), science policy and innovation research (e.g. Freeman 1982; 1987; Perez 1983; Teece 1986; Coombs *et al.* 1987), industrial relations/labour process analysis (e.g. Braverman 1974; Zimbalist 1979; Wood 1982; Wilkinson 1983; Noble 1984; Bouitelaar 1988; Knights and Willmott 1988), and in the sociology of science (Bjiker *et al.* 1987; Callon 1986; Callon *et al.* 1986).

By contrast, the literature on information technology (IT) suffers from a dearth of theoretical reflection especially with respect to its failure to concentrate specifically on information (MacDonald 1983; Coombs *et al.* 1991) as opposed to the technology that is seen to deliver such information to the user. Our concern is to examine the political character of IT systems development through the presentation of an empirical case study of a life insurance company conducted within the context of a sectoral analysis of the industry in which it is located. Because our principal focus is the social and political process through which markets, information technology, and other organizational phenomena are constituted and constructed, we have to draw upon studies from fields (e.g. strategy and organizational politics and change) that are only peripherally concerned with the development and management of IT.

The chapter is organized into two main sections followed by a summary and conclusion. Section 3.1 is made up of three subsections all of which focus on different literatures of relevance to the management of information systems with financial services markets: first, a review of the information technology literature to find that it is limited in facilitating an analysis of the politics of IT management and development; secondly, an examination of financial services markets and labour processes as these constitute the two principal conceptual tools around which the empirical analysis of the management of IT, pursued in the second part of the chapter, is framed; thirdly, an examination of managers in the context of an analysis of power relations. Section 3.2 presents the empirical account of an IT systems application to product development in a life insurance company. Prime attention is given to the social contexts and complexities of information technology, market relations, and the strategic planning to which management subscribes. Finally, an extended summary and conclusion seeks to draw out the implications and significance of the case-study analysis for the debate on the management of IT examined in the first part of the chapter.

3.1 MANAGING MARKETS AND INFORMATION TECHNOLOGY

3.1.1   *Information Systems and Organizational Politics*

Despite theoretical limitations already noted, a literature has proliferated in response to the development of microelectronic technology and its capacity to advance the production and use of information (e.g. Benjamin *et al.* 1990; Bessant *et al.* 1985; and Loveridge 1990). Mostly, this literature either subscribes to a prescriptive managerialism wherein it claims to offer advice on how to manage IT or it adopts a descriptive norm of simply recording the diverse range of systems and applications in organizations. Neither makes reference to, or seems aware of, the political character of particular IT developments and applications (cf. Mosco 1984; Finlay 1987; Bouitelaar 1988) and, therefore, their 'essential contestability' (Benton 1981).

By contrast, more critical labour process accounts tend to view IT as a control technology often investing management with an omniscience and infallibility (Braverman 1974; Zimbalist 1979) that is simply not evident in the field. For when we begin to look more closely at the development or use of particular information systems we see problems and failures as much as success (Lucas 1975; 1984).

Research conducted on computer system developments in the financial services sector highlights how the management of IT in organizations is fraught with difficulties, tensions, and contradictions (Knights and Murray 1994). Drawing upon and developing that thesis, a central argument of this chapter is that the tensions surrounding IT management are systematically related to complex sets of power, managerial, and market relations. They cannot simply be reduced to their technical or administrative dimensions nor managed by purely technical or communication solutions, as much of the prescriptive literature suggests. It is not just a matter of awaiting the advance of technical knowledge or the improvement in communications whereupon systems problems will, at a stroke, disappear.

This tendency to reduce problems to a technical-administrative dimension is illustrated in the rise of an 'IT-strategy' discourse and the identification of a 'communication problem' in systems development. First, with respect to 'strategy', the potential of IT applications in a multiplicity of spheres has been viewed as a factor in gaining competitive advantage in rapidly changing markets (Knights and Murray 1990). In order to placate senior executive anxieties concerning the high costs of IT investment, consultants have increasingly been imposing a concept of 'IT strategy' on their clients in the belief that coherent and long-term planning of IT investments is the only way to secure adequate returns on such capital expenditure (Coopers and Lybrand 1988).

The rationale behind IT strategies is that they are designed to achieve an integration between corporate strategy and IT use such that the selection and development of IT applications is 'business-' or 'market-driven'. This is expected to maximize economies of scale and scope through the adoption of organizational IT standards while at the same time simplifying the prioritization of competing demands made on the organizational IT resource.[2]

In broad terms the preoccupation with IT strategy is an understandable reaction to the problems that have historically plagued business organizations which find huge capital investments in technology failing to live up to their promise. However, of itself IT strategy cannot resolve the various difficulties surrounding the application and development of IT to specific business uses.

Secondly, with regard to 'communications', among the consultants and practitioners whom we have interviewed, there is a tendency to identify many problems as revolving around the 'communication' gap between IT specialists and IT users. Although at one level quite plausible, the tendency to attribute organizational problems too readily to a failure to communicate is to 'cut off' analysis precisely at the point where it should begin. Typically, then, solutions are concentrated on removing the information 'gap' between IT specialists and users by improving communications without much attention to the conditions that give rise to the failure of communications in the first place. So, for example, a number of studies simply argue that communication problems can be overcome by appropriate organizational structural change and learning (Scarbrough and Lannon 1988), better interpersonal communication and appreciation of mutual problems (Mumford and Henshall 1979), and the cross-fertilization of business and IT skills (Friedman and Greenbaum 1984).

There is no doubt that a concentration on improving communications will have some impact on the interactive competence of an organization and this can always be interpreted as beneficial.[3] But what the communications literature neglects is the way in which organizations both reflect and reproduce the major social inequalities in society and hence the essentially contestable nature of organizational relations. A result of this neglect is the failure to examine the activities and practices of members of organizations in terms of their participation in the exercise of power in pursuit or defence of specific identities and competitive material or symbolic advantages.

When power relations are taken into account, it is clear that improvements in communications alone will not guarantee the resolution of problems in the use and development of IT. Indeed since skilled communicators are effective and shrewd political operators, the opposite may well be the case; that is, improvements in communications can result in an intensification of the conflict and competition of career politics. Although career interests are pursued openly rather than in the name of the organization's strategic goods, the deflection of energies and skills along political channels can be extremely damaging to the 'productive power' or effectiveness of an organization (Knights and Roberts 1982; 1983).

This is not to suggest that communication skills should be ignored in an analysis of IT and organizational change; merely, that they cannot be seen as a prescriptive panacea, as is often the case in the managerialist literature.

3.1.2   Financial Service Markets

Until comparatively recently financial service corporations were not subjected to the same competitive pressures as the rest of the UK economy. Even economic deregulation in the 1980s did not disrupt the sector to anything like the same extent as manufacturing, largely because the market for financial products continued to expand. Indeed, as many commentators have argued (e.g. Rajan 1987), it is precisely the growth of this and related service sectors that offset the worst effects of British de-industrialization.

Notwithstanding the Third World debt problem, the financial services sector in many respects maintained the outward appearance of a haven of economic order and stability in the 1970s and early 1980s. The relative stability and rapid growth of retail financial service markets is particularly striking. Until recently the comparative stability of these markets and the social and institutional relations underpinning them has been a condition and consequence of the predominance of continuity, rather than change in managerial and organizational practice within the financial services sector. This is perhaps nowhere more apparent than in the UK life insurance sector where our case study company is located. In terms of premiums of around £12m collected annually, the life insurance industry represents around 5 per cent of the UK gross national product (McRae and Cairncross 1985: 161–2).

However, the financial services sector either in Britain or elsewhere is not immune to tensions and contradictions arising from dynamic changes in domestic and international socio-economic relations. Indeed, the recent governmental concern that Britain have a place in the current globalization of financial markets largely stimulated the timing and the character of the City's 'Big Bang' and the subsequent Financial Services Act during the 1980s. In addition, the break-up of the postwar consensus centred on Keynesian welfarism prompted by the fiscal crisis of the state (O'Connor 1973), inflation, industrial decline, demographic change, and the rise of neo-liberalism (Offe 1984) has led to an increasing 'privatization' of welfare provision and a growing liberalization of retail and other financial services through economic deregulation (Knights 1996). The privatization of welfare is evidenced in the 1986 Social Security Act which encourages UK citizens to contract out of the State Earnings-Related Pensions Scheme (SERPS) and divert a proportion of national insurance contributions to a private pensions policy. According to the Social Security Minister, Peter Lilley (Radio 4 interview 29 Sept. 1995) more than 75 per cent of those entitled to contract out of the state scheme have done so and this, he argued, placed the UK at a considerable advantage over other countries in terms of future liabilities to the Social Security Budget. This has been particularly advantageous to Pensco, the case-study company examined later. Deregulation has occurred through the attack on restrictive practices in the Stock Exchange and the opening up of the City to international competition. Legislation has also enhanced the financial role of the building societies and created a blurring of many of the once clearly demarcated divisions between banks, building societies, and insurance companies. In effect, the financial services industry has witnessed a major and significant upheaval in the 1990s as competition has intensified at the same time as market growth has shown signs of slowing down and even shrinking. This has occurred in the mortgage market owing to falling house prices and consumer confidence, in insurance because of scandals and regulatory difficulties, and in banking more generally as a result of the building societies diversifying their activities so as to compete fully with the banks.

These regulatory acts are perhaps the most apparent sign of change in financial services markets. However, there have also been changes of an equally dramatic nature generated by organizational and technological innovations. 'Big Bang' itself was as much a technological and organizational revolution as a radical transformation of markets as the traditional circus ritual performed by jobbers on the stock exchange floor was displaced by TOPIC—an information technology system of price quotations and market information. Banking has witnessed a self-service revolution as a result of the introduction of Automatic Telling Machines (ATMs) and home computer banking. In the life insurance industry the development of investment products directly linked to share prices (unit-linking) and the emergence of companies employing aggressive marketing and sales techniques have had a major impact on the form and selling of life and pensions products. Furthermore, the rapid take-up of data processing, and latterly information technology, has created another source of dynamic change and uncertainty throughout financial services and, in particular, within the insurance industry which is the focus of the case study at the end of this chapter. All of this change has been taking place against a background of structural transformation in the industry as the larger players have sought to take over other companies as part of a strategy either of vertical integration (e.g. Lloyds–Abbey Life) or horizontal integration (e.g. Lloyds–Cheltenham & Gloucester; Halifax–Leeds) and as medium-sized players (e.g. Alliance & Leicester–Giro) have sought mergers in order to remain in the big league or smaller players (e.g. Northern Rock–Newcastle Building Society) to climb into it. It could be argued that the industry is currently experiencing a merger mania as not only domestic but also foreign predators seek new and speedy opportunities for growth in a comparatively de-regulated UK market.

These changes generated both from within and outside the life industry have been important factors in stimulating change in managerial and organizational practices. The increasing instability and unpredictability of markets and tech-nologies in the 1980s has caused growing uncertainty in the industry. This has tended to intensify managerial competition for scarce material and symbolic resources and well-being and this is addressed in the next section.

3.1.3   Managers and Power Relations

This third theme concerns the problematical nature of managerial and labour processes. As is clear from the above conceptualization of market relations, there is no simple and clear-cut means of establishing precisely what message the market conveys. Partly this is owing to the complexity of the aggregated out-comes of discrete players but, much more, it is because markets and information regarding the state of particular markets do not exist independently of the con-ceptualizations and interpretations that organizational actors have of them. In this sense, markets are not merely a force to which individuals or organizations have to respond; they are actually constituted by the interpretations and actions of those who participate in them. This is equally the case in the market for labour (i.e. managers and staff) as for products (i.e. goods and services).

To a considerable degree then, the activity generated by and reproduced through managers who represent 'knowledgeable agents' (Giddens 1984) is rooted in market relations. In contemporary Western markets, labour as a productive potential assumes the form of a commodity to be bought and sold. This com-modification and specialization of managerial (as well as non-managerial) labour informs the actions, and in part constitutes the identities, of the agents of produc-tion and distribution. It tends to transform individuals who might otherwise be communally creative into subjects who are individualistically instrumental with respect to their career and commitment to organizational activities.

It means that collective cooperation is constrained by an individualistic striv-ing for, and defence of, relatively scarce material and symbolic security and suc-cess. Particularly in the case-study company presented later, this tension between cooperation and competition is reflected in, and reinforced by, the growing technical division of labour into routine, specialist, and managerial functions which give differential access to organizational resources.

What is being argued here is that labour markets and the system of inequality in the broader society has the effect of constructing managers as subjects who secure their sense of themselves predominantly through the instrumental pursuit of career 'progress' and economic advantage. This subjectivity, in turn, is ex-pressed in the exercise of power by these managers, having not dissimilar effects on non-managerial employees. It may already be clear that the conception of power deployed in this analysis is distinct from that which perceives power as wholly negative and repressive (Lukes 1974) or as the source of ideology, to be eradicated if truth is to prevail (Marx 1971). This latter individual conception of power (Foucault 1980) generally views it as a property of individuals or institutions not predominantly of social relations.

This is not to argue that juridical conceptions of power are unsophisticated; quite the contrary. Take, for example, Lukes (1974) account of the three dimensions of power. The first involves power as decision-making where the existence of conflict makes the power visible in behavioural terms. The second points to power that is exercised in the absence of decision-making, where it is expressed as an ability to prevent certain issues from entering the public arena of debate. The third dimension of power refers to the whole institutional framework of life that defines individuals' interests in ways that are compatible with prevailing systems of power. While there are elements of all these three dimensions present in power relations, an analysis drawing upon Foucault (1980; 1982) departs from Lukes and similar perspectives in refusing to perceive power as wholly negative, repressive, and incompatible with the development of true knowledge. On the contrary, power is seen as positive as well as negative, productive as well as repressive, constitutive of rather than seen as a mere constraint upon subjectivity, and is in an intricate and inescapable relationship with knowledge. Power is synonymous with social relations (Foucault 1982), it cannot be seen as incompatible with, or a distortion of, knowledge. Rather, it is inextricably bound up with the production of knowledge such that wherever power is exercised one finds knowledge produced both directly and indirectly within, and as an outcome of, the exercise of power. And knowledge, in its turn, facilitates the exercise of power. While power often represses or constrains individuals, especially when exercised in the form of physical punishment, a major feature of modern economies of power is their targeting of subjects and populations so as to be productive of subjective well-being through strategies of educational and material wealth.

The tensions between individualistic orientations and collective action or class solidarity have been given some attention through studies of the privatized or affluent worker (Brittan 1977; Goldthorpe *et al.* 1969). Similarly sectional divisions and fragmentations within the working class based on craft, technical, or specific union membership have been widely studied within industrial relations (e.g. Armstrong *et al.* 1986; Hyman and Price 1983; Smith 1987). However, the tensions and divisions within management have received less attention (cf. Dalton 1959; Burns and Stalker 1961; Sayles 1964; Pettigrew 1973). Yet they have a crucial bearing on the constitution of managerial identity and the range of intentions that inform managerial action and the structure and performance of organizations.

Overall, then, the general intent of managerial action can be described as an individual and collective struggle characterized by cooperation, competition, and conflict to secure and solidify a given identity[4] through the control of material and symbolic resources. In general, people's identities are precarious because they are dependent on the judgements and evaluations of others which are by definition unpredictable and beyond any individual's control. However, managerial identities are even more precarious since they are based upon ordering and controlling the activities and identities of a whole range of employees, the predictability of which is uncertain. The allocation of managerial positions through internal and external labour markets is largely predicated on changing definitions of 'competence' and mediated by perceptions of 'assessed stature' (Pettigrew 1973) in the organization and broader business community. Such competence is organically linked to the ability to generate 'success' which may have as much to do with the articulation of dominant managerial discourse and technique (Knights and Morgan 1991) as it does with 'bottom line results'.

Managers live out their lives and reproduce themselves while caught between overriding tensions. The identities of managers are contingent on their fulfilling hierarchical expectations regarding managerial competence through demonstrating the effectiveness of their practices as goal-oriented and quantifiable activities. Such activities are continuously subjected to real or threatened disruptions by market forces. As collectivities, managers are charged with the coordination of extremely complex operations that develop their own specialist and professional means of exercising power. The hierarchical organization of management and unequal access to resources is an attempt to resolve this dilemma by investing senior management with the authority to control and coordinate the centrifugal forces of competing specialist and career interests.

While promising to secure the achievement of a rational technical administration of the organization, however, the hierarchy of managerial control and power tends systematically to distort the 'open communication' that is the basis for rational and efficient administration. As managers exercise power through the mobilization of resources or access to knowledge of perceived internal or external realities such as 'strategy', 'markets', and 'technology', they frequently advance their own career position without necessarily contributing significantly to the productive potential of the organization as a whole.

Although sympathetic to Brissy (1990) in his critique of cybernetic rhetoric, we disagree with his view that the 'datocratic ideology permits the merging of administrative authority *and* professional authority . . . [thus] . . . yielding automatic legitimacy' (234–5) or a 'polity without politics' (Jamous and Gremion 1978, quoted in Brissy (1990)). Far from it being difficult to challenge the authority of the datocrats, it is clear that there is considerable conflict surrounding the use of IT and 'IT strategies' (Knights and Murray 1994). Furthermore, the resolution of such conflicts cannot be achieved through technocratic-administrative reasoning whereby solutions are simply 'read off' from the market, prevailing social relations, or technological developments. On the whole, conflict is conditioned by, and regulated through, the exercise of material and symbolic power. This power can be used to mobilize particular views of the market and technology in order to legitimate choices that may have more to do with specific individual and/or collective preoccupations and pursuits than corporate objectives.

The formulation and implementation of IT strategies is a social process in which the intensity of political activity is related to the types of choices being made (Hickson *et al.* 1986), existing structures of organizational control and coordination, and changes taking place within the organization's broader operating environment. And as our case study illustrates, the formulation of strategy based on distorted information is but a moment in a revolving cycle of decision-making and implementation, each stage of which necessarily generates unforeseen consequences and open-ended social interactions and developments.

3.2 UNCERTAINTY, INFORMATION TECHNOLOGY AND ORGANIZATIONAL POLITICS IN A LIFE INSURANCE COMPANY

The tendencies outlined so far are clearly illustrated in the following case study of a long-established and prosperous mutual life office—Pensco. Before moving directly on to the empirical research, it is important to indicate that both a sectoral analysis and a one-off case study using a qualitative but diverse set of methods including in-depth interviews, non-participant observation of several decision-making meetings, and documentary and newspaper research were deployed. Research in the company continued over a period of approximately three years and at no time were the researchers prevented from attending a meeting, committee, or interviewing a manager or member of staff. The research took the form of a longitudinal approach with some retrospective reconstruction of events. Fieldwork consisted of approximately 40 in-depth interviews with senior management throughout the company followed by attendance at 12 senior executive strategy and policy-making meetings (Knights and Willmott 1987a; 1987b). Within the IS Division, 15 members of the pensions systems project and its steering committee and another 14 senior and middle management who had involvement with some stage of the project were interviewed, as well as 5 managers and clerical supervisors within the administrative division which was ultimately responsible for operating the system. Attendance at various IS steering and project meetings provided an observational content to the research. All members of the staff were also subjected to a large-scale attitude questionnaire but such data is only loosely connected to the content of this chapter.

The sectoral and broader company analysis involved 17 visits to different insurance company IS divisions and considerable secondary research. Despite a heavy research involvement in the whole of the financial services sector throughout, the usual qualifications regarding single case studies clearly applies to this research. In support of the method, however, the concern is not to establish empirical facts to generalize to a wider population of organizations; rather it is to develop theoretical insights that may be applied in varying contexts. No doubt in such applications, results will differ but it may be anticipated that certain aspects remain pertinent regardless of circumstance. This is because power and identity relations prevail in almost all humanly organized endeavours.

Having outlined and justified the particular methods of research, the chapter turns first to a brief examination of the historical development of IT use in the life insurance industry.

3.2.1 Information Technology Use in Life Insurance

In the early days of computing, related managerial decision-making largely concerned the question of whether or not to invest in this new technology. Once this decision had been made the application of computing to the business was restricted by the limited range of possibility of early computers and the extremely specialized knowledge required to program these particular machines. Thus mainframe computing was initially used to deal with standard accounting and administrative procedures. The sheer size of this task in the financial services industry effectively excluded other potential uses of computing in the sector for some time. The predominant use of early computing also created important organizational relations between computing and administrative functions. Managers in these functions have often resisted attempts by other departments to encroach on this relationship. Furthermore, the particular uses made of early computing technology, the specialist mathematics-oriented knowledge required, and the organizational position and professional culture of these technologists helped to constitute and reproduce technological identities based on a notion of superior technical rationality. This was supplemented by a strong sense of distance or 'other worldliness' from the field of business which itself increasingly was becoming dependent on the specialist knowledge that these technologists were assumed to possess. Their particular culture and identities, however, remained somewhat marginal to it and were often seen to be something of a threat.

As computing technology has developed so its range of possible application has expanded. This has been facilitated by the emergence of on-line and distributed processing, the creation of relational databases, and the reduced cost of computer hardware. Perhaps surprisingly, given this enlarged range of technological possibility, life companies have until recently used information technology with remarkable similarity. This similarity of use may in part be explained by a technological trajectory of computing (see Barras and Swann 1983). An alternative argument is that the particular character of the life sector and its managers' attitudes to IT are more important than any imputed technological determinant in understanding the contemporary history of technological use and development.

As has been suggested, the life industry enjoyed great stability and growth in the postwar period and internal change has been largely incremental and piecemeal. The control of competition through state and self-regulation combined with a rapidly expanding market for life insurance products created conditions amenable to the survival and growth of the great majority of companies regardless of their size and strength.

The absence of a perceived or substantive crisis in the life industry facilitated the survival of managerial cultures and practices that were challenged, and in part ousted, in the very different conditions experienced by the UK manufacturing sector in the 1970s. This continuity of practice appears to have been facilitated by the tight-knit character of managerial groupings within the industry, the overwhelming predominance of the actuarial profession, and the marked tendency for internal promotion and single-organization managerial careers. Nowhere is this continuity more evident than in the world of the mutual life companies who, due to their legal status, are free from the 'interference' and pressures emanating from institutional shareholders and less threatened by corporate predators. This is not to suggest that they are entirely immune as several building societies with mutual status (e.g. Cheltenham & Gloucester, National & Provincial) have been the target of takeover bids in recent time.

Until recently senior managers in the financial services have regarded IT as a crucial weapon in increasing the administrative efficiency of their corporations at the lower end of labour costs. Accordingly, the vast bulk of IT investment in the life industry has been made in the area of administrative systems.

However, some of the changes now taking place in the financial services industry are at least in part a condition and consequence of changing managerial attitudes to IT. That is to say, much of the liberalization and intensification of internal and cross-sectoral national and international competition has been facilitated by, but in turn increased the demand for, information systems innovation and development. It was soon realized that because of the ease with which systems advantage could be copied by competitors, IT could not necessarily be the key factor in strategic competition. None the less, without efficient systems other means of securing a competitive advantage such as customer service, cost constraint, or quality would be impossible.

Still the gap between the rhetoric of strategic IT use and managerial practice with regard to IT is often considerable. This is not particularly surprising given that IT strategy formulation is being sold precisely as a tool to impose order and coherence on rapidly escalating and diverging IT investments. This search for technology strategy is also fuelled by a more global quest for sustainable business strategies in rapidly changing markets.

3.2.2   *The Search for Strategy at Pensco*

As a mutual company Pensco has tended to rely on the sale of up-market insurance and investment products through independent financial intermediaries, mainly insurance brokers and accountants. In order to sustain the support of independent intermediaries, even before the Financial Services Act reduced their number, Pensco management have tried to provide a comprehensive range of insurance and investment products. The arrival of a new Chief Executive Officer (CEO) in the early 1980s placed particular emphasis on the rapid development of sophisticated and flexible investment products.

Up until this time, IT spending had been largely targeted at the development and updating of Pensco core administrative systems. Indeed, when the new CEO arrived, the company was in the middle of a five-year project to bring its entire range of administrative systems on-line. This project has been largely devised and run by the Data Processing Division and their colleagues in Customer Services. The CEO's decision to develop new products and the systems necessary to administer and produce quotations for these rather disrupted the on-line project. Although the new executive pensions product developed at the CEO's behest sold well, its administrative costs were considerably above the industry average. This could well be a consequence of its prioritization having the effect of sacrificing the full development of the on-line administrative system for all Pensco's products.

This change in the planned use of the IT resource did not come about without conflict. Indeed, the new CEO brought about an almost complete turnover in the senior management team. This included pushing the head of Information Services sideways to take over the management of Customer Services. In his place the CEO brought in the head of the IS Division from a previous employer where both had worked.

Given this radical restructuring of senior management to match the CEO's objectives and ambitions we might have expected conflict over the use of IT to subside. However, in the event it intensified. This intensification of inter-managerial conflict was clearly illustrated during the development of the new products and systems that the CEO felt were necessary to meet likely changes in the pensions market as a consequence of the 1986 Social Security Act (see Knights and Murray 1990). The intention here is briefly to render intelligible the problems surrounding this intensification of inter-managerial competition.

Currently, changing markets are beginning to have a major impact on the intensity of inter-managerial competition for scarce material and symbolic resources throughout Western economies. In his discussion of the intensification of inter-firm competition Auerbach (1988) argues that a primary effect of this historical tendency is an ever-increasing pressure on employees to maximize their productive potential. This increase in the pressure for results is perhaps even more strongly experienced by managers under the watchful eye of organizational superiors, competitors, peer groups, financial intermediaries and journalists, and institutional shareholders.

In periods of relative stability when organizational practices and decision-making procedures are well established inter-managerial competition may be muted and decision-making relatively straightforward, particularly if it does not threaten the existing distribution of resources, influence, and status between managers. However, these periods of relative calm will tend to be punctuated by periods of overt conflict as markets and technologies and managerial perceptions of these change, along with the career interests and perceptions of how to pursue them.

3.2.3 *Mobilizing Markets at Pensco*

At Pensco a number of vital changes were under way at the time of the pensions system and product development. These concerned the manner in which senior

48

Strategies and Markets

managers perceived technology and markets, the changing character of Pensco itself under the leadership of the new CEO, and presumably the more secretive, or tacit, considerations being made by managers concerning personal strategies to sustain their own renumeration, advancement, and subjective well-being.

The Financial Services Act (1986) has had a major impact on the constitution and functioning of financial services markets. Similarly, the Social Security Act (1986) itself created an expectation of what Pensco's CEO called 'a bloody big pensions boom' in the private sector of the pensions market. The expectation of this boom and the possibility of gaining substantial corporate advantage from it led the CEO to suggest that his Board would think 'his head needed examining' (see Knights and Willmott 1987b) if he did not place Pensco in a position from which it would be able to reap those benefits.

The CEO argued that this entailed revamping and redeveloping Pensco's existing pensions products to meet the new markets. However, from the start there was great uncertainty as to the shape and extent of these new markets and the 'best' strategy to prepare for them. This uncertainty was further heightened by a lack of clarity in the Social Security legislation itself, and the shifting interpretations of that legislation made by the regulatory authorities and the Inland Revenue.

These externally generated uncertainties were added to by the anxiety and fear amongst the company's managers. The CEO had shown on his arrival that he was prepared to use his dominant position to hound unsuitable senior managers out of the company and that he had little sympathy for managers who made mistakes or were responsible for organizational failings. And in the IS division the CEO's trusted colleague at the head of the division behaved in such a way as to create a climate of fear and apprehension despite his professed aim to run an 'open door policy'.

The high profile given to the pensions development suggested that managers associated with a 'successful' completion of the project could expect to benefit from it. On the other hand, managers seen to be obstructing the project, or failing to meet its objectives, were liable to meet with considerable approbation or worse.

Yet in order to meet with the objectives laid down in the project planning documents with regard to sales, cost, and potential profits managers had to secure a share of a project budget that turned out to be a woeful underestimate of the resources required. Thus, throughout the project there was intense competition between the divisions over the control and allocation of this resource between competing areas of systems requirements. This competition was exacerbated by the IS division's estimates of system development times and resources which in hindsight were seen to have gone 'haywire'. Tensions were particularly marked between the expanding Sales and Marketing Division and the Customer Services Division. Marketing wanted to create a wide range of products to maximize the possibility of benefiting, both personally and corporately, from the pensions boom. By contrast, the objective of Customer Services was in part to continue to put core administrative systems on-line while ensuring that systems back-up for the launch and administration of the new products was sufficient to process them at the costings given in the project plans.

During this competition the Sales and Marketing Division was particularly adept at mobilizing its, and what it claimed was the industry's, changing perception of the potential pensions 'market-place'. This had the effect, intended or not, of legitimizing its demands for the prioritization of the development of new products over the development of cost-saving or service-improving administrative systems. In this it was greatly helped by the CEO's objective of prioritizing the development of Pensco's 'marketing flair' over the improvement of the cost performance of its products, despite these costs being well above the industry average and of considerable concern to the Finance Division.[5]

In this example, then, contested perceptions of the market are shaped and mobilized to pursue internal and politically loaded objectives. Yet the sum of those internally contested views of the market have a profound impact on organizational strategy and the dynamic shaping of the market.

3.2.4 Politics and Software

As already mentioned, managerial perceptions of the potential benefits of IT investment are undergoing important changes with regard to IT's strategic potential. However, the perceived need for strategy, where *ad hoc* decision-making once sufficed, is in part indicative of the potential confusion surrounding the prioritization of competing IT investments. In particular, the growing demands being made of IS divisions to develop product and marketing systems is leading to difficult management decisions.

At Pensco the decision to prioritize product development over the renewal of core administrative systems had implications that no manager was particularly keen to champion. It was also something that less senior staff in IS would, but for decisions from 'above', have been prepared to fight over for; like R&D staff (Loveridge 1990: 11), their values differed substantially from those of marketing personnel. The result was that the development of the products systems and the limited revamping of existing administrative systems was seriously compromised by the need to 'bolt on' additional processes to ageing Pensco systems. This not only affected the design of the product systems and their hoped for flexibility and 're-usability' but also created a substantial volume of development work around the duplication of systems to communicate with Pensco's older tape and disk databases. Given the CEO's reorganization of the senior management team and the marginalization of the two most experienced systems managers from the systems area it is perhaps not surprising that the substantial financial, and perhaps strategic, cost of the CEO's decision to develop products rather than administrative systems, which was vociferously supported by the new head of the IS division, has remained largely hidden.

During the pensions project itself the rational prioritization of demands on the limited IT resource appears to have broken down. What began as a series of steering committee meetings to prioritize a particular mix of product-related and administrative systems degenerated into a free-for-all where additional systems demands were simply added to an already over-burdened development schedule. This led to sharp interchanges between Sales and Marketing and Customer Services managers as the latter fought a rearguard action to secure an IS division commitment to develop the administrative systems necessary to process the new products at the projected costs developed at the beginning of the project.

These conflicts over the use of the IT resource were not limited to an initial period of negotiation at the outset but continued throughout the development of the project. Furthermore, the conflict was not something to which the IT specialists who were developing the systems simply had to react for they were also active participants in its construction and continuity. This was in part because the conflict was reproduced with greater and lesser degrees of intensity at all levels of the project where system developers and potential users met. It was also because the IT specialists were anxious both collectively and individually to enhance their division's rather tarnished reputation as well as protect themselves from the stigmata of failure that at times threatened the pensions project.

Despite, or perhaps because of, the compromised and shaky systems that were produced, the budget overshoot, and the massive amount of development work shifted into the 'post-launch' phase of the project, senior management went to considerable lengths and expense to convince their staff of the great success of the new systems and their associated pensions products.

3.3   SUMMARY AND CONCLUSION

This chapter has attempted to theorize the relationship between technological innovation and organizational change as a complex historical process within financial services. In particular, it has examined markets, managers, and messages or information through the theoretical lens of power and identity.

3.3.1   *Messages*

The development and use of information systems is neither determining nor determined. Thus the process of organizational change cannot simply be read off from technological developments just as the use of technology cannot simply be read off from socio-economic structures. The use to which information systems are put depends upon the exercise of managerial choice. Technologies and the systems they enable open up a range of organizational possibilities. A central focus of this research has been to understand how and why one choice is taken rather than another with regard to the use of IT in the financial services industry. If both the idea that the technology determines its own use and that socio-economic imperatives unproblematically determine the use of information systems are rejected, it is necessary to provide another account of how choices are made and how they affect organizational change. This was the focus of the first part of the chapter where markets and managers as well as technologies were examined.

3.3.2   Markets

In examining markets it was suggested that they are not only unpredictable and precarious but also cannot be treated as an external reality to which managers must simply respond, for markets are actually constituted by the interpretations and actions of those who participate in them. They can be rendered more stable and predictable in the short run through the combined regulatory efforts of their participants but in the longer run markets often operate in ways that undermine the managerial attempts at control they engender. This is partly because the attempts by one group of managers to control are bound to counter or undermine the control design of another. Consequently the rational designs of managers can only be operationalized through what might be defined as the 'irrationality' of the market.

If markets are not a uniform and external reality but rather are constituted through the perceptions and actions of their participants, there is no one single message that the market conveys. Perceptions of the market will depend upon one's position in the market and position in a particular organization. But this is not all. Particular accounts and interpretations of the market are also strongly linked to the attempts by managers to advance or maintain their own material and symbolic security.

3.3.3   Managers

It has been argued that the use of IT in organizations is systematically linked to complex sets of market and power relations. For this reason it is important to avoid studying the development of information systems as if they were independent of the power relations of the managerial labour process. The historical development of capitalism has given rise to the growing treatment of managerial as well as non-managerial labour as a commodity. These processes inform the actions, and in part constitute the identities, of managers. Managers must strive for material power and symbolic success if they are to survive in a managerial world characterized by the contradictory forces of competition and cooperation and personal and collective or corporate objectives. As such it is not possible to conceive of management as an embodiment of systematic imperatives or unproblematic corporate objectives. Rather, management and managerial labour processes need to be seen as a hierarchical power/knowledge arena in which individuals and groups are in a continuous and competitive struggle for stability, security, and success that is itself often self-defeating because it stimulates an ever more precarious and uncontrollable set of working conditions.

From the foregoing it may be concluded that there is no one best or objective use of technology or systems. Choices regarding their use are conditioned by perceptions of labour and product markets, of technologies themselves, and by the exercise of power within managerial labour processes. This is necessarily problematic because markets are unstable and unpredictable, perceptions depend on organizational and market position, and the resources that are drawn upon in the exercise of power are unequally distributed between managerial actors. Furthermore these managerial actors are locked into competition to gain access to the positions which confer the greatest access to, and control over, material and symbolic rewards.

There are then considerable and shifting tensions between socially constructed organizational goals and individual and group objectives within the labour of management. These tensions create potential conflict around the management of the organizational IT resource, as illustrated in this brief case study, because different managers and operating divisions will perceive and pursue distinct IT priorities by invoking particular views of 'markets', 'technology', and 'organization'.

The case study illustrated how Pensco's CEO and the Sales and Marketing Division promulgated particular views of the life insurance market to legitimize their IT objectives. This in part rested on the CEO making use of his coercive potential, as conferred on him by his organizational position, to force through particular organizational changes. He effectively defeated opposition and resistance to his objectives by the virtual replacement of the senior management team and the reorganization of Pensco operating divisions.

Having apparently secured the control of the IT resource, the CEO began to make particular demands of it in terms of product-related systems development. But as the pensions fiasco only too clearly illustrates, the generality of these demands, and the lack of cohesion of the Pensco management team around particular IT priorities, led to a proliferation of demands on the IT resource that, although accepted by the head of the IS division, could simply not be met. This situation led to a growing disparity between the appearance of an apparently well-ordered and controlled software development project and the chaos, and frantic efforts to displace blame, that characterized the project.

It may be suggested that Pensco's IT problems are typical of much systems development. The undoubted technical complexities notwithstanding, this is owing in the main to the character of managerial labour processes and markets, tensions between individual and collective goals, and the very organizational uncertainties that are reproduced through markets. Therefore, the prescriptive literature which advocates 'IT strategies' and greater 'communication' between systems users and developers, although bolstering the semblance of purposive-rational managerial technique in the use of IT serves in part to reproduce, as it simultaneously obscures, precisely the conditions that generate and sustain the problematical and precarious character of IT management.

In other words, the management of IT can first and foremost be understood as a process of organizational and extra-organizational politics responding to, and acting upon, perceived imperatives generated through the socially constructed phenomena of 'markets', 'technologies', and 'organizations'. These phenomena appear to take on a life of their own and the individual confronts them as a constraining or facilitating reality. The asymmetrical distribution of power as access to, and control over, material and symbolic resources allows certain individuals, groups, and classes to dominate a socially constructed development, design, use, and management of specific technologies. But tensions between managers locked into particular labour processes and the very unpredictability of markets suggest that this domination cannot necessarily guarantee the successful use and development of IT.

This analysis would suggest that the role of IT in organizational change is neither pre-ordained nor predictable. There are strong structural constraints on the use to which IT is put. Through markets and labour processes, these constraints present a range of political, as opposed to technical, limitations on the possible uses and quality of application to which IT may be directed. However, within these dynamic and changing ranges of technical and political possibility, the clash of competing managerial objectives and the unpredictability of market outcomes serve to render the development and implementation of IT choices a continuing source of tension and difficulty for managers.

NOTES

1. See Loveridge (1990) and Coombs *et al.* (1991) for a similar view of the literature on new technology.
2. The need for an acute analysis of the constraints and opportunities inherent in particular technological developments and the decision-making processes around the use of technology, appears particularly pressing because technologies have become more flexible with the advent of microprocessor electronics and the increasing sophistication and speed of computers and their associated software. Thus, the range of technological possibility has expanded, particularly in areas of information gathering and processing. Multiple information technology applications give rise to large, integrated, and extremely complex software systems requiring costly and labour-intensive development, enhancement, correction, and maintenance. While the accelerating speed of IT innovation tends to reduce the effective lifespan of hardware and software (Mandel 1975), these linked developments have tended to increase the need for coherent, proactive decision-making regarding IT use and application.
3. Indeed, in the 1960s and early 1970s, group psychologists could earn considerable consultancy fees running encounter groups, transactional analysis workshops, and other interpersonal training sessions in industry precisely with communication problems as the main training agenda item.
4. While there is not space to discuss identity in detail here (cf. Knights and Willmott

1983; 1985), the concept is being used as shorthand for the sense that an individual has of her or himself—a sense that is uncertain and precarious in so far as it is dependent upon the judgements and evaluations of others which can never be precisely predicted or controlled.

5. The senior executive of Finance had instigated the development of an expenses control system as early as 1984 to try and bring costs down at least to the market average.

REFERENCES

Armstrong, P., Carter, B., Nichols, T., and Smith, C. (1986) *White Collar Workers, Trade Union and Class* (London: Macmillan).

Auerbach, P. (1988) *Competition: The Economics of Industrial Change* (Oxford: Blackwell).

Barras, R., and Swann, J. (1983) *The Adoption and Impact of Information Technology in the UK Insurance Industry* (London: Technical Change Centre).

Benjamin, R. I., de Long, D. W., and Scott Morton, M. S. (1990) 'Electronic Data Interchange: How much Competitive Advantage', *Long Range Planning*, 23(1): 29–40.

Benton, T. (1981) 'Objective Interests and the Sociology of Power', *Sociology*, 15: 161–84.

Bessant, J., Guy, K., Miles, I., and Rusk, N. (1985) *IT Futures* (London: NEDO).

Bijker, W., Hughes, T., and Pinch, T. (eds.) (1987) *The Social Construction of Technological Systems* (Cambridge: Mass.: MIT Press).

Blauner, R. (1964) *Alienation and Freedom* (Chicago: University of Chicago Press).

Bouitelaar, W. (ed.) (1988) *Technology and Work* (Aldershot: Avebury).

Braverman, H. (1974) *Labour and Monopoly Capital: The Degradation of Work in the Twentieth Century* (London: Monthly Review Press).

Brissy, J. F. (1990) 'Computers in Organizations: The (White) Magic of the Black Box', in B. A. Turner (ed.), *Organizational Symbolism* (New York: De Gruyter).

Brittan, A. (1977) *The Privatised World* (London: Routledge).

Burns, T., and Stalker, G. M. (1961) *The Management of Innovation* (London: Pergamon).

Callon, M. (1986) 'Some Elements of a Sociology of Translation: Domestication of the Scallops and Fishermen of St. Brieuc Bay', in J. Law (ed.), 'Power, Action and Belief: A New Sociology of Knowledge', *Sociological Review Monograph*, 32 (London: Routledge).

—— (1990) 'Techno-Economic Networks and Irreversibility', paper delivered at the conference on Firm Strategy and Technical Change: Microeconomics or Microsociology Manchester School of Management, UMIST 27–8 Sept.

—— Law, J., and Rip, A. (1986), *Mapping the Dynamics of Science and Technology: Sociology of Science in the Real World* (London).

Child, J., and Loveridge, R. (1990) *Information Technology in European Services: Towards a Microelectronic Future* (Oxford: Blackwell).

Coombs, R., Knights, D., and Willmott, H. C. (1991) 'Culture, Control and Competition: Towards a Conceptual Framework for the Study of Information Technology in Organisations', *Organization Studies*, 12(3): 51–72.

—— Saviotti, P., and Walsh, V. (1987) *Economics and Technological Change* (London: Macmillan).

Coopers and Lybrand (1988) *IT in Insurance* (with Bristol Business School) (London: Coopers and Lybrand).

Dalton, M. (1959) *Men Who Manage* (New York: Wiley).

Finlay, M. (1987) *Powermatics: A Discursive Critique of New Technology* (London: Routledge & Kegan Paul).

Foucault, M. (1980) *Power/Knowledge*, ed. by C. Gordon (Brighton: Harvester Press).

—— (1982) 'The Subject and Power', in H. L. Dreyfus and P. Rabinow (eds.), *Beyond Structuralism and Hermeneutics* (Brighton: Harvester Press).

Freeman, C. (1982) *Economics of Industrial Innovation* (London: Frances Pinter).

—— (1987) *Technology Policy and Economic Performance* (London: Frances Pinter).

Friedman, A., and Greenbaum, J. (1984) 'Wanted: Renaissance People', *Datamation*, Sept.

Giddens, A. (1984) *The Constitution of Society* (Cambridge: Polity Press).

Goldthorpe, J., Lockwood, D., Bechoffer, F., and Platt, J. (1969) *The Affluent Worker: Industrial Attitudes and Behaviour* (Cambridge: Cambridge University Press).

Hickson, D., Butler, J., Gray, D., Mallory, G., and Wilson, P. (1986) *Top Decisions: Strategic Decision Making in Organisations* (Oxford: Blackwell).

Hyman, R., and Price, R. (eds.) (1983) *The New Working Class? White Collar Workers and their Organisations* (London: Macmillan).

Knights, D. (1997) 'An Industry in Transition: Regulation, Restructuring and Renewal', in D. Knights and T. Tinker (eds.), *Financial Service Institutions and Social Transformations: International Studies of a Sector in Transition* (London: Macmillan).

—— and Morgan, G. (1991) 'Strategic Discourse and Subjectivity: Towards a Critical Analysis of Strategy in Organizations', *Organization Studies*, 12(3).

—— and Murray, F. (1990) 'Information Technology and The Marketing-Driven Firm: Problems and Prospects', *PICT Policy Research Paper* No. 9 (Oxford: Economic and Social Research Council).

—— —— (1994) *Managers Divided: Organisational Politics and Information Technology Management* (London: Wiley).

—— and Roberts, J. (1982) 'The Power of Organisation or the Organisation of Power?: Management-Staff Relations in Sales', *Organization Studies*, 3(1): 47–63.

—— —— (1983) 'Understanding the Theory and Practice of Management Control', *Employee Relations Monograph*, 5(4): 41 pages.

—— and Willmott, H. C. (1983) 'Dualism and Domination', *Australian and New Zealand Journal of Sociology*, 19(1): 33–49.

—— —— (1985) 'Power and Identity in Theory and Practice', *Sociological Review*, 33(1): 22–46.

—— —— (1987a) 'The Executive Fix: Strategic Decision Making in the Financial Services Industry', in J. McGoldrick (ed.), *Teaching Case Studies in Behavioural Management* (London: Van Nostrand).

—— —— (1987b) 'Organisation Culture as Management Strategy', *International Studies of Management and Organization*, 17(3): 40–63.

—— —— (eds.) (1988) *New Technology and the Labour Process* (London: Macmillan).

Loveridge, R. (1990) 'Apolyptic Change, Normative Uncertainty and the Control of Knowledge', paper delivered at the conference on Firm Strategy and Technical Change: Microeconomics or Microsociology, Manchester School of Management, UMIST 27–8 Sept.

Lucas, H. (1975) *Why Information Systems Fail* (New York: Columbia University Press).
—— (1984) 'Organisational Power and the Information Services Department', *Communication of the ACM*, Jan.
Lukes, S. (1974) Power: A Radical View (London: Macmillan).
MacDonald, S. (1983) 'Technology beyond Machines', in S. MacDonald, D. McL. Lamberton, and T. Mandeville (eds.), *The Trouble with Technology* (London: Frances Pinter).
McRae, H., and Cairncross, F. (1985) *Capital City: London as a Financial Centre* (London: Methuen).
Mandel, E. (1975), *Late Capitalism* (London: Verso).
Marx, K. (1971) *Capital*, trans. by S. Moore, ed. by F. Engels. (London: George Allen & Unwin).
Miller E. J., and Rice A. K. (1967) *Systems of Organisation* (London: Tavistock).
Mosco, V. (1984) *Pushbutton Fantasies: Critical Perspectives on Videotex and Information Technology* (New Jersey: Ablen).
Mumford, E., and Henshall, D. (1979) *The Participative Design of Computer Systems* (London: Associated Business Press).
Noble, D. (1984) *Forces of Production: A Social History of Industrial Automation* (New York: Knopf).
O'Connor, J. (1973) *The Fiscal Crisis of the State* (Oxford: Blackwell).
Offe, C. (1984) *Contradictions of the Welfare State*, ed. by J. Keane (London: Hutchinson).
Perez, C. (1983) 'Structural Change and the Assimilation of New Technologies in the Economic and Social Systems', *Futures*, 15(4): 357–75.
Pettigrew, A. (1973) *The Politics of Organisational Decision-Making* (London: Tavistock).
Rajan, A. (1984) *New Technology and Employment in Insurance, Banking and Building Societies* (Aldershot: Gower).
—— *Services—The Second Industrial Revolution?* (London: Butterworths).
Sayles, I. (1964) *Managerial Behaviour: Administration in Complex Organisations* (New York: McGraw-Hill).
Scarborough, H., and Corbett, J. M. (1992) *Technology and Organization: Power, Meaning and Design* (London: Routledge).
—— and Lannon, R. (1988) 'The Successful Exploitation of New Technology in Banking', *Journal of Management*, 13(3).
Smith, C. (1987) *Technical Workers: Class, Labour and Trade Unionism* (London: Macmillan).
Teece, D. J. (ed.) (1986) *The Competitive Challenge* (Cambridge, Mass.: Ballinger).
Trist, A., Higgin G., and Murray, H. (1963) *Organisational Choice* (London: Tavistock).
Turner, H. A. (1963) *The Trend of Strikes* (Cambridge: Cambridge University Press).
Wilkinson, B. (1983) *The Shopfloor Politics of New Technology* (London: Heinemann).
Wood, S. (1982) *The Degradation of Work? Skill, Deskilling and the Labour Process* (London: Hutchinson).
Woodward, J. (1958) *Management and Technology* (London: HMSO).
—— (1965) *Industrial Organisation: Theory and Practice* (Oxford: Oxford University Press).
Zimbalist, A. (1979) *Case Studies in the Labour Process* (New York: Monthly Review Press).
Zuboff, S. (1988) *In the Age of the Smart Machine* (London: Heinemann).

4

Paradigm Thinking and Strategy Development: Marketing Strategy in Information and Communication Technology Sectors

DOMINIC WILSON, DALE LITTLER, AND MARGARET BRUCE

4.1 INTRODUCTION

This chapter discusses research by the authors into the development of marketing strategies within organizations competing in fast-moving information and communication technology sectors. They discuss the observed processes of marketing strategy development in terms of paradigm thinking and argue that the problems of developing marketing strategy in fast-moving environments require a greater emphasis on collaborative relationships and 'relationship marketing'.

The influence of paradigm thinking has been discussed within the general strategy literature (e.g. Johnson 1988) and in the context of technology development (Dosi 1982) but has received much less attention in the marketing strategy literature which remains largely dominated by a structural-functionalist perspective (Deshpande and Webster 1989). This perspective has tended to perpetuate a view of marketing strategy development in which the manager is still often seen as a proactive 'planner' identifying opportunities and threats, evaluating strengths and weaknesses, and devising seemingly rational responses which are then implemented by subordinates (McDonald 1992). This perspective of planning has been comprehensively criticized in the corporate strategy literature (Pettigrew 1977; Mintzberg 1990) where it has been largely supplanted by the image of organizations as 'learning' systems which engage incrementally with perceived stimuli from their competitive environments, guided by an overall sense of strategic 'vision', and mediated through socio-political processes and cultural constraints. Nevertheless, marketing managers continue to make decisions which (other explanations notwithstanding) they regard presumably as sensible and which reflect their understanding of the competitive environment. The concept of paradigm thinking provides a useful integrating element in explaining how strategy emerges from this interaction of socio-political processes, cultural constraints, and managerial comprehension.

The authors' research has generated insights into the apparent influence of paradigm thinking in strategy development and into the ways in which paradigms may change in fast-moving sectors. These insights are illustrated through case studies of how two market-leading computer suppliers came to terms with the collapse of their competitive positions. Our research uses an integrated mix of interviews and surveys with senior marketing managers working mainly in rapidly evolving ICT sectors—especially those involving computer systems, electronic data interchange (EDI), and mobile telephones. These sectors were chosen because the scale and speed of their development seemed likely to highlight the problems of a traditional approach to marketing strategy, while the potential size of the markets involved seemed to offer powerful incentives to those organizations which were able to develop successful competitive positions.

The rest of the chapter is in four parts. First, we discuss the different approaches to understanding the process of marketing strategy formation offered in the literature, including consideration of the more recent idea that paradigms may be an important factor in understanding strategic marketing decision-making. Secondly, we discuss briefly those features of fast-moving ICT sectors which have particular significance for marketing strategy. Thirdly, we present some of the empirical evidence derived from our research, in the form of two case studies, which help to provide insights into how marketing strategy is formed by organizations competing in ICT sectors. Fourthly, we discuss the implications of our research findings for a better understanding of marketing strategy formation processes, and for marketing management.

4.2 DIFFERENT APPROACHES TO EXPLAINING THE FORMATION OF MARKETING STRATEGY

The marketing strategy literature offers several different accounts of how strategy is formed within organizations.[1] The earliest of these accounts started from the position—implicitly or explicitly—that the process of strategy formation is, from the perspective of those involved, a logical and factually based sequence of discernible steps (e.g. setting objectives, collecting and analysing data, generating options, and making logical decisions). This 'planning' approach remains highly influential amongst practitioners but has been challenged by more recent attempts to understand strategic decision-making in terms of perceptual, cultural, political, and environmental constraints. A somewhat artificial and overpolarized debate (Wensley 1996) has emerged between proponents of the 'planning' approach,[2] who see the organization's leadership as the key to understanding the strategy formation process, and proponents of what might be termed the 'behaviouralist' approach,[3] who regard the decision context as the key. Interest in the underlying issue in this debate—how an organization's strategy is formed and developed over time—has been driven more recently by concern that the prescriptive recommendations of the planning literature are increasingly questionable in the growing uncertainty and turbulence experienced in many competitive environments of the 1980s and 1990s. On the other hand, the ability of some companies, with or without the benefit of good fortune, to achieve and sustain competitive success—even in these environments—gives prima facie support for the argument that it may be possible to analyse some aspects of volatile environments and to plan and implement strategies accordingly (Collis 1992; Slater 1993).

The effect of the burgeoning research into strategy formation has been to identify a wide range of factors which expose and reject many of the implicit assumptions concerning the assumed 'rationality' of managerial strategic decision-making. From this research has emerged an approach which regards strategy formation generally as a function of socio-political processes by managers with limited discretion, varying cognitive capacity, and preoccupations which go well beyond the strategic agenda under the spotlight on any one occasion.

A useful overarching concept which helps to explain many of the cognitive aspects of strategic decision-making is provided by the notion of 'paradigms', popularized initially by Kuhn in the early 1960s (Kuhn 1962). Application of the paradigm concept to the context of strategy formation in organizations dates at least from the innovative work of Grinyer and Spender (1979), Sheldon (1980), and Huff (1982). Johnson (1988) later integrated the concept with related issues in organizational culture and strategy formation, referring to the 'cultural web' which he sees as comprising aspects of organizational culture, structure, control systems, and socio-political systems which collectively support what Johnson refers to as the 'organizational paradigm' or collective, taken-for-granted, set of beliefs and assumptions describing the organization's view of itself within its environment.

Other researchers have noted the natural conservatism of such organizational paradigms which makes them particularly resistant to change (Freeman 1984; Harrison and Carroll 1991). This may be partly because such a paradigm is supported by the inertia and resilience of the 'cultural web', and partly because, being 'taken-for-granted', the paradigm is rarely challenged. It is also worth noting that individuals may avoid questioning the organizational paradigm, consciously or unconsciously, because this can have the effect of undermining the political *status quo* within the organization. Paradigms are also thought to be slow to change because they tend to generate their own criteria of relevance, resulting in a tendency within organizations to ignore, deny, discredit, or minimize disruptive environmental signals while endorsing and highlighting supportive signals (Johnson 1988; 1990; Johnson and Scholes 1988).[4]

Quinn (1980) recognized the need to manage the potential ambiguity between the natural conservatism of organizational behaviour and the changing environment within which the organization operates. This ambiguity may gradually become much greater than the organization realizes because of the tendency for paradigm thinking to overlook and dismiss disruptive environmental signals. So an organization's managers may make occasional incremental adjustments to strategy in line with what they perceive as *relevant* environmental changes, yet the environment may be moving further away from managers' perception of it than they realize. Johnson (1988) describes this phenomenon as 'strategic drift' and argues that this will eventually produce a situation where adverse signals from the environment can no longer be explained within the paradigm, leading to a loss of faith in the paradigm and in its supporting 'cultural web'. The resulting changes in the paradigm can be dramatic as the organization questions its most fundamental beliefs in the attempt to realign itself with its environment. Where the paradigm is particularly strong and/or the environment is particularly uncertain, it can be expected that the need for radical organizational realignment will be more frequent and/or more dramatic.

The concept of the paradigm is now broadly accepted in principle but less attention has been given to how paradigms evolve and adapt to change and how they are manifested in specific decision instances. One important contribution to explaining how paradigms influence strategic decision-making comes from the continuing discussion of 'industry recipes', sometimes referred to also as 'rules of the game', or 'strategic formulae' (Porter 1979; Grinyer and Spender 1979; Thomas and Soldow 1988; Loveridge 1990). There are many obvious affinities between the 'recipe' concept and the 'planning model' of strategy formation. For example, reference to recipes/rules/formulae clearly implies a process which can be repeated with predictable results, and that successful strategy is made up from the 'ingredients' of 'objective' analysis of the environment.

Essentially then, the paradigm perspective suggests that organizations are 'rooted in the interpretation of events in terms of the recipe' (Johnson 1986) leading to 'muted' interpretation of environmental stimuli, management complacency,[5] and a tendency to preserve the dominant recipe to which managers have become most accustomed (Johnson 1986). As Johnson argues, the shared beliefs and assumptions comprising an organizational paradigm are 'self-evident to "insiders"' (Johnson 1988) even when seemingly inexplicable to external observers, and these assumptions can serve to distort environmental signals and ultimately may affect the company's performance. In fast-moving uncertain sectors, however, it seems unlikely that managers will have time to 'become accustomed' to their environments in the way that advocates of paradigm interpretation imply, resulting in analytical distortion and greater likelihood of reduced organizational performance. If paradigms are indeed a natural cognitive feature of organizational life then it will be particularly challenging—and important—to explore their influence in marketing-strategy formation in the sort of fast-moving, highly competitive markets which seem to be increasingly typical of contemporary sectors.

To conclude, the process of strategy formation, is perhaps best viewed as essentially one of political and cultural change carried out within the constraints of the organizational and sectoral paradigms, *as well as* one of structured analysis and option selection carried out within the dynamics of competition and demand. When dramatic strategy change is required, it may be that this will only be achievable through the partial destruction of the prevailing paradigms and their associated strategic perspectives and formulae.

Finally, another obvious, if infrequently mentioned, point is that many of the fundamental concepts of marketing strategy formation—such as 'market', 'market share', 'demand', 'competitiveness', 'strategy', 'organization'—still lack universally accepted definition and are socially and individually constructed by managers in terms of how they are understood. In fast-moving and uncertain sectors these terms become even more problematic, as the next section shows, making the formation of marketing strategy especially difficult to explain.

4.3 FEATURES OF FAST-MOVING INFORMATION AND COMMUNICATION TECHNOLOGY SECTORS WITH SIGNIFICANCE FOR MARKETING STRATEGIES

We have argued that fast-moving ICT sectors may provide insights into marketing strategy formation processes because of the intermittent volatility typical of such sectors. This reflects the logic that unpredictable sectors do not generally provide the time or the level of reliable information implicitly required for structured strategy analysis, and so they may increase reliance on informal information and accelerated decision-making, thereby exposing some of the more 'behavioural' influences on strategy formation. We also argue that other features of these sectors (outlined below) bring into question the meaning of several fundamental concepts in marketing strategy. These questions have important implications for the formation of marketing strategy. In this section we discuss briefly the features of fast-moving ICT sectors while their significance for marketing strategies is discussed in Section 4.5 below, drawing on the material in the case studies in Section 4.4.

There is no convenient definition of 'ICT sectors' though the term seems to be associated in popular usage with computer-based products and services. The term also seems to have acquired a set of strategic, managerial, political, social, and even moral issues which can greatly complicate the formation of marketing strategy in ICT sectors. One might also distinguish between those sectors which produce and distribute the computer-based offerings which are at the core of this popular perception (e.g. computer and communication systems, software and services) and those sectors where such offerings play a supportive, though increasingly fundamental, role (e.g. publishing, entertainment, manufacturing). While this distinction may still seem discernible in the 1990s, the self-evident universal relevance of technologies based on information and communication will, sooner or later, make it more sensible to think of ICT offerings as an integral aspect of *all* sectors rather than as separate sectors. This trend can be seen clearly in the increasing restructuring of traditionally product-oriented computer markets (e.g. the mainframe market; the graphics software market) into a structure based on the differentiated needs of customers in, for example, financial services or health-care sectors.

Box 4.1. Sample quotes describing the perceived impact of IT on management, the economy and society

---

The most visionary of science-non-fact writers could not have predicted the transformation wrought by a mere forty years of micro-technology development. The scale and speed of change has produced every response from terror to intoxicated optimism. (Neil Kinnock, 'Foreword' to Large 1984)

The information revolution is sweeping through our economy . . . not only transforming products and processes but also the nature of competition itself. (Porter and Millar 1985: 150)

We are now a few years into a staggering efflorescence of information technology made from components that are simultaneously increasing in variety and power . . . A result of this technology push is the possibility of creating a virtually complete spectrum of products for handling in any conceivable way all forms of information—numerical data, text, physical measurements, sound, graphics and images both fixed and moving, analogue and digital. (Anderla and Dunning 1987: 161)

There can be no disputing the fact that IT has illustrated more rapid technological improvement than any other part of the productive process in the last 25 years. (Stoneman 1988: 143)

Technology is yet another wild card affecting every aspect of doing business. It has revolutionized financing . . . [and] forever changed manufacturing . . . design . . . distribution . . . [and] product definition. (Peters 1988: 10)

In the technological environment of the 1990s, the automation of sales and marketing is no longer an option—it is a necessity. Moriarty and Swartz 1989)

What children do at school was the province of post-doctoral intellectuals just a few years ago. Seldom can there have been such a rapid de-mystification of skills. (Henderson 1991: 12)

IT is reshaping the basics of business. Customer service, operations, product and marketing strategies, and distribution are heavily, or sometimes even entirely, dependent on IT. The computers that support these functions . . . have become an everyday part of business life. (Keen 1991: 23)

New technology has become the key to competitiveness in international markets and to economic growth. (Ball 1991, p. xxvii)

. . . in five years time there will be two types of company—those who use the computer as a marketing tool and those who face bankruptcy. (Gorski and Ingram 1993)

IT and the computer are transforming what marketers do, how they do it, and how they organise themselves to do it. (Mitchell 1994)

Many researchers and commentators have been impressed with this pervasive and fundamental quality of ICTs and have referred to the potential of ICTs to revolutionize the managerial, economic, and social structure of society (see Box 4.1). Although this potential of ICTs seems indisputable in the longer term it is, of course, important not to underestimate the costs involved (Leverick *et al.* 1995) for example, in disruption, learning processes, and enforced obsolescence. Thus ICTs can both reduce and generate complexity; they can liberate people from drudgery through automation while at the same time making them dependent on ICTs through the very ubiquity and importance of their applications. Yet ICTs are not unique in these respects—much the same could be said for earlier equally revolutionary technologies such as the internal combustion engine, electricity, and radio telephony.

As with all such enabling technologies, the effectiveness of ICTs depends on an infrastructure of 'network externalities' (e.g. electricity supply, microelectronics, software engineering, training, capital availability) on which the ICT products and services themselves are dependent. The efficient management of these network externalities raises a number of important commercial and political issues, for example, the need for universally agreed technical standards within the network, the need for a critical mass of users in applications such as telecommunications, and the need for a critical mass of data in databases to enable the optimal use of ICTs in society (while not encroaching unduly on organizational confidentiality or personal privacy).

A useful illustration of the implications of these network externalities for marketing strategy is provided by the development of satellite TV in the UK where Rupert Murdoch subsidized the consumer entry cost to the market (the purchase of satellite-receiving equipment and decoding machines) in order to accelerate the achievement of the critical mass of subscribers necessary for commercial viability. Murdoch also standardized the market around a relatively uncomplicated version of the available technological approaches to satellite TV broadcasting, while investing heavily in the necessary compatible software, to ensure the reliability of the service and the satisfaction of subscribers. Murdoch's was an entrepreneurial, high-risk, long-term strategy taken at a time when he could not have known—other than intuitively—that these would be appropriate or sufficient measures to achieve his objectives. A similar strategy of establishing critical mass in an emerging market was followed by Bill Gates of Microsoft through his decision to make the MSDOS operating system for personal computers freely available to software writers, thereby encouraging the development of software applications and so encouraging hardware suppliers to design their PCs around MSDOS rather than the many rival operating systems then available. Gates has now repeated this strategy by making Microsoft's World Wide Web (WWW) browsing software package—*Internet Navigator*—freely available in an effort to accelerate a critical mass of WWW users while also ensuring Microsoft's dominance in providing software systems for various WWW services. Murdoch and Gates have been successful because they invested not only in the products and services in question but also in the network externalities necessary to provide the infrastructure on which these offerings relied.[6]

In summary, while many factors and issues might be suggested as being typical of ICT sectors, there appears to be nothing that differentiates IT sectors *per se*. We might conclude that there are no absolute differentiating features of ICT sectors though there may be features which are perhaps *more* apparent in these sectors than in others. More accurately, what differentiates ICT sectors is perhaps the collective effect of a *cluster* of features which characterize the sector, rather than any individual feature—coloured, in the case of ICT sectors, by the all-important widespread belief by many participants that ICT sectors *are* different, even to the extent of being revolutionary. Finally, the perception of revolutionary change, coupled with the uncertainty generated individually and collectively by this cluster of features, has lead to a feeling amongst many observers of anticipation, even of excitement, at the prospects which ICTs seem to hold for profound change in the many aspects of society which can be influenced by more efficient processing and distribution of information. This sense of excitement and anticipation has become—for some more than others—a notable feature of ICT sectors.

4.4   EMPIRICAL EVIDENCE FROM OUR RESEARCH

Our PICT-funded research over the period 1987–95 has explored many aspects of marketing strategy and management in ICT sectors—especially those sectors involving computer systems, electronic data interchange, and mobile phones. The research has involved interviews and surveys with a wide range of organizations and has focused on product development, collaboration, strategic analysis and planning, and competitiveness. The discussion below draws directly on only a small part of this extensive research portfolio. The case studies describe how two market-leading organizations with a predominantly proactive and 'planning-oriented' approach to forming marketing strategy responded to increased uncertainty in their markets. Both case studies are based on interviews conducted over the period 1988–94 with senior managers responsible for strategic planning and marketing, together with extensive secondary material.

4.4.1   *Case Study 1:* Boss Systems Ltd. (BSL)

The following brief case study provides an illustration of how an organization (referred to here discreetly as 'Boss Systems Ltd.') attempted to develop its marketing strategy while competing in fast-moving and uncertain sectors within the UK computer industry. An important issue in this case is the way that information was apparently regarded as 'factual' or as 'non-factual' by different individuals involved in the process of strategic marketing analysis and decision-making. The extensive research[7] from which cases 4.4.1 and 4.4.2 are drawn provides ample evidence that the specifics of this case are by no means unique in this sector.

In 1985 Boss Systems Inc.—a global supplier of computer systems—experienced a sudden decline in its normally strong rate of sales growth. These results deteriorated dramatically in 1986 with only 2 per cent growth in sales and a fall of 27 per cent in reported profits. The reasons behind this trend were complex but were closely linked both to the recent success of suppliers of rival offerings in PC and mainframe markets, and by Boss Systems' apparent inability to perceive the competitive importance of these dynamics. Boss Systems Inc.'s senior management in the USA decided to put increased pressure on national subsidiaries to develop sales and improve profitability by devolving responsibility for competitive marketing strategy to these national subsidiaries.

Consequently, Boss Systems Ltd.—the market-leading UK subsidiary of Boss Systems Inc.—convened a major strategic planning conference in 1986 with the aim of developing a revised marketing strategy for achieving the new corporate objectives. One of the most significant outcomes of this conference was the decision to set up long-range marketing planning systems. Previously, Boss Systems Ltd. (BSL) had planned largely on the basis of accounting data, technical product development schedules, and sales management routines—sources providing highly quantitative 'factual' information. The conference prompted the realization that in order to meet its new responsibilities for competitive marketing strategy, BSL would have to make a transition to a system of planning based around rigorous and comprehensive competitive analysis. To achieve the transition, it was decided that the new system would also reflect a perspective of computer markets that was based on 'customer segments' (known as vertical markets, e.g. financial services, government agencies) rather than on the previously used 'technology segments' (known as horizontal markets, e.g. mainframes and PCs).

The design of BSL's new strategic marketing planning system clearly reflected BSL's entrenched culture and paradigms, and required a huge volume of carefully structured quantitative data which would then be analysed through BSL's mainframe computers. The new system provided input to a range of planning horizons: 10 years for technology issues; 5–7 years for issues in *business areas* (in effect, 'vertical markets'); 2–5 years for competitive marketing strategy assessment; and 3 years for financial planning. The length of these horizons now seems surprisingly optimistic in such an uncertain environment but reflects BSL's deep-seated confidence that their historic domination of many computer markets would continue into the future. Meanwhile, collecting information, managing the database, and analysing data for these horizons was to be the sole responsibility of a new unit within BSL—the Commercial Analysis Group (CAG)—the mission of which was:

[To] be the sole centre of competence on all aspects of the competitive marketplace, the individual competitors, their strategies, performance, and offerings and [to] use this

---

Box 4.2. Information sources scanned for the BSL Commercial Analysis overview

Internal Sources	External Sources
Visit Reports	Surveys (Romtec, IDC, Datamation)
Contact Reports	Computer Users' Yearbook
Monthly Highlight Reports	Stockbroker Reports and Annual Reports
Key Wins and Losses Reports	Press and media reporting
Market research data	Customer contacts
Manufacturing data	Competitor contacts
Finance data	Dealer and consultant contacts
Technical and engineering data	Seminars and exhibitions

Sources: Interviews with BSL managers and BSL documents referred to in these discussions.

---

competency to support the [BSL] business goals and processes. (BSL 1989—internal company document)

This new Commercial Analysis Group was located as a free-standing department equidistant between the four areas of 'marketing, business [i.e. operations] staffs, executive management, and European HQ' (BSL 1989) in an apparent attempt to enhance its objectivity through structural independence. Nevertheless, it was obvious from interviews with BSL managers that in practice there were very close cultural, personal, and organizational links between the CAG and the marketing function in particular, reflecting what were seen as the natural responsibilities of marketing for competitive analysis. Thus, the logic of structural and budgetary independence was circumvented by the 'behaviouralist' influences of custom and practice and of personal relationships.

Meanwhile, information for the new planning system was gathered from many different sources through 'vast reading' by CAG analysts (see Box 4.2 for an indication of the scale of this reading) and either rejected or included as a data 'cell' in the database. The database covered '100 vendors' operating in twenty-four market sectors each with three subdivisions (mainframe, mid-range, PC), and extended to '120 fields' (e.g. revenue, profit, channels used, resources used)—amounting to almost a million 'factual' data inputs for any single time period. The intention was to develop historic data for the previous five years (where possible) to assist the annual mid-September exercise of calculating forward estimates in support of the various planning horizons. Each of the items of information recorded in the database was assessed by analysts in terms of one of four 'credibility factors: factual (1); high credibility (2); believed, but not sure (3); no clear evidence or basis for belief (4)'. Analysis was generally in the form of trend projection and two-dimensional matrices, focusing on correlation of 'key measures' (such as sales and revenues, market share, profitability, cost efficiency in production and distribution, and cost and revenue per employee). It was evident that, for BSL managers, 'factual' information was the most desirable and highly regarded form of information for strategic analysis.

BSL's attempt to develop a fresh understanding of its markets and competitors was, perhaps inevitably, built on its deeply engrained culture of respect for IT and this attempt illustrates some of the difficulties involved in such a transitional process. For example, at first inputs to BSL's new planning systems were only accepted where they could be expressed quantitatively (e.g. the 'credibility' grading system), and all information had to conform to the technical requirements of the computerized database system (e.g. in the number of letters which each data 'cell' could accommodate; and the need for quantitative expression of the data for processing and analysis). Subsequent analysis was then computerized using spreadsheets, regression techniques, and matrices and presented to managers. By 1989 these changes in information analysis had begun to generate a degree of returning confidence and managerial intuition started to question some of the conclusions of this analysis. It became apparent to BSL senior managers that the system's insistence on 'factual' analysis could limit or even distort understanding. BSL then abandoned credibility ratings and started to experiment with slightly more qualitative methodologies such as customer satisfaction surveys and a case-study approach to the analysis of lost contracts.

It is noticeable that BSL's history and culture seemed to affect not only the systems of data capture and analysis in UK markets but also the identification of the organizations to be analysed, tending to prioritize global rivals familiar to Boss Systems Ltd. in US markets at the expense of smaller competitors, even where the latter were much more important as rivals for BSL itself in UK markets. This problem of monitoring global rivals rather than local rivals became obvious as early as 1989, when, for example, BSL realized that Nintendo had secured a very substantial share of the UK PC market without being 'observed' by BSL's commercial analysis system, and that McDonnell Douglas had emerged as an unnoticed yet serious rival in local and central government markets in the UK.

Recognizing such problems was made even more difficult by the inflexibility of BSL's planning systems. For example, despite the accelerating competitive pace and intermittent volatility of UK computer markets in the late 1980s, BSL continued its practice of conducting strategic assessment only on an annual basis and at a time (just prior to the mid-September strategy planning meetings) which was determined more by the easing of other pressures on key managers and the necessary lead-time for data analysis, than by the needs for timely competitive response.

Nevertheless, by 1990 this system had undergone various reforms and it had begun to forecast several key strategic issues for BSL in the early 1990s. The emerging Single European Market and adoption of Unix (the industry standard computer operating system) were agreed as the two prime strategic opportunities for BSL—'Unix kept cropping up in the top right hand corner' (the optimum position in BSL strategic analysis matrices). The two major strategic threats were 'the Japanese' (once alerted to this issue by BSL, and not before, Boss Systems Inc. had counted nineteen $1-billion-IT Japanese rivals already competing in US markets), and hidden protectionism in European government markets through 'bureaucracy'. It is significant that all four of these key opportunities and threats emerged strongly from 'qualitative' analysis (discussions with customers and distributors) but were undetected by previous quantitative analyses.

In conclusion, BSL responded to increased uncertainty in its markets by first regrouping its planning systems around what it considered to be 'factual' data, then adapting this system in line with its experience in what Mintzberg describes as a 'learning' process (Mintzberg 1990). In the course of this learning process BSL moved from predominantly 'factual' towards more informal information sources. It is also important to note that the simultaneous shifts in the BSL paradigm which enabled this learning process were generally achieved only through replacing key personnel, including the appointment of one manager specifically recruited to manage the process of strategic planning.

4.4.2   Case Study 2: Tile Systems Ltd. (BSL)

Tile Systems Ltd. was the UK subsidiary of a major US-based supplier of mid-range computer systems which were initially marketed to specialist engineering and scientific markets before becoming widely adopted for more general commercial computing applications because of their reliability and low cost. Formal strategic-marketing planning systems were introduced at Tile Systems Ltd. as part of a major strategic reorientation in the mid-1980s following the appointment of a new managing director (MD) and some twenty years after Tile's entry to UK markets. The new structured planning system replaced an informal pattern of impromptu strategic-marketing decisions with little integration and no formal long-term analysis. For example, one interviewed source described how in the late 1970s he recalled that Tile had examined UK commercial computing markets to see if Tile products were suitable for these markets. Tile's UK management found that a significant competitive position had already been built up without any marketing effort and without any real awareness: 'it was a sudden startling shock'. Nevertheless, at a later stage in the interview, the same source referred to 'the decision many years ago to move into commercial systems rather than stick to Tile's traditional scientific and engineering markets'. This apparent contradiction shows not only how competitive positions can 'emerge' without any conscious marketing strategy, but also how such 'emergent strategies' can become 'planned' either by a process of retrospective rationalization, or by the planned development of *de-facto* situations.

Tile's new planning system was strongly influenced by Michael Porter's (1980; 1985) current work on competitive strategy (which praised aspects of Tile's management) and especially by his 'value chain' analysis. For example, following analysis by the new planning system, Tile's distribution strategy was reformed in recognition of the value-added importance of Tile's channel agencies—a clear example of formal structured analysis leading directly to strategy formation (and, significantly perhaps, one which was unlikely to have encountered cultural resistance).

However, sudden and unexpected losses in 1988/9 persuaded the MD that the benefits of the new planning system were not being achieved and that further reforms were necessary. It was clear that the strategic planning changes of the previous year had not been as successful in terms of practical implementation as they had been in managerial conception. Tile marketing strategy managers acknowledged that 'it could be almost as difficult to manage changes in the Tile culture as it was to shift Tile's competitive position'.

In the 1989 reform of strategic planning, Tile decided that what it needed was not so much a system to generate a 'strategic plan' as an ability to 'accommodate the market'. By this Tile meant that it was simply not possible to 'anticipate' or forecast markets as broad as the ones addressed by Tile, and that it was impossible to 'drive' these markets or 'manipulate' them. Therefore it was unrealistic to imagine that a corporate marketing strategy could be based on traditional market-centred proactive assumptions. The best that could be done with respect to strategic marketing was to watch market developments very carefully for changes and then to try to accommodate those changes as swiftly as possible in a strategy of 'guided flexibility' and 'opportunism'.

In terms of the necessary strategic planning for this more flexible and interpretive process, Tile's Director of Strategic Planning and Marketing stressed that what was needed was an 'antiseptic backdrop' of formal information integrated from various sources, against which strategic planning discussions took place with occasional reference to the 'backdrop' as necessary. However, he continued, 'the backdrop must remain in the background . . . the last thing you do is listen to experts'. He described the process as one of 'intuitive distillation' involving logical criteria, weighting, and careful analysis, though the 'rationality' of the process need not be immediately apparent to those collecting and analysing the information since strategic policy considerations were often much broader than the remit of analysts.

Tile now regards progress towards the achievement of strategic objectives as an 'organic' process whereby incremental (even nominal) improvements were made in many different aspects and on many different fronts such that there was an overall effect of organic progress. It was not possible to be sure in which areas progress would be achieved at any particular time, nor in which aspects there would be competitive equilibrium, or even erosion—this was a reflection of the complexity of Tile's scale of operations and of the environments in which Tile competed. But above all, the Strategic Planning and Marketing Director at Tile felt that any strategic progress would depend crucially on convincing Tile's managers of the priorities of customer needs. It was acknowledged that there were particular difficulties in communicating this marketing message amongst Tile's non-marketing executives, nor were conventional planning data (such as market share and contribution data) thought to be sufficient to communicate what was essentially a cultural message. What was really needed was a change in the broader 'engineering paradigm' prevailing in Tile Inc., which was only achieved two years later with the reluctant departure of the ageing founder of the organization.

4.4.3 Discussion

There are obvious similarities between the BSL and Tile cases. Both organizations responded to competitive uncertainty and threat by adopting formal structured-planning systems which focused on what those involved considered as 'objective' information; and both discovered that a less formal, more subjective, and heuristic approach was more suited to the learning processes involved in adapting to their rapidly changing competitive environment.

The BSL and Tile cases suggest that managers within organizations tend to react conservatively to unexpected change, seeking reassurance in the face of uncertainty and attempting to understand change within the terms of reference of their accustomed paradigms. This observation is supported by some of our earlier survey research into the use of collaborations in product development (and is discussed further in the following section). This research found, *inter alia*, that organizations tend to use financial measures to assess the success of their collaborations until they become more familiar with collaboration management, at which point less formal assessments of the collaboration tend to get more sympathetic consideration (Littler *et al.* 1993). Thus formal information consistent with the paradigm may be perceived as being more credible and reliable than more innovative informal information, even when the formal information in question is less directly related to the situation at hand. In other words, the difference between formal and informal information may be less to do with the perceived accuracy of the information than with the paradigms, comfort, and risk-perception of managers engaging with the information.

4.5 IMPLICATIONS FOR UNDERSTANDING MARKETING STRATEGY FORMATION PROCESSES

The cases described above, and our research into marketing strategy more broadly, raise a number of implications for a better understanding of marketing strategy and how it is formed in fast-moving sectors. Some of these implications have been raised by previous studies of strategy processes more generally, though without specific attention to the context of marketing. Seven of these implications are discussed here.

4.5.1 Formal and Informal Information

Our research suggests that one method of gaining insight into how paradigms change in the light of adverse signals from the competitive marketing environment may be to consider the way in which marketing managers use relatively formal and informal information in strategic analysis. The issue of how information is used has received little attention so far in this debate over strategy formation. Advocates of strategic-marketing planning seem to imply that the most appropriate information for strategy decisions is formal factual data while those who prefer a processual explanation of strategy formation seem to attach greater significance to the role of more informal information sources such as casual conversation (Sapienza 1987), previous experience (Bowman and Daniels 1995), intuition (Pondy 1983; Parikh *et al.* 1994), and learning (Shrivastava and Grant 1985). 'Planners' seem to overlook the obvious point that even 'formal' information is received and processed by managers through filters (e.g. of perception, prejudice, cultural association) which can radically change the way in which superficially 'objective' information is understood by different individuals.

It is worth noting that some organizations or individual managers seem to reveal a cultural predisposition for certain types of data.[8] So the probability of further investment in an ongoing innovative strategy (e.g. a new product) may be undermined by monitoring its success through conservative formal data (e.g. sales) rather than through more innovative informal data (e.g. effect on brand perception; level of customer satisfaction). This important effect of cultural predisposition towards formal or informal information was noted also in our earlier research into collaborative product development where survey respondents found that the success of collaborations was often difficult to gauge with the conventional formal measures used such as the achievement of agreed goals within allocated budget and time constraints (Wilson *et al.* 1995; Bruce *et al.* 1995).

4.5.2 The Role of 'Myths' in Marketing-Strategy Formation

Evidence from our research shows how myths—or commonly held beliefs—can be an important part of making sense of novel, complex, and/or unpredictable situations, even though they may turn out to have been wrong—as 'draft versions of reality' or 'working hypotheses' perhaps (e.g. that mobile phones are universally desirable; that PCs are getting cheaper; that only the most advanced technology can compete successfully; that organizations must be global competitors to be commercially viable in computer markets; that strategy formation is characteristically 'rational'). The scale and rapidity of change in many ICT sectors tends to leave managers with little time for extensive information searches and in such circumstances a risk-reducing strategy may well be to accept unquestioningly a belief commonly held by colleagues or sectoral opinion leaders.

It seems possible that these sorts of myths might provide vivid insights into the broader paradigm from which they derive legitimation and to which they give support. Therefore further research into the emergence and disappearance of 'myths' in organizations and sectors may be valuable in illuminating the important processes of paradigm change. Explanations of how organizational paradigms evolve and adapt to changed environments might refer to the way in which organizations seem to 'build bridges of meaning' between their current situation and where they think they have to be in order to be successful in their vision of the future. One might also think of paradigm evolution as a process of building continuity between previous experience and perceived future opportunity. A crude model for understanding the process of paradigm evolution is suggested below (point 5.4), following a broader discussion of the significance of paradigms in the formation of marketing strategy (point 5.3).

4.5.3 Organizational and Sector Paradigms

In ICT sectors we have observed paradigm-type influences at work amongst cultural and functional subgroups of managers within organizations. For example, the paradigm influences amongst marketing personnel can often be markedly different to those evident amongst technical staff, even though everyone might subscribe also to the same broader organization-wide paradigm. Using the same logic, it is also possible to refer to sector-wide paradigms which help to distinguish the 'industry recipes' favoured within one sector from those predominating in another. This would still allow for considerable variation amongst participating organizations with respect to their own interpretation and expression of the sector paradigm. Paradigms seem to be built up gradually over time—whether at the level of the subgroup, organization, or sector—by managers and organizations, in terms of psychological commitment and resource investment (e.g. in technology, markets, training, product design).

With respect to marketing strategy formation, perhaps the important issue is that the assumptions inherent in these paradigms can act as 'blinkers', limiting the criteria of validity and the perceived options of those involved. Furthermore, in situations of high perceived risk and uncertainty, a low-risk strategy may be to define the world as others do, and so avoid innovative strategies. The effect of this 'cultural conservatism' is very different to the image of dynamic entrepreneurialism often associated in the popular media with fast-moving ICT sectors.

4.5.4 A Multi-Stage Learning Process

Reflecting on our observations, it may help to understand managers' response to environmental uncertainty in terms of a pattern of responses which might be summarized crudely as following at least five 'stages': first, by attempting to re-establish certainty (more accurately, 'familiarity') where possible—often through a renewed emphasis on established planning systems. When this strategy fails to resolve uncertainty, sometimes even revealing further areas of uncertainty, a second 'stage' (though this may sometimes be a 'first' stage) becomes discernible where the criteria of information validity are gradually eased to allow more informal information or unconventional sources to influence the analysis. Where this more innovative information still fails to bring the level of perceived environmental uncertainty within the tolerance levels of the organization, then a third 'stage' tends to emerge of fundamental debate whereby, in effect, the internal paradigms of the organization and the mind-sets of its most influential managers begin to be challenged. This can result in a fourth 'stage'— the replacement of key managers as the organization 'hunts' heuristically for a revised paradigm or 'working hypothesis' representing a viable compromise between the organization's objectives and its perception of its environment. A final 'stage' of adjustment then follows as the revised paradigm adapts to the lessons learned by managing in an environment which may still seem uncertain in many respects—if more tolerable. The various stages will, of course, vary considerably in terms of duration, sequence, and stage-separation according to contingent circumstances and the degree of cultural embeddedness of the prevailing paradigm. However, this crude model is broadly consistent with the literature and provides a convenient structure for understanding much of the change observed in our research of organizations attempting to manage marketing strategies in uncertain environments.

4.5.5 Strategic Myopia

There are many examples in the computer industry of major strategic developments which were ignored or not noticed by market leaders—even where rivals, customers, or industry observers had already concluded that the developments were important. These might be seen as examples of organizations which were unable to adapt their paradigms gradually and so were faced with potential competitive disaster. For example, IBM was late to develop a minicomputer despite the clear success of DEC in doing so in the early 1960s, something which IBM nearly repeated following Apple's development of the personal computer in the early 1970s. More dramatically, one of the leading global suppliers of office computer systems (especially word processing systems) completely failed to appreciate the significance of industry-standard personal computers as a generic platform for mass-market office software systems. The company subsequently went into bankruptcy. In the words of one of its senior executives:[9] 'We missed the PC revolution and, having missed it, we missed everything else . . . To survive you have to be open and into selling knowledge. We had closed products and sold boxes. We even brought out proprietary PCs.'

Such strategic myopia underlines the importance of understanding the perceptual filters through which managers view the competitive environment. What is considered by those involved as 'objective' information for strategic analysis and decisions clearly depends on the perceptual filters through which such information is received, filters which reflect a range of influences such as individual and organizational culture, education, experience, capability, work pressures, and motivation systems. It is also possible to regard these filters as reflections of the paradigms held within the organization and by the managers involved. Thus a paradigm which prioritizes technological issues is likely to be reflected in greater sensitivity to technological signals from the environment and—given the limited resources, time, and cognitive capacity of all managers—this presumably must displace or discount some other signals to which different organizations might be more sensitive.

4.5.6   *Fundamental Concepts in Marketing Strategy*

An important effect of environmental uncertainty is to question assumptions not only in management practice, for example about the validity of information and the relevance of previous experience, but also concerning more fundamental concepts in marketing strategy, including the meaning of such key terms as market, organization, and competitive analysis, each of which is touched on briefly below.

4.5.6.1   *Market*

Defining and segmenting markets is a crucial aspect of strategic marketing planning yet, at least in fast-moving ICT sectors, it is often difficult to identify and analyse markets unambiguously. This may partly reflect the technological fascination of many ICT suppliers which can eclipse the often very different perspective of the customer, who is generally more concerned with a narrow range of actual product applications than with the full technical potential of the product. Clearly these different perspectives can also be seen as aspects of 'rival' paradigms. Thus many multi-featured products have failed *inter alia* because they were over-engineered for their markets. Nor can demand be assumed to be related exclusively—or even predominantly—to the technical features of the product. For example, image, lifestyle, and fashion are clearly important issues in the demand for mobile phones and notebook computers. The problem of market definition may also reflect the novelty of many ICT offerings where the nature of demand is difficult to assess (and impossible to forecast with confidence) because users are unfamiliar with the products in question, leaving analysis of demand open to indirect inference, intuition, and personal conviction. Furthermore, the interdependence of many ICT offerings (e.g. in terms of network externalities) poses problems in analysing potential usage and demand.

  If, as marketing theory suggests, a market should be considered as a set of related exchange relationships, then a great deal more analysis is needed of such relationships in ICT sectors before markets can be confidently defined and segmented. Indeed, the rapid pace of technological and competitive development, and the continuing growth of demand for many ICT offerings, suggest that any market definition and segmentation could rapidly become anachronistic. Meanwhile, there is at least a clear trend in some ICT sectors (e.g. computer systems) away from 'horizontal' product-based definitions of markets towards user-focused 'vertical' market definitions such as EPOS (electronic point of sale) systems and security surveillance systems.

4.5.6.2 *Organization*
The increasing use of inter-organizational collaborative relationships in many sectors has been widely documented (e.g. Littler and Wilson 1991; Lamming 1993; Jorde and Teese 1989; Håkansson 1990). An important consequence of this trend is that boundaries of individual organizations can become blurred with respect, for example, to competitive analysis and discretion over strategic decisions. Organizations such as Olivetti, IBM, and Groupe Bull have chosen to engage in a very wide range of collaborations and are consequently well placed to move promptly in whatever directions their numerous technology collaborations suggest are most promising, and can enter new markets and segments quickly through their channel collaborations with distributors. But in each case the 'organization' pursuing this strategy would, more realistically, be a loose alliance of collaborators and their related suppliers and customers. The question remains open as to how we might most appropriately conceptualize such an extended notion of 'organization'—whether legally, socially, commercially or competitively—but it is certainly no longer appropriate (if it ever was) to regard them as atomistic entities as is implied in many analytical techniques of marketing strategy. The growing literature on network theory and organizational interaction (e.g. Ford 1990) seems relevant here but this literature has yet to develop a viable set of analytical techniques for the formation of marketing strategy.

4.5.6.3 *Competitive Analysis*
Competitive analysis in many ICT sectors is complicated by the development of collaborations to the extent that competition may be, in effect, between networks of organizations as well as between individual organizations. So organizations may be active competitors in some markets or operations while active collaborators in others.

It is clear that the contemporary relevance of many competitive analysis techniques is being increasingly questioned (Collinge 1991; Greenley and Bayus 1993; Crainer 1996) because *inter alia* they require the sort of information, time, clarity of focus, and separation of issues which are simply unavailable for real-time managers. Managers are relying more on intuition, experimentation, and the comforting realization that rivals face similar difficulties.

4.5.7 *Implications for Marketing Management*

Much of the marketing management literature tends to suggest that marketing is (or should be) conducted in an ordered, sequential, formalized process (e.g. McDonald 1992; Kotler 1994; Dibb *et al.* 1994) where there is little allowance for the influence of preconception, paradigms, and the politicization of strategy-formation processes. In many respects this suggestion does not comply with our observations of marketing management in ICT sectors, though it is partially recognizable from the descriptions of these processes by participants. For example, the problems of segmenting markets which defy conventional definition and research have already been noted, nevertheless many managers felt able to discuss in some detail how they approached segmentation (e.g. through analysis of vertical markets). There are similar problems in researching, understanding, and targeting customers who may have significantly different perceptions of the function and role of ICT offerings compared to those held by suppliers, but these problems are much diminished where the managers involved recognize, and accept as potentially valid, the different perceptions held by customers.

Both Boss and Tile achieved substantial profit margins while they remained largely unchallenged by competitors in their markets. However, both companies shared a perception, common amongst many other successful ICT-pioneering firms in our research, that it was they (rather than customers) who held the expertise necessary for product development. Therefore, for example, Boss and Tile pursued proprietary-product development strategies in mainstream markets while tending to leave third parties (e.g. software houses and value-added resellers) to develop software applications for specific niche markets. Encouraged by the commercial success of Boss and Tile in mainstream markets, rivals developed niche market offerings which were more closely built around perceived customer requirements and less dependent on previous investments in proprietary technologies. As the increasing power and sophistication of ICTs allowed greater customization of ICT offerings to individual user requirements, niche markets grew rapidly at the expense of the traditional mainstream markets dominated by Boss and Tile. Furthermore, many users within all markets soon began to develop extensive expertise in the application of ICTs to their particular circumstances, encouraging a collaborative approach to further product development amongst those suppliers untrammelled by the perception that technological expertise was something that belonged primarily to proprietary suppliers.

These processes can be seen in terms of competing paradigms. The dominant paradigm in Boss and Tile was apparently that the locus of technological expertise and market power was within the market-leading proprietary suppliers. By contrast, many other companies following niche strategies seemed to regard the customer (and other organizations within the value chain) as having important areas of expertise and market power. The case studies show how, when Boss and Tile saw their profits collapse, they were forced to re-evaluate their basic understanding of their markets and of their own organizational self-worth, and to question many of their assumptions about the nature of demand, supply, and competition in ICT markets. It is difficult to capture the scale and significance of this process of re-evaluation from within the traditional perspective of the marketing literature. The considerable cultural shifts involved include, for example, relative re-orientation from R&D towards customer needs, from product issues to service issues in product development, from internal proprietary technical development to collaboratively developed industry-standard technologies, from differentiation through product/service specifications to differentiation through branding and marketing communications, and from mass-market centralized strategic-marketing decision-making to more targeted and flexible strategies involving considerable local discretion. Managing any of these shifts individually would be problematic but engaging with all of them (and more), while continuing with the day-to-day management of the relationships with customers and suppliers, has posed enormous difficulties for many long-established companies in ICT markets.

The general recommendation in the marketing management literature tends to be that marketing problems should be analysed and prosecuted as individual issues and that organizations should seek to retain direct control over what are perceived as the most important elements of marketing strategy. However, our observations suggest that these issues are often best managed and developed iteratively, and in collaboration with important suppliers and/or customers. Many of the strategic marketing problems encountered by the organizations we observed in our research arose because the organizations became locked into their own perspective of their competitive environment and lost sight of their dependency on other organizations, a perspective which failed to keep pace with developments. It may be that flexibility of perspective, or paradigm, can be stimulated by a more collaborative approach (internally and externally) to the development of marketing strategy—echoing the emerging concept of relationship marketing (Evans and Laskin 1994) which owes so much to the interorganizational network theory of the IMP Group (Ford 1990).

4.6 CONCLUSION

This chapter has examined some of our research in marketing strategy formation in fast-moving ICT sectors with a view to commenting on the influence of paradigm thinking on marketing strategy formation processes. It was concluded that the nature and practice of marketing strategy in fast-moving ICT sectors—and perhaps more broadly as the characteristics of these sectors become more universal—is significantly different to that implied in much of the marketing strategy literature. To understand how marketing strategy is developed (both proactively and reactively) in these, and other, sectors we have found that it is particularly productive to think in terms of paradigms—at the level of the organization and of the sector, as well as at the level of the individual. Finally, many organizations are adopting a more collaborative approach to marketing strategies and an additional benefit of such strategies may be to expose an organization to different paradigms and thereby discourage the otherwise natural conservatism of more independent paradigm development.

NOTES

1. For a brief but thought-provoking review see Wensley (1994*a*).
2. e.g. in the corporate-strategy field: Ansoff and McDonnell (1990); Hamel and Prahalad (1994)—or in the field of marketing strategy: Greenley and Bayus (1993); McDonald (1992); Piercy (1991).
3. e.g. in the corporate-strategy field: Mintzberg (1990); Johnson (1987)—or in the field of marketing strategy: Wensley (1994*b*); O'Shaughnessy (1995).
4. Clearly, the concept of paradigms can help to explain differing perceptions amongst organizations participating within a sector (the 'organizational paradigm'), or between sectors participating within an economy or region (the 'sectoral paradigm'), or even between individuals within an organization (where reference might be made to a range of overlapping and iterative paradigms such as 'professional paradigms', 'functional paradigms', 'structural paradigms' (worker/mananger/executive), 'gender paradigm' (male/female), and so on). Thus any particular decision-making occasion might be interpreted in terms of a kaleidoscope of inter-mingling paradigms—in addition to other factors and variables (including the data relevant and available to the occasion).
5. Because managers think they have responded to environmental stimuli when, more accurately, they have often only responded to signals which coincide with (and so are recognized by) the dominant 'recipe' or 'paradigm'.
6. e.g. through: affordable and reliable PCs, (e.g. Microsoft's alliance with IBM); software programs running on MSDOS (e.g. Microsoft's collaboration with software houses); the approval of regulatory authorities (e.g. Murdoch's lobbying activities); the availability of distribution channels (e.g. Murdoch's collaboration with leading UK electrical retailers); encouraging the use of the WWW (e.g. through Gates's public speeches and writings); access to a library of programmes for broadcasting (Gates's purchase of photography archives); adoption of penetration pricing strategy (because of the need to attract the critical mass of users necessary for commercial viability).
7. This 'extensive research' includes wide-ranging secondary research as well as personal semi-structured interviews with Boss Systems Ltd. personnel (Senior Manager, Business Plans; Manager, Strategic Analysis, Commercial Analysis Group; Manager, Local Government, Health and Utilities; Manager, Retailing and Banking; all of Boss Systems Ltd., September 1989) and Tile Systems Ltd. personnel (Director, Strategic Planning and Marketing; Strategic Planning Process Manager; May and July 1989). The case analysis is also informed by the broader research context of about 200 hours of interviews over the period 1987–94 with 87 respondents from 55 organizations, including most of the leading suppliers of computer systems in UK corporate markets and many of their major customers.
8. e.g. product quality may be measured by numbers of defects found by quality inspections (formal data) or through customer complaints records (informal data). Measurement should, of course, involve both aspects but one form of information may well dominate the assessment because of the real—or perceived—information preferences of the managers involved.
9. Ken Olisa, Wang's Director of Worldwide Marketing and of European Operations, ruefully reflecting on Wang's collapse as he became part of the Wang staff cutbacks in 1992 (cited in J. Evans 'Wang's Catalogue of Disasters', *Computing*, 3 (Sept. 1992: 11).

REFERENCES

Anderla, G., and Dunning, A. (1987) *Computer Strategies, 1990–1999; Technologies, Costs, Markets* (Chichester: Wiley).

Ansoff, H. I., and McDonnell, E. J. (1990) *Implanting Strategic Management*, 2nd edn., (London: Prentice Hall).

Ball, D., and Wilson, H. (eds.) (1991) *New Technology: Implications for Regional and Australian Security*, Canberra Papers on Strategy and Defence No. 76, Strategic and Defence Studies Centre, Research School of Pacific Studies, Australian National University, Canberra.

Bowman, C., and Daniels, K. (1995) 'The Influence of Functional Experience on Perceptions of Strategic Priorities', *British Journal of Management*, 6(3), 1995: 157–67.

Bruce, M., Leverick, F., Littler, D. A., and Wilson, D. F. (1995) 'Success Factors for Collaborative Product Development: A Study of Suppliers of Information and Communication Technology', *R&D Management*, 25(1), (Jan.), 33–44.

Collinge, P. (1991) 'Marketing in the IT Industry: A Review of the Applicability of Standardised Techniques in a Dynamic Business Environment', in D. F. Wilson (ed.), *The Marketing of IT Products and Services*, Manchester School of Management, UMIST, Apr.

Collis, D. (1992) 'The Strategic Management of Uncertainty', *European Management Journal*, 10(2) (June), 125–35.

Crainer, S. (1996) 'The Rise of Guruscepticism', *Management Today*, (Mar.), 48–52.

Deshpande, R., and Webster, F. E. Jr. (1989) 'Organizational Culture and Marketing: Defining the Research Agenda', *Journal of Marketing*, 53(1) (Jan.), 3–15.

Dibb, S., Simkin, L., Pride, W. M., and Ferrell, O. C. (1994), *Marketing—Concepts and Strategies (European Edition)*, 2nd edn. (Boston: Houghton Mifflin).

Dosi, G. (1982) 'Technological Paradigms and Technological Trajectories', *Research Policy*, 11.

Evans, J. R., and Laskin, R. L. (1994) 'The Relationship Marketing Process: A Conceptualization and Application', *Industrial Marketing Management*, 23(5), (Dec.), 439–52.

Ford, D. (ed.) (1990) *Understanding Business Markets: Interaction, Relationships and Networks*, (London: Academic Press).

Freeman, C. (1984) *The Economics of Industrial Innovation*, 2nd edn. (London: Frances Pinter).

Gorski, D., and Ingram, J. (1993) *The Price Waterhouse Sales and Marketing Software Handbook*, 2nd edn. (London: Pitman Publishing).

Greenley, G. E., and Bayus, B. L. (1993) 'Marketing Planning Decision Making in UK and US Companies: An Empirical Comparative Study', *Journal of Marketing Management*, 9: 155–72.

Grinyer, P. H., and Spender, J.-C. (1979) 'Recipes, Crises and Adaptation in Mature Businesses', *International Studies of Management and Organisation*, 9(3): 113–23.

Håkansson, H. (1990) 'Technological Collaboration in Industrial Networks', *European Management Journal*, 8(3): 371–9.

Hamel, G., and Prahalad, C. K. (1994) *Competing for the Future*, (Boston: Harvard Business School Press).

Harrison, J. R., and Carroll, G. R. (1991) 'Keeping the Faith: A Model of Cultural

Transmission in Formal Organizations', *Administrative Science Quarterly*, 36(4) (Dec.), 552–82.

Henderson, J. (1991) 'Is There a Computer Science?' *The Computer Bulletin*, 3(1) (Feb.), 12–14.

Huff, A. S. (1982) 'Industry Influences on Strategy Reformulation', *Strategic Management Journal*, 3: 119–31.

Johnson, G. (1986) 'Managing Strategic Change: The Role of Strategic Formulae', in J. McGee and H. Thomas (eds.), *Strategic Management Research: A European Perspective*, (Chichester: Wiley), 71–90.

—— (1987) *Strategic Change and the Management Process*, (Oxford: Blackwell).

—— (1988) 'Rethinking Incrementalism', *Strategic Management Journal*, 9(1): 75–91.

—— (1990) 'Managing Strategic Change: The Role of Symbolic Action', *British Journal of Management*, 1: 183–200.

—— and Scholes, K. (1988) *Exploring Corporate Strategy*, 1st edn. (London: Prentice Hall).

Jorde, T. M., and Teece, D. J. (1989) 'Competition and Cooperation: Striking the Right Balance', *California Management Review*, 31(3) (Spring), 25–37.

Keen, P. (1991) *Shaping the Future: Business Design Through Information Technology* (Boston: Harvard Business School Press).

Kotler, P. (1994) *Marketing Management: Analysis, Planning, Implementation and Control*, 8th edn. (Englewood Cliffs, NJ: Prentice Hall).

Kuhn, T. S. (1962) *The Structure of Scientific Revolutions* (Chicago: University of Chicago Press).

Lamming, R. (1993) *Beyond Partnership* (Hemel Hempstead: Prentice Hall).

Large, P. (1984) *The Micro Revolution Revisited* (London: Frances Pinter).

Leverick, F., Littler, D. A., Bruce, M., and Wilson, D. F. (1995) 'A Revolution Unrealised, Promises Unfulfilled: Information Technology in Marketing', in D. Bennet and F. Steward (eds.), *Technological Innovation and Global Challenges*, Proceedings of the International Association for Management of Technology (IAMOT) European Conference on the Management of Technology, Aston University, Birmingham, July, 612–20.

Littler, D. A., Leverick, F., and Wilson, D. F. (1993) 'Collaboration in New Technology-Based Product Markets', *Technology Analysis and Strategic Management*, 5(3): 211–33.

—— and Wilson, D. F. (1991) 'Strategic Alliancing in Computerized Business Systems', *Technovation*, 11(8): 457–73.

Loveridge, R. (1990) 'Footfalls of the Future: The Emergence of Strategic Frames and Formulae', in R. Loveridge and M. Pitt (eds.), *The Strategic Management of Technological Innovation* (Chichester: Wiley), 95–124.

McDonald, M. H. B. (1992) 'Strategic Marketing Planning: A State-of-the-Art Review', *Marketing Intelligence and Planning*, 10(4): 4–22.

Mintzberg, H. (1978) 'Patterns in Strategy Formation', *Management Science*, 24(9) (May), 934–48.

—— (1990) 'Strategy Formation: Ten Schools of Thought', in J. W. Frederickson (ed.), *Perspectives on Strategic Management*, (New York: Harper Business), 105–35.

Mitchell, A. (1994) 'The Hi-Tech Hybrid', *Marketing Guide to Marketing Technology*, 23 June, pp. v–vi.

Moriarty, R. T., and Swartz, G. S. (1989) 'Automation to Boost Sales and Marketing', *Harvard Business Review*, 67(1) (Jan./Feb.), 100–8.

O'Shaughnessy, J. (1995) *Competitive Marketing: A Strategic Approach*, 3rd edn. (London: Routledge).

Parikh, J., Neubauer, F., and Lank, A. (1994) *Intuition: The New Frontier of Management* (Oxford: Blackwell).

Peters, T. J. (1988) *Thriving on Chaos: Handbook for a Management Revolution* (London: Macmillan).

Pettigrew, A. M. (1977) 'Strategy Formation as a Political Process', *International Studies of Management and Organisation*, 7(2): 78–87.

Piercy, N. (1991) *Market-Led Strategic Change* (Glasgow: Harper-Collins).

Pondy, L. R. (1983) 'Union of Rationality and Intuition in Management Action', in P. Shrivastava (ed.), *The Executive Mind* (San Francisco: Jossey Bass).

Porter, M. E. (1979) 'How Competitive Forces Shape Strategy', *Harvard Business Review*, 57 (Mar.–Apr.), 137–45.

—— (1980) *Competitive Strategy: Techniques for Analysing Industries and Competitors*, (New York: Free Press).

—— (1985) *Competitive Advantage—Creating and Sustaining Superior Performance*, (New York: Free Press).

—— and Millar, V. E. (1985) 'How Information Gives You Competitive Advantage', *Harvard Business Review*, 63(4) (July/Aug.), 149–60.

Quinn, J. B. (1980) *Strategies for Change: Logical Incrementalism*, (Englewood Cliffs, NJ: Irwin).

Sapienza, A. M. (1987) 'Imagery and Strategy', *Journal of Management*, 13(3), (Fall), 543–56.

Sheldon, A. (1980) 'Organisational Paradigms: A Theory of Organisational Change', *Organisational Dynamics*, 8(3): 61–71.

Shrivastava, P., and Grant, J. H. (1985) 'Empirically Derived Models of Strategic Decision-Making Processes', *Strategic Management Journal*, 6: 97–113.

Slater, S. F. (1993) 'Competing in High-Velocity Markets', *Industrial Marketing Management*, 22(4) (Nov.), 255–63.

Stoneman, P. (1988) 'Information Technology', in P. Johnson *The Structure of British Industry*, 2nd edn. (London: Unwin Hyman), 140–63.

Thomas, G. P., and Soldow, G. F. (1988) 'A Rules-Based Approach to Competitive Interaction', *Journal of Marketing*, 52(2) (Apr.), 63–74.

Wensley, J. R. C. (1994*b*) 'Strategic Marketing: A Review', in M. J. Baker (ed.), *The Marketing Book*, 3rd edn. (Oxford: Heinemann), 1994, 32–53.

—— (1994*a*) 'Making Better Decisions: The Challenge of Marketing Strategy Techniques', *International Journal of Research in Marketing*, 11: 85–90.

—— (1996) 'Fallacies and Fantasies', *BAM News*, 6: 6–9.

Wilson, D. F., Littler, D. A., Leverick, F., and Bruce, M. (1995) 'Collaborative Strategy in New Product Development—Risks and Rewards', *Journal of Strategic Marketing*, 3(1): 1–22.

PART 2

Integrating Technology and Organization

5

Paper Traces: Inscribing Organizations and Information Technology

BRIAN P. BLOOMFIELD AND THEO VURDUBAKIS

5.1 INTRODUCTION

Recent work in the Sociology of Scientific Knowledge (SSK) and Social Studies of Technology (SST) have contributed to an understanding of technology as an integral part of social life. In the actor-network approach of Latour (1987; 1991), Callon (1986; 1990), Akrich (1992), and others (for example: Law 1986; 1994), technological innovation is viewed as an attempt to build and stabilize a diffuse system of allies composed of both human and non-human entities (such as texts, artefacts/machines, or natural forces).[1] The construction of a working machine is not just a 'technical' matter but also requires the simultaneous construction of human actors—in short, the development/building of an actor-network within which the technology can operate. In this way the heterogeneous engineering inherent within the building of a network in which a technology develops and can function, is constitutive of that technology.[2]

One of the strengths of the actor-network approach is the systematic avoidance of what we might call 'methodological dualism': the making of a priori distinctions between what is 'technical' and what is not (and is therefore by implication 'social'). Instead the focus of such investigations is on those processes through which 'socio-technical' networks are (or fail to be) created, sustained, and dismantled.[3] Particular attention is paid to the key role played by various *intermediaries* in the (always provisional) construction and stabilization of such networks. This role consists in designating and (re)defining the various elements that make up a network, and in setting up the relations that hold them in place.

the notion of intermediary . . . serves to designate everything which passes from one actor to another, and which constitutes the form and the substance between them—scientific

We would like to acknowledge the contribution of Ardha Danieli who was a member of the Intermediaries Project team, and the useful comments of Chris Westrup and Hugh Willmott. We are also indebted to the firm of management consultants (Manex) and the NHS staff who allowed us access in order to study their IT project.

articles, software, disciplined human bodies, technical artefacts, instruments, contracts, money and so on. (Callon 1990: 5)

Intermediaries, in other words, constitute the means for bringing together (and we would add keeping apart) various heterogeneous entities thereby construct-ing the form and the substance of the relations set up between them—for in-stance, what, in any given context, counts as 'technical' or 'social' (Bloomfield and Best 1992; Bloomfield and Danieli 1995; Bloomfield and Vurdubakis 1997).[4] In this chapter we are interested in the tasks, techniques, and operations involved in the accomplishment of intermediation.[5] In the context of the development of IT systems in organizations, this includes everything and everyone (management consultants, commentators, manuals, development methodologies, and so on) deployed as part of attempts to ensure the optimal integration or mixture of 'technical' and 'social/organizational' elements.

In the circumstances of technological development and implementation, texts and, more generally, all sorts of literary inscriptions, constitute a particularly potent set of intermediary devices. Technological artefacts for instance tend to be accessed through the appropriate textual material which routinely defines their content and dictates the conditions of their effective deployment and use (Bloomfield and Vurdubakis 1994*b*). Examples would include manuals, text-books, consultancy reports, popular guides to choosing the right technology, and so on. Here we are specifically interested in those texts involved in the devel-opment and implementation of information systems. A systems development project is an endeavour which, in Callon's terms, requires a complex hetero-geneous network—of people, machines, texts (such as installation and training manuals, Gantt charts and other project management tools, contracts), flows of money, ideas, aspirations, concerns about the risks of project failure, and so on—to be assembled over time and actively held together. Thus to a significant degree systems development is enabled and mediated by an exercise on paper: that is, the construction of a system on paper is a precursor to its situated realization in the organization concerned. The discursive work involved shapes the form and content of the project and, typically, takes place before a single item of equipment or software is purchased, unpacked, or put in place. In the terminology of Callon and Latour, the role of texts is that of representing and thereby mobilizing the heterogeneous human and non-human actors and mater-ials constitutive of an IT system.

It can be argued that as a rule IT is known and made available for action predominately through the deployment of various inscription devices which therefore operate as intermediaries between the 'technology' and its 'users'. In recent years, a number of scholars (Hoskin and Macve 1986; R. Cooper 1992; Kallinikos 1994) have investigated the documentation of human activities as a process of construction as much as description.[6] The significance of this literat-ure for our purposes is that it involves a wider methodological shift from a view of textual accounts as (more or less) partial and incomplete representations of real world objects, people, and events, which exist outside those texts, to a view that 'cultural objects and events exist in and through the texts which represent them' (Gephart and Pitter 1995: 328). What are the consequences of this theoretical move? Given that the manner in which professions, organizations, and institutions in all areas of social life approach their tasks is heavily dependent upon the representations of the real world of activities, objects, and events which appear in documents of various kinds, this means that all forms of administrative, political, and managerial intervention are not reactions to reality 'as such'[7] but to a reality socially and discursively constructed within documents. What one might call a 'textual reality' (for example: Bloomfield and Vurdubakis 1995*b*; 1994*b*; Smith 1984; 1978; 1974; Green 1983). Consequently the various techniques (for selecting, transcribing, editing, encoding, highlighting, and so on) and the forms of language utilized in this 'construction work' constitute, at least in part, the ways in which reality is known for purposes of organizing, administering, managing, and other kinds of 'knowledgeable' intervention in the world. What this means of course is that such constructions tend not to remain 'on paper' but are through administrative practices 'returned', as it were, to the world which they purport to render knowable. Documents, such as reports, files, folders, and dossiers, are created with a view to their eventual deployment and mobilization in the shaping of what they describe. Textual production must therefore be conceived as part of a circuit: Bruno Latour (1987) for instance, has analysed the construction of texts and other textual and graphical constructs— inscription devices—such as maps, statistical tables, and so on, in terms of network creation involving the institution of a two-way traffic between a decision-making 'centre' and a 'periphery' about which decisions are made.

In what follows we illustrate our argument by reference to a typical exercise in intermediation initiating a six-stage plan to implement a hospital information system for the purposes of Resource Management (see below). More specifically, we examine a document known as a readiness review which was produced by a leading firm of management consultants—Manex[8]—specializing in IT systems. Its objective was to assess the preparedness of the particular hospital to implement Resource Management using an IT system already developed by the management consultants at another hospital site, Newtown.[9] The Resource Management Initiative was a program set up within the National Health Service (NHS) with the aim of using IT systems to inform decision-making on the allocation of resources (Bloomfield *et al.* 1992). Although initially developed at some six pilot sites Resource Management was subsequently extended with the intention that it would be implemented in over 250 general hospitals. Thus the readiness review discussed here was but one typical example of a genre produced by a range of consulting firms and others (e.g. hardware/software suppliers) claiming expertise in the area of organizations and technology. What we are interested in is the *specific* way in which it enables IT to be known: both as the means for fulfilling the information requirements of doctors and managers—as established by the review—and as instantiated in the particular information system which is to be implemented within the organization by following the required method-ology prescribed by Manex. (Later stages of this particular systems development project have been reported elsewhere (see Bloomfield and Best 1992; Bloomfield and Vurdubakis 1994*a*; Bloomfield and Danieli 1995).) Thus we are interested in how knowledge of the technical is produced, and how technology comes to be put in place—in short, how a particular 'presence' is created for IT within the readiness review executed and reported by Manex. The next section introduces some general issues regarding reading and writing as a prelude to a fuller con-sideration of the specific work of intermediation carried out by the readiness review.

5.2   READING TECHNOLOGY

In James Thurber's satirical 'Macbeth Murder Mystery' (1984) an American tourist in search of a detective mystery, buys the Penguin edition of *The Tragedy of Macbeth* under the misapprehension that it belongs to that genre (the covers were similar). Having read the play, she comes up with the solution: Macduff done it! Given the conventions of the detective novel, she argues, Macbeth could not be the murderer: that would have been too obvious and the reader's interest would flag. It must therefore have been Macduff (who discovers the body), subsequent actions being explainable in terms of Macbeth and Lady Macbeth trying to shield one another. Having recovered from the initial shock, her trav-elling companion produces an even more convoluted 'solution' before suggest-ing they turn their attentions to solving the crime in *Hamlet*.[10]

   In terms of our concerns, Thurber's amusing story draws attention to the interpretive conventions—reading practices—for eliciting the 'content' of a given text. Any text can of course be read in a number of ways and as such cannot be said to have a fixed and immutable meaning. A text, Terry Eagleton (1983: 119) argues, is:

subject to the 'reinscriptions' and reinterpretations of many different readers. The work itself cannot 'foresee' its own future history of interpretations, cannot control and delimit these readings . . . Its 'anonymity' is part of its very structure not just an unfortunate accident which befalls it; and in this sense to be an 'author'—the 'origin' of one's own meanings with 'authority' over them—is a myth.

Thus, not unlike the American tourist's companion, the academic community has for some time been pondering over the interpretive vacuum opened up by the so-called 'death of the author'.[11] By way of summary, we might say that communicative objectives though 'embodied' in particular instances of written discourse, are conceived and (re)defined within the parameters of specific inter-pretive communities (Fish 1980). Thus, any text is meaning-full only within particular frames of reference and the 'recovery' of that meaning can be viewed as constituting a community performance (Cooper and Woolgar 1994), in the sense that correct interpretation both constitutes membership and is instantiated by members. In view of the task undertaken in this chapter, this reminds us of the need to simultaneously attend to the co-production of content and context. Foucault's (1973: Appendix) rejoinder to Derrida's review of *Madness and Civilization* provides us with a lead by drawing attention to the points where, and the manner in which texts—in our case technological accounts—enter networks of social applications and relationships of instrumentality (Kallinikos 1994); and, one might add, how the social practices in which texts are implicated will rely upon and be reflected in the specific features and conventions defining their content (Bloomfield and Vurdubakis 1995*b*; 1994*b*). This is an issue we take up below.

As we have seen, the comic effect in the Macbeth murder mystery is derived from a misapplication of the reading conventions appropriate to the mystery story to a text outside that genre. As Fowler (1982: 359) has put it, the notion of genre is of value not so much in its role as a classificatory device, but rather in terms of the communicative function it performs: the recognition/imputation of genre supplies what he calls an interpretive 'horizon' for the construction and reception, writing and reading, of a text. The question then is what makes the readiness review recognizable as an authoritative text about technology? The answer we suggest lies not so much in its declared subject as in the particular way this subject is written 'about'.[12] That is to say, the practices and conventions of a particular writing genre and the 'reading positions' set up by them.

5.3   INTERMEDIATION AS NARRATIVE ORGANIZATION

In what sense can the readiness review text be considered as an intermediary? In other words, what is the intermediation 'work' carried out by the text; what are the specific intermediations performed/attempted by the review and how are they discharged? Given our PICT-related focus on organizations and IT, we will concentrate on two central interlinked intermediations: between the domain of technology and the (social) world of the organization; and between the two professional groups of management and clinicians, together with the rationalities (medical/administrative) these are held to embody. Thus in addition to constituting/negotiating the boundary between the 'technical' and the 'social' (Bloomfield and Vurdubakis 1994*a*), as an intermediary device the review must effect translations between the worlds of management and medicine, the commercial ethos of management consultancy and the public service orientation of the NHS.[13] We see these intermediations as translated in the text in terms of three self-imposed tasks: first, to assess the state of readiness of the hospital; secondly, given a positive evaluation, to provide a detailed plan of how implementation can be achieved; and thirdly, to address the practical issues of how specific pieces of equipment are to be 'matched' to specific organizational needs.

In terms of structure, the review falls into two halves followed by a series of detailed appendices. The first half sets out the background, gives a management summary, surveys the information requirements of doctors, and is followed by an assessment of the existing and planned IT systems at the hospital. The second half proposes a specific IT systems architecture for Resource Management and sets out planning details such as time-scales, the implementation team, and detailed costings of all the equipment (hardware, software, and communications infrastructure) and work involved. At the beginning of the review we have statements regarding the stark reality of tight health-care resources and the nature of relationships between doctors and managers; by the end we have a detailed list of technological artefacts (hardware and software), a costed specification. Within the confines of the review then, the organization (e.g. information requirements, the goals of service efficiency and effectiveness, and so on) is rendered or translated into the 'technical' (a list of equipment). Thus the initial problematic which authorizes the report (that is, how to interrelate the organization and IT) finds its symbolic resolution in its textual organization.

In what follows we address these issues through an examination of the narrative organization of the text. It is perhaps unusual to speak of narrative in association with an IT consultancy text.[14] In this connection, Myers (1990) can be seen as providing what we might call a minimal definition of narratives as 'the selection and sequencing of events so that they have a subject, they form a coherent whole with a beginning and end, and they have a meaning that is conveyed by the sequence as a whole'.[15] The readiness review accordingly identifies itself as constituting the starting-point of a six-stage sequence, the other five stages—which are set out in the review—being ordered as follows:

(2) prepare implementation plan;
(3) complete design of new system for the hospital;
(4) customize standard Manex system;
(5) carry out site preparation and installation;
(6) implementation of system.

The report is represented in other words as a sort of obligatory passage point, since without the completion and acceptance of the review no further work could be carried out. The review is therefore singularly important because it enables, sets out, and authorizes the later stages of the project.

We can map the discursive space occupied by the review in terms of a number of interrelated concepts which it deploys. These are a means by which it establishes its mode of reasoning. Here we will begin by listing five of them and then discuss how their key status is conveyed. The concepts are: patient care, Resource Management, dialogue, information needs/requirements, and information systems. These provide the means of organizing the text in terms of a logical and temporal sequence. The list is in a specific order representing the relative importance of the concepts both in terms of understanding the text—the work it has to do—and in respect of the particular moral order which is enacted or performed by the ordering inherent in the list.[16] Thus the most important item is that of patient care. The whole *raison d'être* of the initiative which the report addresses—the introduction of Resource Management—is centred on patient care. The care of patients is the ultimate end to which all actions must be seen to be subordinated. Put another way, at the end of the day, whatever decisions are taken they must be represented in terms of a net contribution to the further-ance of patient care. Next comes *Resource Management* itself. This is an initiative which aims to generate information about medical activity and costs and connect them together with a view to making decisions about the most efficient and effective allocation of resources in order to further patient care.

A related concept is the notion of dialogue. In this context dialogue be-tween doctors and managers reflects the inherent ambiguity which surrounds the decision-making subject of Resource Management.[17] That is, Resource Manage-ment has no well-defined subject who will receive the information generated by the new information system and manage accordingly. If no one group is to gain pre-eminence in matters of resource allocation then dialogue appears to fill the void. This brings us to the fourth concept: for a dialogue to take place about decisions regarding resource allocation there must be information which in turn presupposes that doctors and managers have information needs or information re-quirements. And lastly, to fulfil these needs one must then have information systems. In summary then, information systems are necessary to meet informa-tion needs in order that an informed dialogue can take place about the manage-ment of resources for the improvement of patient care.

5.4 EPISTEMOLOGICAL AND ONTOLOGICAL CONCERNS IN THE REVIEW

Following Latour (1992), we can see the foregoing concepts deployed in a range of narratives, texts, and subtexts—that are either enacted or negated by the readiness review. For example, as a review the text represents an investigation which seeks to apply a test of readiness on the part of the organization apropos of the implementation of Resource Management. However, this is not the only dramatic structure or narrative which can be discerned within it. To see why, let us consider some of the reasons which could be said to have brought the review about. There are in fact a variety of different accounts of the hospital's relation-ship with Resource Management, and Manex's IT product in particular. For example, our research indicated that the Regional Health Authority wanted to know if the proposed IT system would interface with the existing Regional Patient Administrative System; in other words, the hospital could be seen as a mere experimental site in the hands of the Region. On another tack, one hospital manager, who was charged with responsibility for the project, made an aside after one interview to the effect that the hospital would be gaining new resources through the Region and so if money was available why shouldn't they have it. Alternatively, Manex could be read as only interested in selling their product and services; or the managers could be seen as interested in a system to impose constraints on doctors. All of these represent factors which could be regarded by the report's 'implied readership' (Eco 1979) as non-legitimate (self-interested) reasons for instigating the readiness review because they would not be seen as directly contributing to the improvement of patient care. Though they were a common means of orientation among staff at the hospital they did not figure as such in that review: its task was to suitably translate if not suppress such concerns as we shall seek to demonstrate below. Indeed, to understand something of the tension between the different narratives, between the 'legitimate' and non-legitimate explanations for its writing, we must bear in mind the wider context within which the review was produced. This was characterized by a deepening sense of crisis in the NHS (despite rising expenditure), worries over the increasing privatization of services, and uneasy relationships between government, management, and medicine concerning control over the allocation of the resources available. Clinical freedom—the right of doctors to decide on the best treatment for their patients—was seen to be under attack and increasingly subject to the discourses of management and accounting.[18] In fact the medical profession had mounted a nationwide advertising campaign to highlight its disquiet at what they saw as the government's reluctance/refusal to listen to doctors.[19]

As indicated previously, documents are a crucial means through which social activities are organized and instrumented—technological practices not excepted. As Latour (1987: 226) puts it, '(m)any things can be done with this paper world that cannot be done with the world'. The ability to more or less freely (re)construct the 'world on paper' is however a mixed blessing. For this very ease may also be seen as a source of ontological insecurity capable of undermining the world so constructed, its authority as a reality account. This problem can be seen as a version of what Edwards *et al.* (1995) have termed the realist's dilemma, namely the inherently representational nature of any invocation of a pre-existing, unconstructed 'external' world. (In our case this would mean external to the report, that is not constructed by it: see Bloomfield and Vurdubakis (1997).) The potential precariousness of 'paper worlds' is demonstrated if we recall the standard realist complaints against social constructivism. For most realists the assertion that an object is socially constructed is tantamount to a claim that it is, by implication, arbitrary, akin to the rules of contract bridge or the length of women's skirts (Weinberg 1993: 149). Resolution of this dilemma has traditionally been sought in the discursive affirmation of some sort of necessary relation between object and linguistic construct. (Rhetorical questions of the kind 'Nothing in Nature Gives Rise to Accounts of Nature?' (Murphy 1994: 957) can be seen in this light.) Accounts should, it is implied, somehow be permeated by the properties of the object they describe. In this vein, Edwards *et al.* (1995) have described the habit of realists of thumping the furniture ('this is NOT a social construction') as a knock-down argument against relativism. This action constitutes the rhetorical introduction of bits of (physical) reality into ontological argument.

Viewed as a practical problem faced by the readiness review this translates into the task of displaying the shaping impact of a reality 'out there' upon its contents. In this respect the readiness review starts with a disadvantage in the sense that Manex had a system which they were interested in selling: on the one hand they had valuable expertise in IT, but on the other they represented private sector interests—the impure world of commerce. The text may thus be read as a misrepresentation, a sales pitch rather than as true knowledge uncompromised by commercial (self) interests.[20]

The review we might say, requires a willingness on the part of the reader(s) to suspend disbelief. To this end it must avoid those factors which would undermine both its own credibility as an objective inquiry and, it might be added, the legitimacy of the proposed implementation of Resource Management. Clearly certain readings are more readily made public—which brings in questions of power and authority. Of course the very fact that we are dealing with a review by a reputable firm of management consultants, and that it was indeed a factual account rather than, say, a work of fiction or an example of Manex's promotional material, lends credibility to the statements contained within it. However, this is by itself insufficient. In order to help secure its legitimate reading the text should also be seen as being authorized by the facts of the matter.[21] On the one hand this authorization represents the rhetorical subordination of the subjective (vested interests) to the objective—that is, there is an implicit commitment to relating reality 'as it is'. On the other it denies any putative contradiction between the interests of the organization (the inside) and those of the consultants (the outside); which in a climate of growing anxiety concerning a perceived creeping commercialization of the NHS was symbolically important. In the final analysis, the review already represents an introduction of 'external' commercial considerations and the only way that this can be construed as legitimate (rather than as pollution) is if it can be seen as in some way furthering 'patient care'. These effects are achieved to the extent that readers feel (or are) powerless to challenge the facts. Let us then proceed to examine more closely the resources utilized by the review in asserting its authority and thereby effecting the various translations constitutive of its task.

5.5 DIAGNOSIS: INSIDER AND OUTSIDE VIEWS COINCIDE

The review contains statements which purport to represent the facts on matters such as: the relationship between doctors and managers; the current state of the hospital's IT systems; the information requirements of doctors and managers; the relationship of the latter to the capacities and functional capabilities of the Manex system; and recommendations as to how the existing IT infrastructure could be augmented in order to enable the implementation of Resource Management. But as already indicated, in order to be perceived as legitimate, any facts stated within the review would have to avoid the implication that they merely masked Manex's desire to clinch another sale. In this connection the staff at the hospital (the pure inside) proved an important source of support and credibility.[22] Specifically, the review appeals to the numerous interviews of staff conducted by Manex—including some thirty doctors, managers, and IT specialists, indexed by name in one of the appendices to the review—as expert witnesses in their own diagnosis of the situation in the hospital:

Interviewes, in general, are of the view that [the hospital], in terms of the current dialogue between managers and clinicians, are well placed to introduce the [Manex system] and realise the potential benefits. On the basis of the enthusiasm and commitment demonstrated during the interviews, and with the general level of understanding shown, we concur with this view.

Manex's view of the situation in the hospital coincides with that of hospital staff;[23] in other words the judgement of the latter (as re-presented in the review) helps to authorize that of the former. The report is a construction by an openly interested actor (Manex) but through the deployment of such discursive moves it attempts to overcome its own construction. In Latour's (1992) terms we might say that the judgement is 'shifted out', delegated to another collection of actors (doctors and managers, and so on). This shifting out can also be seen in the invocation of the Regional Health Authority as an advocate of the proposed new IT system: 'Recognising the potential benefits to be gained from the [Manex system] implementation within Newtown, [the Regional Health Authority] now wish to establish the feasibility of introducing the system in other districts within the Region.'

In this context the support of the Region was doubly important: first in terms of delegating the decision about the need for the new IT system; and secondly because it controlled the financial resources available through the Department of Health. Furthermore, it is worth noting that the review makes rhetorical use of the hospital staff as witnesses to the reality of developments outside, including those at Newtown where the Manex system was originally developed: 'many clinicians and managers have kept themselves informed about developments at the Resource Management pilot sites and . . . [have made] . . . visits to Newtown and elsewhere.' In other words, 'many' doctors and managers have already seen the future and it works. They have seen the reality of how better patient care and improved resource allocation can be achieved through the use of IT.

We also find the assertion of expertise or a technical knowledge claim on the part of the management consultants:

Based on our experience of implementing [the Manex system] . . . and the findings of the [review] . . . we have concluded that [the hospital] is an appropriate site for the successful implementation of [the Manex system] and offers considerable potential to realise the benefits in terms of better Resource Management and improved patient care.

Thus, Manex have experience in certain technical matters beyond those of the hospital staff. The notion reinforced by these textual moves is that Manex and their review are merely the means (providing an IT system) to an end (improved patient care) which managers and clinicians have freely chosen and which has not been manipulated in any way by Manex.

Having thus discussed some of the ontological concerns of the readiness review let us now proceed to examine the processes of intermediation in more detail. We will do so by considering the narrative organization of the review reflected in the interrelationship between the five concepts referred to earlier.

5.6 PATIENT CARE

As indicated previously 'patient care' constitutes a key term representing the *raison d'être* not only of Resource Management—which is the information system's task to render operable—but also of the health service as a whole: 'the overriding aim of the [Manex system] is to provide clinicians with the information they need to manage clinical resources effectively in the cause of improving patient care.'

In a sense then, the concept of patient care can be thought of as a form of 'boundary object', something which inhabits 'different social worlds' (Bowker and Leigh Star 1991; Fujimura 1991)—in this case management and medicine. As a boundary object it has related but different meanings for doctors and managers with each professional group taking part in its construction and maintenance. The role and functions of a boundary object have been variously conceived within different analytical strategies. Atkinson and Parsons (1995: 18) for example argue that boundary objects 'are therefore objects of use by different occupational groups, specialisms and the like, and are used to articulate the work and the meanings of the respective groups'. However, we would wish to stress the need to not lose sight of the exercise of power which is inherent in all works of intermediation. In this sense 'boundary objects' become such by virtue of being (appropriated and) deployed within specialist language games. We can illustrate our use of the term by means of an analogy with the apostle Paul's strategy for persuading his Athenian audience on the merits of what in their eyes could appear as a mere cultural curiosity: the teachings of an obscure Jewish sect.

And they took hold of him and brought him to the Areopagus saying, 'May we know what this new teaching is which you present? For you bring some strange things to our ears; we wish to know therefore what these things mean.' . . . So Paul standing in the middle of the Areopagus said: 'Men of Athens, . . . as I passed along, and observed the objects of your worship, I found also an altar with this inscription, "To an unknown god." What therefore you worship as unknown this I proclaim to you'. (Acts 17: 19–24)

Paul's problem can perhaps be described as one of paradigm incommensurability. The unknown god is strategically deployed as an instance where the concerns of the two world-views meet: a boundary object. In this sense the altar to the 'unknown god' is rhetorically construed as the site of a self-acknowledged gap in Greek knowledge. With this move Pauline discourse is (self) defined as an obligatory passage point to full knowledge of the divine. It is however used in an attempt to induce a fundamental *break* with existing religious practice and not to merely 'supplement' the Athenians' state of knowledge.

We would therefore see the discussion of the concept of patient care in the readiness review as not unlike the deployment of the concept of the 'unknown god' in Paul's speech to the Areopagus. Just as the latter is a means through which Christianity is introduced in order to redefine the *weltanschauung* of the Athenians, so is the former employed to transform the work philosophy of clinicians. During an interview one of the senior management consultants from Manex (re)interpreted the notion of clinical freedom in the context of Resource Management by arguing that a given patient being seen by a consultant doctor was in reality the person currently at the head of a queue of people awaiting a consultation.[24] In this context, it was suggested, Resource Management enabled the greater care of all the patients in the queue including the individual patient presenting to the doctor at a fixed point in time. Thus, in the context of 'patient care' Resource Management does not simply involve a form of two-way translation or communication between management and medicine: inscribing medical activity into costs or, conversely, mapping available resources into different packages of clinical treatments and care. Rather, Resource Management can be seen as something which displaces or at least radically redefines the notion of clinical freedom: doctors will continue to make decisions about which, and how, patients are treated but such decisions are no longer merely 'clinical'—there are also decisions about resource allocation—and should therefore be made against an *informed* picture of available resources and the relative costs of treatment. As a boundary object then, patient care as mobilized by Resource Management constitutes a breach in the previously relatively closed world—as far as management were concerned—of medical practice and expertise.

5.7   RESOURCE MANAGEMENT

As indicated earlier, intermediaries can be seen to perform a dual role: they bring certain categories together but also keep them apart. While effecting translations between different categories, their identity must not be compromised.[25] Intermediaries must accordingly be understood as simultaneously performing the (related) 'labour of division' (Kallinikos 1994), of preventing those same elements from collapsing into one another and producing undifferentiated chaos. Resource Management is a potential site of conflict between clinical autonomy and management accounting. For the purposes of Resource Management, medicine and management must be brought together as must managers and IT, doctors and IT, doctors and managers, medical activity and costs, and so on. However, though medical activity can be seen in terms of costs it must not be reduced to them: Clinical practice must not degenerate into accounting. Similarly, the power and status of doctors must not be seen to be usurped by that of management. Accordingly, the review makes it clear that the whole purpose of Resource Management is to seek the betterment of patient care. 'The principal objective . . . is to introduce a new approach to resource management and to demonstrate whether or not this results in measurable improvements in patient care.' Moreover, while the review reaffirms this objective it also indexes support for the initiative from amongst the hospital staff: 'Based on our interviews with managers and clinicians within [the hospital], it is clear that there is considerable support for the aims and objectives of the Resource Management Initiative.'

Our own interviews at the hospital revealed quite some variation in doctors' awareness and attitude towards Resource Management. While some doctors voiced their own particular reservations, the varying degrees of acceptance and distrust among doctors was a topical trope amongst certain other staff. Similarly, the review also identifies a certain 'lack of awareness' among doctors. 'Our interviews, however, also identified a lack of detailed awareness by some clinicians about the objectives and strategies of Resource Management and the operation of the [Manex system].' Notably, this does not acknowledge hostility, scepticism, or a begrudging willingness to see how things work out. The problem is not conveyed in political terms, such as the struggle between managers and doctors *vis-à-vis* clinical freedom (Bloomfield and Coombs 1992), but is instead constituted as one of knowledge, as a deficit in awareness among 'some' clinicians within the hospital. None the less, this revelation may serve to indicate Manex's professional standards and independence in 'telling it like it is', which in turn bolsters rather than undermines their final conclusion. Moreover, that this problem is not seen as an insurmountable obstacle to implementation is to be discerned in the fact that a solution is ready to hand: 'We therefore recommend that seminars are arranged for clinicians to raise awareness of Resource Management generally, and to deal specifically with the issue of clinical review.' Interestingly, it is couched in terms designed to appeal to the particular status and norms of dialogue assumed to be prevalent among doctors as a professional community. Thus a deficit in awareness (lack of knowledge) can be eradicated through a dissemination of the missing knowledge in the appropriate social context. A seminar presupposes a meeting of equals in the sense that what differentiates the individuals concerned is a matter of diverging knowledge/expertise; a seminar is not meant to be a forum in which self-interests or power are manifest; the framing of a seminar is meant to allow all such aspects to be distanced in order to allow rational discussion. In contrast, one would not hold a seminar to decide on a fundamentally political matter such as the allocation of resources.

5.8 DIALOGUE: TRANSLATING BETWEEN MANAGEMENT AND MEDICINE

The review portrays a strong image of ongoing dialogue between doctors and managers.

Both groups are keen to follow the Resource Management approach in order to gain access to the scope, content and format of information needed to sustain and improve the dialogue on the best use of resources in patient care.

Managers emphasised a need to have an integrated and credible source of both activity and financial information. This is required to build upon the quality of dialogue that exists currently in [the hospital] between clinicians and managers.

Consultancy discourse has traditionally appealed to imagery of the rational organization as a unitary entity directed by an authoritative subject (management) (Bloomfield and Vurdubakis 1994*b*). In the case of the NHS inhabited by a variety of professional groupings, all with their own potentially conflicting goals and agendas (Bloomfield *et al.* 1992), the impossibility of such a direct appeal is in this sense a problem which the concept of dialogue aims to circumvent. In the context of the review, dialogue is a means of recovering the potential of unity and order out of the possibility of fragmentation and disorder. Thus the notion of dialogue is important because in narrative terms it does not elevate any one group at the expense of others. Though distinct professional groups,[26] doctors and managers are seen in cooperative discourse. Manex's IT system is not identified with the interests of one group rather than another. Indeed the review identifies the 'greatest benefit' of the new IT system as being an enhanced opportunity for a 'balanced dialogue' on the management of resources. Notably, this suppresses that reading of Resource Management which equates it with attempts at managerial control over doctors. Thus, improved management will better support medical activity but such activity will not be subordinated to (corrupted by) managerial imperatives. Indeed, although the national launch of Resource Management had been couched in terms which identified it as an initiative which would lead to information systems owned by doctors and nurses—in an attempt to signal a break from the previous Clinical Budgeting initiative—none the less significant numbers of doctors remained wary if not cynical about the motives behind it.

The review focuses on the dialogue between doctors and managers and reflects a commitment to its ongoing improvement. Intertwined here are claims about matters of epistemology and the future. That is to say, knowledge about 'the best use of resources in patient care' can be achieved through dialogue mediated by the information which the new IT system will make possible in an 'integrated and credible' way. As for the future, this in turn is portrayed as centred on dialogue over resource allocation. In fact, though the goal of instituting Resource Management was clearly stated, it was largely a step into the unknown: that is, no one could say with any certainty what the future of the hospital would be like in terms of organizational practice, the profile of treatments offered, or other consequences which Resource Management might give rise to. Against this uncertainty and lack of definition, the notion of dialogue takes on an enhanced importance and meaning, for whatever the future might bring it is presupposed that it will be subordinate to the rigour and legitimacy of (rational) debate. Amidst the vision of a changing landscape, dialogue thereby emerges as a kind of touchstone, an icon of permanence which none can resist because to oppose it would be to run the risk of being seen as self-interested or irrational and thus undermining patient care. Thus improved dialogue will drive the future rather than any partisan agenda.

5.9   INFORMATION REQUIREMENTS

'Information requirements' identify a need which is both anterior to and necessitating the introduction of the Manex system. The concept of information needs/requirements allows the review to outline a virtual presence in recording the details of a declared absence. If the hospital is ready, if it is in a position to bridge the gap between its existing organizational procedures and IT infrastructure, and the aims of Resource Management, then the information requirements identified during the review must be translatable within its terms. This is important because the representation of the information requirements of the staff, as revealed by the review, do not centre on a Resource Management system *per se* but, rather, the sorts of information they would like access to. If their perceived information needs can be seen to correspond to those addressed in the aims of Resource Management, and the design and functional capabilities of the Manex system in particular, then this lends yet further support to the assertion of *readiness*. Similarly, given that Resource Management called for information systems that were owned by doctors and nurses, and which could address both clinical and management information requirements, it is further necessary that the revealed needs of management and doctors be deemed compatible with each other.

The types of information requirements identified above are wholly consistent with the aims of Resource Management. Furthermore, the different information requirements stated by clinicians and managers at [the hospital] have consistent and complementary objectives. We therefore firmly believe that the benefits to [the hospital] of implementing [the Manex system] will be to secure better Resource Management with better patient care.

One of the key issues revealed by this extract is the assertion that the information requirements of doctors and managers are 'identified': it is presupposed that these people have information requirements and that these are capable of being recognized. In other words, information requirements are objectively given and pre-date the review. Indeed, the review goes on to assert: 'The system has been developed in conjunction with clinicians and in recognition that clinicians have been badly served in the past in terms of their information needs.'

Because of who clinicians are, that is their expert status, the review cannot be seen to undermine or in any way challenge their information requirements. On the contrary, the authority of the doctors again reinforces the authority of the review. The implication is that Resource Management and the new IT system are not Trojan horses (sources of contamination) to be foisted on the unwilling constituencies of either doctors or managers. On the contrary, they will enable the fulfilment of the expectations regarding information management which these groups *already* have. Purportedly then, the review is not arguing for a radical change as far as organizational practices are concerned. Rather it is reaffirming that which is already taking shape, addressing information needs which have been badly neglected in the past.

It is clear that the requirements analysis in the review constitutes a gloss on the (ontological) claim implied in the notion of identifiable pre-existing information needs that are brought to light. The interviews reported by the review, and further indexed by a list in an appendix, lend credence to the view that reality is reported as it is. This can only be the case if the methods employed are neutral—a matter of methodology—and can be trusted to lead to the production of valid knowledge—a matter of epistemology. Furthermore, the interview is an interesting technique because it too represents an intermediation: in this case between the world of the management consultant (the outsider) and the doctor (the insider). The discourses of information technology, commerce, and medicine can be brought together (and kept apart) in the institutionalized social setting of the interview which must reproduce the sovereign status of its subjects. This must be done both for the sake of the organizational *status quo* within the hospital, which in this case requires that the machiavellian interpretation of Resource Management must be denied, and the authorization of the report. More specifically, the interview is meant to objectively reveal what doctors need in terms of information. It is to be understood as simply documenting these requirements and not, for example, as a means whereby doctors are drawn into a *particular* understanding of Resource Management or *constituted* as users with information needs.

5.10   INFORMATION SYSTEMS

As we suggested earlier, the IT system enjoys what one might call a special relationship with Resource Management. Its role as depicted in the review is one centred on the improvements and furtherance of a 'balanced' dialogue between doctors and managers. A corollary of this is that IT must be neutral politically speaking (see Bloomfield 1995). Thus the review authorizes the introduction of the new IT system by subordinating it to the cause of dialogue between doctors and managers. The review represents the information requirements of hospital doctors and management and thereby portrays the IT system as fulfilling a pre-existing need. The narrative structure here is founded on the discovery of a state of readiness on the part of the hospital followed by the production of a detailed system architecture, specification, and implementation plan. The review presents Manex's own IT system as *the* solution which bridges the gap between the current state of affairs and the implementation of Resource Management. In displacing the tensions or politics (seen as) inherent in the relationship between management and medicine, the 'politics' of IT are also displaced. In other words, the presumed a-sociality of the 'technical' is deployed here as a resource.

As we have already seen in our discussions of patient care, Resource Management, dialogue, and information requirements, and so on, the review's standard rhetorical move is to attempt a harmonization of potential oppositions by (re)defining opposites as interdependent. The system therefore can be viewed as the material expression of such interdependencies.

However the technology—the system—is not presented as the sole solution to the problems of organization. Although the review identifies the benefits of the proposed IT system in terms of the efficient allocation and use of resources, it stresses the risks associated with implementation and sets out measures which may be enacted to avoid them: 'The costs of getting the implementation wrong are enormous and care must be taken to ensure that these are avoided and that benefits are maximised.' But in casting the spotlight on such risks the review underscores rather than undermines its authoritative status: its authors stand as bona-fide management consultants rather than as equipment purveyors (Bloomfield and Danieli 1995). The alternative reading which would depict Manex as merely seeking another sale is again thereby countered. The upshot is that a particular knowledge of IT is fostered; a failed implementation can be costly in more than just monetary terms; it can lead to: 'loss of service effectiveness, because information is unavailable, inaccurate or out of date'. In other words the purported virtues of IT—more effective organizations, greater access to information, more timely information, and so on—are mirrored by a set of corresponding vices. Moreover, it is not sufficient merely to pursue the former: for their negative counterparts have to be actively suppressed through adherence to an approach which is 'thorough and well organised'—namely, the five stages of the implementation plan which the review seeks to authorize and set in train.

Another feature of the review is the emphasis it places on the need for hospital staff to participate in all stages of the project (though it is worth recalling, not the actual writing of the review), from design through to implementation. In particular, it identifies a need to develop staff skills in using the new information system, with report generation using the specialist software incorporated in the information system seen as a key feature of implementation.

there will be a continuous requirement for two full time staff to assist in the training and support of users, particularly in terms of . . . report writing.

the real power of the system is in the facilities it provides for users to define their own reports.

This conveys the strong message that the development and use of IT is a necessarily active process on the part of the user organization. First, it has to be tailored to the specific organizational context: without staff involvement throughout the systems-development life cycle failure lies beckoning. Secondly, no matter how comprehensive and reliable the *data* on the systems's database may be, it cannot produce *information* automatically. Rather, users have to be trained how to produce reports detailing information appropriate to their particular requirements. In other words, the data gathered by the information system has to be structured through the report writing process in order to produce information. 'The . . . system is based on . . . relational database technology. As a result . . . [it] has sophisticated facilities for storing, organising and manipulating data to meet the reporting needs of a wide range of users.'

It is clear then that the system is not to be used for simply automating existing procedures. Though part of the hospital's paper trail of information management would be rendered in electronic form, new organizational practices centred on dialogue, decision-making, and planning *vis-à-vis* Resource Management are to be instituted. The system represents a technology to enable this change; it is to be delegated the task of data gathering and consolidation but decisions about resource allocation will be displaced to the medicine–management interface. Both doctors and managers are to remain the sovereign subjects of decision-making.

5.11   DISCUSSION

A number of recent studies of technology (for example, Cooper and Woolgar 1993; 1994; Woolgar 1991; Hill 1988) have argued that technological artefacts such as machines, could—and should—be 'read' as texts.[27] The analogy, it is argued, 'highlights the social contingency of the process of both designing (writing) and using (consuming, interpreting, reading) technology' (Cooper and Woolgar 1993: 3). In particular the aim is to show how '(t)he technology text makes available a particular reading which can be drawn upon by adequately configured users' (Cooper and Woolgar 1993: 3; see also Cooper and Woolgar 1994: 55–7). Software for example, 'is authored/designed, on the one hand, and read/interpreted/used, on the other', intermediaries being understood as interventions in this process (Cooper and Woolgar 1994: 55).

In terms of our concerns here, the notion of 'technologies as texts' has much to recommend it. Among other things it calls attention to the crucial dependence of supposedly asocial technological artefacts on social processes of interpretation.[28] Moreover, the Woolgar *et al.* thesis appears to fit neatly with our own emphasis on technological practices as 'grammatocentric' activities (Hoskin and Macve 1986). Since it might be argued that sophisticated technologies tend to be available only through the appropriate texts (such as manuals, guides, reports, and the like) they are thus 'read' as a matter of course: as we have tried to demonstrate through our analysis of the readiness review, 'reading' can be seen to describe a crucial aspect of the practical knowledge and use of such artefacts (Bloomfield and Vurdubakis, 1994*b*).

Why then resist stepping into the theoretical space of technology *as* text? To show that something more than academic hair-splitting is at stake it is necessary to review some of the sources of our disquiet. Critics of the extension of linguistically inspired metaphors to cover the domain of material objects have traditionally bemoaned the perceived subordination of 'object' qualities to symbolic properties. They thus protest at what they see as a wilful conflation of two distinct ontological orders—texts and machines, words and things (e.g. Sismondo 1993; O'Neill 1995). More subtly, it is argued that objects are thus rendered passive reflectors of social meaning.[29] Our own objection however is rather different: briefly, it is that the metaphorically asserted identity between reading/writing and other forms of practice obscures their specificity. For instance, although Woolgar and others do not elaborate the practice of reading, their references to it tend to be dominated by expressions like 'reading/interpretation', 'read/interpreted/used' (Cooper and Woolgar 1994: 56) suggesting that they see reading as a metaphor for (all?) interpretive practice. Nevertheless 'interpretation', however defined, is practised via a diverse array of socially and historically situated activities. We should therefore resist this premature subordination of all interpretative practice to reading. In addition, were reading and writing to be treated as umbrella concepts in the manner suggested by Woolgar *et al.* their specificities as social practices become harder to recover. A rather more precise specification of such activities is therefore required. We see the specificity of such activities (reading and writing in this instance) as being of definitive relevance to our argument in terms of (at least) two sets of issues.

Firstly, the practices and techniques of 'writing' (like those of, say, cooking, metal-working, winemaking, or wood-carving) must be seen as socio-historically specific activities for eliciting the perceived possibilities and limitations of a particular working medium. Consequently, as Green (1988: 24) points out, 'the methodological and substantive content of an art form, and what it means to be a practitioner there, will be shaped by a compositional medium as a point of departure and return'. Secondly, and following from the above, there is the question of any particular text's specific social location. As Foucault (1973)[30] has argued, documents enter social life as conductors, mediators, and exchange points within power–knowledge networks. Networks that—as Latour (1987, 1992), Green (1988; 1983), and Hoskin and Macve (1986) argue—pass as it were in and out of writing. In this sense, different types of text would constitute and occupy specifiable positions in such networks.[31] For analytical purposes, we might view the work performed by a report of the sort examined here, in terms of two inter-linked processes of translation (Bloomfield and Vurdubakis 1994*b*; 1995*b*):

(i) the (re)construction of people, objects, and events 'on paper'; that is, the creation of a textual reality where, for example, the facts of the matter can be set out, and what needs to be done can be authoritatively decided, with the confusion and ambiguity of contrasted versions (at least in principle) overcome. It is also the place where the world is re-ordered, objects and acts orchestrated and instrumented as the occasion demands;

(ii) a corresponding movement 'back to the world' in the form of informed/ knowledgeable action.

As we have seen, in our case the culmination of this 'move back' is a material artefact in the form of an information system. Thus in terms of the Woolgar *et al.* notion of 'technology as text' we understand particular texts as occupying specific positions in this process. Rather than being interchangeable, the terms reading/use, and so on represent concrete moments in the process of engagement with objects (Collins 1985). Accordingly, the readiness review can be seen as the site where specific translations of the organization—the hospital—and of the technology—the Manex system—are brought together and rendered compatible. In other words, organizational tasks and activities are translated in terms of the information system (information requirements and so on) and vice versa.

In our discussion of the readiness review, the concern to keep in focus both the particular strategies for attaining credibility and persuasion and the possible authorized and non-authorized readings of the text, was in part driven by the need to understand the social locations and interpretive communities within which they operate and which in turn indicate the specific work of intermediation that had to be carried out. In this sense alternative (deviant) readings would constitute 'mistranslations' which would subvert the orderly integrations the review aims to achieve on paper. For example, if the review were seen as little more than a sales pitch for the Manex system then there would be no *necessary* correspondence between what the organization needs and what the system can deliver. To speak of the processes of narrative construction (e.g. the investigation, identification of requirements, test of readiness, recommendations), and narrative suppression (e.g. the non-legitimate accounts of the role of Manex or the purpose of their system at the hospital) is to reinforce the importance of power/knowledge relations and the struggle between different actors to assert the 'truth' or 'reality' of things.

In this chapter we have been concerned with elucidating the processes of textual intermediation in the context of the development of IT systems in organizations. We have sought to highlight the specific characteristics of the practices of reading/writing through which knowledge and the use of technology is made available in a given genre, and how the work of intermediation serves to constitute as well as delimit the interpretations or meanings of technology that are publicly available in a given setting. Expressed differently, the meaning of an artefact for 'relevant social groups' (Pinch and Bijker 1987), or its identity (Callon 1986), must be considered in relation to the various discourses and social practices within which the artefact becomes an object. In general terms, we may assert that there is a form of reciprocal interdefinition at work in projects which envision the 'development' of IT in organizations. Paraphrasing Latour (1991) we might say that technology is (a particular version of) organization made durable. For example, an apparently mundane 'technical' *list* of equipment may be read as being simultaneously 'social' (the specific organization for particular purposes embodied in the list).

5.12 CONCLUSION

As indicated in the introduction to this volume, until relatively recently, most work on 'Organizations and Technology' had tended to be couched in dichotomous terms, treating technology as in some way 'other' than social—and vice versa (Bloomfield and Vurdubakis 1994*a*). Consequently much intellectual effort and academic ink were expended in attempts to better specify how the two 'come together'—this being already implicit in the very formulation 'IT and Organizations'. The conjunctive *and* represents in this sense a logic of addition. Our focus on the means and practices of intermediation can thus be seen as an attempt to explore how the conceptual space demarcated by this 'and' is filled. As we have argued with respect to intermediaries, it brings the two terms— 'Organizations' and 'Technology'—together while at the same time keeping them separate; thereby preventing the creation of undifferentiated chaos (in which for instance clinical decisions are made by accountants or technical decisions by the inexpert).[32] Thus the technical and the organizational, insiders and outsiders, medicine and accounting, must all be brought together and at same time kept separate so that the potential to pollute is contained. Such distinctions, we have suggested, function at the same time as discursive resources (Bloomfield and Vurdubakis 1994*a*, *b*) and are drawn upon in the accomplishment of intermediation. In this light the division of the technical from the social, the technology from the organization, is as much an accomplishment of the review as their ultimate reconciliation.

NOTES

1. Thus the term 'actant' is used to refer to all such entities which can be attributed with agency.
2. In order for an actor to secure or win the support of others (potential allies) it must in some way make itself indispensable to them by translating their interests; it must become an 'obligatory passage point' (Callon 1986). In one strategem to achieve this the actor may suggest that it shares a 'common' problem with putative allies: that is, it may draw an equivalence between its problem and the problems which preoccupy others. This is known as problematization. If the actor can convince the allies that it has the necessary skills, knowledge, or other resources to devise a solution to their 'common' problem then it may come to be seen as indispensable. It will have translated both the allies and their problem: that is, both become different or have

a new identity. The original problem is renegotiated while the allies become actors within a network defined by their common ownership of the translated problem.

3. For a critique of certain assumptions made in this work see Bloomfield and Vurdubakis (1995*a*).

4. The negotiation of the identities of the various actors inside and outside an actor-network—'interessement'—is an intrinsic part of network building. It is: 'the group of actions by which an entity . . . attempts to impose and stabilize the identity of the other actors it defines through its problematization' (Callon 1986: 207–8). In practical terms identities are negotiated through the deployment of various human and non-human intermediaries which thereby mediate the relationships between actors. Expressed another way, intermediaries are passed between actors, constituting the interactions between them. This can imply a distinction between actors who have agency and intermediaries which are seen as essentially passive (Law 1994: 70). However, it should be noted that attributions of agency versus passivity are context dependent, made for particular purposes (see Bloomfield and Vurdubakis 1995*a*).

5. Taking this as a starting-point we have employed the notion of the intermediary in order to explore intermediation as a social accomplishment in specific settings. For example, we have spent a great deal of time studying the work of management consultants specializing in IT. We regard such consultants as intermediaries who aim to speak for technology; they seek to provide expert advice on organizations/management *and* IT to their clients. In doing so they may deploy various discursive resources to depict a role as purveyors of truth or, at least, best practice and not, for example, as self-interested. That is, in speaking for technology, or organizations, they can appear as mere conduits: as intermediaries. In this connection they may choose to differentiate themselves from sellers of hardware and software (Bloomfield and Danieli 1995).

6. The focus on the production of documents as an integral part of practices of 'organizing' has of course been a long-held concern of ethnomethodology (Zimmerman 1969; Garfinkel 1974).

7. However this 'reality' may be defined.

8. A pseudonym.

9. Again, a fictitious name.

10. The American woman's reading of *Macbeth* appears of course highly eccentric. This is after all a comic tale. 'Competent' readers are not supposed to read Shakespeare as if it were Agatha Christie. Textual aids such as learned introductions or illuminating commentaries aim to produce the competent reader required by the text. However it is worth remembering that 'deviant' readings can also be institutionalized in a similar manner. The establishment of competing literary associations dedicated to proving that the works of Shakespeare were in fact pseudonymously authored by someone else—Christopher Marlowe, Francis Bacon, and Edward de Vere the Earl of Oxford, being the most popular candidates—may be cited in this context. A 'competent' reading from any of these viewpoints is one that yields the desired clues such as stylistic similarities with Marlowe, cryptic references to Bacon's work, and so on (Michell 1996).

11. See also the debate between Searle and Derrida over what constitutes an acceptable interpretation of Austin (Derrida 1977; Fish 1982).

12. A simple declaration to the effect that this is a 'true account' of this or that is clearly not enough. It is the concept of genre which allows the reader to distinguish, for

example, the 'fictional' story of Robinson Crusoe from the 'true' story of Alexander Selkirk.

13. A conflict which was seen as particularly acute at the time.

14. Except in so far as these include examples or case studies of the success or failure of IT in particular organizations (e.g. those analysed by O'Connor (1995)).

15. Also quoted in G. Cooper (1992).

16. All technologies can be considered to be inscribed with a particular moral order regarding their legitimate use (Akrich 1992).

17. For further discussion of the Resource Management Initiative see Chapter 6 of this volume.

18. Mannheim (1971) has distinguished between two kinds of challenge to reality accounts operative within social theorizing. In our terms these would constitute different (resistant or unauthorized) readings of the review. One is to question the moral character of the writer in order to show an intent to deceive and expose the account as a lie or misrepresentation. The other form of questioning aims to expose the account as an ideological construct. Thus one way of challenging the review's status as an authoritative account about technology would be to expose is as a sales pitch by Manex; the other would be to show it as permeated by an accounting 'mentality' and hence unreliable as an account of what really goes on.

19. 'What do you call a man who ignores medical advice?' ran the gist of one billboard advertisement, with 'Mr [Kenneth] Clark' (the encumbent secretary of state for health) being the answer.

20. If the recommendations of the review, and the discursive moves which frame them, were not appealing to staff at the hospital then such a reading might be publicly aired. Such a possibility is precisely what underscores the need to understand the work carried out by the review in attempting to prevent such occurrences. The discursive moves involved represent exercises of power, attempts to construct a particular understanding of Resource Management and institute it within organizational practice via the deployment of the Manex information system (Knights and Vurdubakis 1994).

21. In this connection we are following Latour's argument regarding Pasteur: 'Pasteur authorizes the yeast to authorize him to speak in its name . . . the text itself will be in the end authorized by the yeast, the real behavior of which will be said to underwrite the whole text.' (Latour 1992: 144.)

22. Thus Manex depend on their informants—the staff at the hospital. This of course is a common trope in fiction, as, for example, when Edgar Alan Poe (1982: 882) attributes the abrupt termination of his *Narrative of A. Gordon Pym* to the 'sudden and distressing death' of his informant which is 'already well known to the public through the medium of the daily press'.

23. Whose views were solicited but not actually involved in the writing of the report.

24. These were conducted by Brian Bloomfield and Ardha Danieli.

25. In fact, not only is the review an intermediary in this sense but so too is the proposed information system.

26. Distinct in terms of ethos rather than personnel; some doctors were already involved in management.

27. A metaphor adapted from (1970s) anthropology (Geertz 1973).

28. Even some of Woolgar's critics acknowledge the concept of 'technology as text' as an important contribution to the sociology of technology (Pinch 1993: 519).

29. In his critique of semiotics, for instance, Scruton (1979: 157–78) uses the case of

architecture's observance of its own conventions and sense of detail to reject the analogy with linguistic domains organized in terms of syntax and grammar.

30. And also Smith (1974); Green (1983); Hoskin and Macve (1986).

31. For example the specific position occupied by anatomical diagrams is illustrated by Hirschauer's (1991) study of surgical practice. Surgeons, he suggests, can be viewed as engaged in a process of 'making anatomy' in the sense of attempting to elicit a correspondence between opened-up body and anatomical diagram. The bloody tangled mess first revealed when the body is opened up is gradually rendered by the surgical team into the orderly, identifiable features of an anatomical map. For a similar study of veterinary surgery see Pinch *et al.* (1996).

32. 'A leading software specialist . . . Brian Warboys, professor of software engineering at Manchester University and consultant . . . said that clinical staff lacked the skills to make working systems and should leave it to Information Technology professionals. "One of the problems of people having their own computers is that they start to take the view that they can do it all themselves" . . . Dr David Patterson, a consultant physician and cardiologist at Bloomsbury and Islington Health authority, speaking at the same conference agreed . . . "We shouldn't meddle ourselves but should simply collaborate and co-operate with experts in the field".' *Health Service Journal*, 4 July 1991, p. 8.

REFERENCES

Akrich, M. (1992) 'The De-Scription of Technical Objects', in W. Bijker and J. Law (eds.), *Shaping Technology/Building Society* (Cambridge, Mass.: MIT Press), 205–24.

Atkinson, P., and Parsons, E. (1995) 'The Professional Construction of Family and Kinship in Medical Genetics', 4th Bath Quinquennial Science Studies Workshop on Humans, Animals, Machines, Bath, 27–31 July.

Bloomfield, B. P. (1995) 'Power, Machines, and Social Relations: Delegating to Information Technology in the UK National Health Service', *Organization*, 2(3): 489–518.

—— and Best, A. (1992) 'Management Consultants, Systems Development, Power and the Translation of Problems', *Sociological Review*, 40(3): 533–60.

—— and Coombs, R. (1992) 'Information Technology, Control and Power: The Centralisation and Decentralisation Debate Revisited', *Journal of Management Studies*, 29(4): 459–84.

—— —— Cooper, D. J. and Rea, D. (1992) 'Machines and Manoeuvres: Responsibility Accounting and the Construction of Hospital Information Systems', *Accounting, Management and Information Technology*, 2(4): 197–219.

—— and Danieli, A. (1995) 'The Role of Management Consultants in the Development of Information Technology: The Indissoluble Nature of Socio-Political and Technical Skills', *Journal of Management Studies*, 32(1): 23–46.

—— and Vurdubakis, T. (1994*a*) 'Boundary Disputes: Negotiating the Boundary between the Technical and the Social in the Development of IT Systems', *Information Technology and People*, 7(1): 9–24.

—— —— (1994*b*) 'Re-Presenting Technology: IT Consultancy Reports as Textual Reality Constructions', *Sociology*, 28(2): 455–77.

—— —— (1995*a*) 'The Outer Limits: Humans, Animals, Machines and Attributions of Agency', 4th Bath Quinquennial Science Studies Workshop on Humans, Animals, Machines, Bath, 27–31 July.

—— —— (1995*b*) 'Paper Worlds: A Note on the Role of Textual Analysis in Technology Research', *Technology Studies*, 2(2): 364–8.

—— —— (1997) 'Visions of Organization and Organizations of Vision: the Representational Practices of Information Systems Development', *Accounting, Organizations and Society*, 22, in press.

Bowker, G., and Leigh Star, S. (1991) 'Situations vs. Standards in Long-Term, Wide-Scale Decision-Making: The Case of the International Classification of Diseases', *Proceedings of the 24th Hawaiian International Conference on System Sciences*, Anaheim Calif. Vol. 4, 73–81.

Callon, M. (1986) 'Some Elements of a Sociology of Translation: Domestication of the Scallops and the Fishermen of St Brieuc Bay', in J. Law (ed.), *Power, Action and Belief* (London: Routledge & Kegan Paul), 196–233.

—— (1990) 'Techno-Economic Networks and Irreversibility', Conference on Firm Strategy and Technical Change: Microeconomics or Microsociology, Manchester School of Management, UMIST, 27–8 Sept.

Collins, H. (1985) *Changing Order: Replication and Induction in Scientific Practice* (London: Sage).

Colquhoun, A. (1981) *Essays in Architectural Criticism* (Cambridge, Mass.: Opposition Books).

Cooper, G. (1992) *Narrative Requirements and Dilemmas in the Construction of a Proposal*, Centre for Research on Innovation, Culture and Technology Discussion Paper No. 29, Brunel University.

—— and Woolgar, S. (1993) 'Software is Society made Malleable: The Importance of Conceptions of Audience in Software and Research Practice', CRICT Brunel University.

—— and Woolgar, S. (1994) 'Software Quality as Community Performance', in R. Mansell (ed.), *Information, Control and Technical Change* (London: A), 54–67.

Cooper, R. (1992) 'Formal Organization as Representation: Remote Control, Displacement and Abbreviation', in M. Reed and M. Hughes (eds.), *Rethinking Organization: New Directions in Organization Theory and Analysis* (London: Sage), 254–72.

Derrida, J. (1977) 'Limited Inc. abc', in J. Derrida *Glyph*, ii (Baltimore: Johns Hopkins University Press).

Eagleton, T. (1983) *Literary Theory: An Introduction* (Minneapolis: University of Minnesota Press).

Eco, U. (1979) *The Role of the Reader* (London: Hutchinson).

—— (1992) 'Overinterpreting Texts', in S. Collini (ed.), *Umberto Eco Interpretation and Overinterpretation* (Cambridge: Cambridge University Press).

Edwards, D., Ashmore, M., and Potter, J. (1995) 'Death and Furniture: The Rhetoric, Politics and Theology of Bottom Line Arguments Against Relativism', *History of The Human Sciences*, 8(2): 1–23.

Fish, S. (1980) *Is There a Text In This Class? The Authority of Interpretive Communities* (Cambridge, Mass.: Harvard University Press).

—— (1982) 'With the Compliments of the Author: Reflections on Austin and Derrida', *Critical Inquiry*, 8: 693–721.

Foucault, M. (1973) *Madness and Civilization* (London: Routledge).

Fowler, A. (1982) *Kinds of Literature: An Introduction to Theory of Genres and Modes* (London: Oxford University Press).

Fujimura, J. H. (1991) 'Crafting Science: Standardized Packages, Boundary Objects, and "Translation"', in A. Pickering (ed.), *Science as Practice and Culture* (Chicago: University of Chicago Press), 168–211.

Garfinkel, H. (1974) ' "Good" Organizational Reasons for "Bad" Clinical Records', in R. Turner (ed.), *Ethnomethodology* (Harmondsworth: Penguin).

Geertz, C. (1973) *The Interpretation of Cultures* (New York: Basic Books).

Gephart, R. P., and Pitter, R. (1995) 'Textual Analysis in Technology Research: An Investigation of the Management of Technology Risk', *Technology Studies*, 2(2): 325–56.

Gibbons, M., Limoges, C., Nowotny, H., Schwartzman, S., Scott, P., and Trow, M. (1994) *The New Production of Knowledge: The Dynamics of Science and Research in Contemporary Societies* (London: Sage).

Golding, W. (1995) *The Double Tongue* (London: Faber & Faber).

Green, B. (1983) *Knowing the Poor: A Case Study in Textual Reality Construction* (London: RKP).

—— (1988) *Literary Methods and Sociological Theory: Case Studies of Simmel and Weber* (Chicago: The University of Chicago Press).

Health Service Journal (1991) 'Software Guru Says "Leave IT to the Professionals"', 8.

Hill, S. (1988) *The Tragedy of Technology* (London: Pluto Press).

Hirschauer, S. (1991) 'The Manufacture of Bodies in Surgery', *Social Studies of Science*, 21(2): 279–319.

Hoskin, K., and Macve, R. (1986) 'Accounting and the Examination: A Genealogy of Disciplinary Power', *Accounting, Organizations and Society*, 11(2): 105–36.

Kallinikos, J. (1994) 'Predictable Worlds: On Writing, Rationality and Organization', Workshop on Writing, Rationality and Organization, 21–2 March, European Association for Advanced Studies on Management, Brussels.

Knights, D., and Vurdubakis, T. (1994) 'Foucault, Power, Resistance and All That', in J. M. Jermier, D. Knights and W. R. Nord (eds.) *Resistance and Power in Organizations* (London: Routledge), 167–98.

Latour, B. (1987) *Science in Action* (Milton Keynes: Open University Press).

—— (1988) 'A Relativist Account of Einstein's Relativity', *Social Studies of Science*, 18: 3–44.

—— (1991) 'Technology is Society made Durable', in J. Law (ed.), *A Sociology of Monsters: Essays on Power, Technology and Domination* (London: Routledge), 103–31.

—— (1992) 'Pasteur on Lactic Acid Yeast: A Partial Semiotic Analysis', *Configurations*, 1: 129–45.

Law, J. (1986) 'On the Methods of Long-Distance Control: Vessels, Navigation and the Portuguese Route to India', in J. Law (ed.), *Power, Action and Belief, Sociological Review Monograph 32* (London: Routledge).

—— (1994) *Organizing Modernity* (Oxford: Blackwell).

Mannheim, K. (1971) 'The Problem of the Sociology of Knowledge', in K. Wolff (ed.), *From Karl Mannheim* (Oxford: Oxford University Press).

Michell, J. (1996) *Who Wrote Shakespeare?* (London: Thames & Hudson).

Murphy, R. (1994) 'The Sociological Construction of Science Without Nature', *Sociology* 28(4): 957–74.

Myers, G. (1990) *Writing Biology: Texts in the Social Construction of Knowledge* (Madison: University of Winsconsin Press).

O'Connor, E. S. (1995) 'Paradoxes of Participation: Textual Analysis and Organizational Change', *Organization Studies*, 16(5): 769–803.

O'Neill, J. (1995) 'I've Gotta Use Words When I'm Talking To You', *History of the Human Sciences*, 8.

Pinch, T. (1993) 'Turn, Turn, and Turn Again: The Woolgar Formula', *Science, Technology and Human Values*, 14(4): 511–22.

—— and Bijker, W. (1987) 'The Social Construction of Facts and Artifacts', in W. Bijker, T. Hughes, and T. Pinch, *The Social Construction of Technological Symptoms* (Cambridge, Mass.: MIT Press), 17–50.

—— Collins, H., and Carbone, L. (1996) 'Inside Knowledge: Second Order Measures of Skill', *Sociological Review*, 44(2): 163–86.

Poe, E. A. (1982) *The Penguin Edgar Allan Poe* (Harmondsworth: Penguin).

Scruton, R. (1979) *The Aesthetics of Architecture* (London: Methuen).

Silverman, D. (1987) *Communication and Medical Practice* (London: Sage).

Sismondo, S. (1993) 'Some Social Constructions', *Social Studies of Science*, 23(3): 515–53.

Smith, D. (1974) 'The Social Construction of Documentary Reality', *Sociological Inquiry*, 44(4): 257–68.

—— (1978) ' "K is mentally Ill": The Anatomy of a Factual Account', *Sociology*, 12(1): 23–53.

Smith, D. (1984) 'Textually Mediated Social Organisation', *International Science Journal*, 34: 79–95.

Thurber, J. (1984) *The Thurber Carnival*, 1st edn. 1945) (Harmondsworth: Penguin).

Weinberg, S. (1993) *Dreams of A Final Theory* (London: Hutchinson Radius).

Woolgar, S. (1991) 'Configuring the User: The Case of Usability Trials', in J. Law (ed.), *A Sociology of Monsters: Essays on Power, Technology and Domination* (London: Routledge).

Zimmerman, D. (1969) 'Record-Keeping and the Intake Process in a Public Welfare Agency', in S. Wheeler (ed.), *On Record: Files and Dossiers in American Life* (New York: Russel Sage), 319–54.

6

Doctors as Managers: Constructing Systems and Users in the National Health Service

BRIAN P. BLOOMFIELD, ROD COOMBS, JENNY OWEN, AND PAUL TAYLOR

6.1 INTRODUCTION

One of the distinctive features of the application of IT in the field of management information systems is that the systems often have a reach and scope which goes across the whole organization and transcends functional boundaries. This has a number of interesting aspects. First, major organizational goals are brought into the frame of reference—existing goals being questioned, or new ones posited/formulated—in the process of designing and constructing such systems. Secondly, sub-units and specialisms within the organization are brought into engagement with each other, and frequently reassess their perceived interests in and through the construction process. Thirdly, the specific informational content of the systems constructed, and the organizational practices they inform, become powerful representations of organizational reality, providing a means of orientation through which that reality is thought about, argued, and renegotiated. Thus, systems development provides the means for questioning inherited organizational structures and practices (Bloomfield and Vurdubakis 1994b). This fact is usually understood by the participants during the development process and thereby shapes their engagement within.

Designing information systems then, is about much more than specifying the particular technological artefacts or equipment. It also about designing, inscribing (Akrich 1992), or configuring (Woolgar 1991) the users. During this process a specific representation of organizational reality—of its constitutive practices and the putative users of the technology—is the focus of ongoing negotiations and is subsequently embedded in the information system. This representation derives from a specific moral order to which the users are expected to conform, with deviations between expected (inscribed) behaviour and actual practice providing a space for admonition.[1] User resistance to computer systems is a commonplace feature of systems development (Hirschheim and Newman 1988);

but the struggle to bring on board and retain the commitment of users may be matched by that directed at the hardware and software components in the search for a functioning system. Thus a project to develop and implement an information system may be understood as an attempt to build a complex and heterogeneous set of alliances between people and machines, between human and non-human actors: an actor-network (Latour 1987).

In this chapter this theoretical perspective is employed to analyse a series of events in the design and development of information systems in the National Health Service.[2] The argument consists of three parts: in the following section we present a brief elaboration of the theoretical approach, signalling its linkages to related arguments in other chapters of the present volume. The subsequent section presents the analysis of the evolution of information systems in the NHS. The final section concludes by drawing out the implications for our understanding of the interactions between organizational change and the development of information systems.

6.2 THEORETICAL PERSPECTIVES

Two issues are addressed in this section. First, in order to develop the notion that building IT systems also involves 'constructing the users', it is necessary to clarify how we view the exercise of power. This relates both to the exercise of power in constructing the systems, and the subsequent exercise of power by virtue of the properties of the system when in use. The second issue to be addressed is the relationship between the machine or artefact that is usually seen as the *IT system*, and the organizational setting in which it is contextualized. An obvious question in this regard is whether these are clearly distinct, with causal links running from one to the other over time; or are they related in a more intimate way, with changes in one being possible only by virtue of simultaneous changes in the other? Rather than assuming that we are dealing with two separate, but related, ontological domains—technology and organization—we propose to regard 'them' as but 'phases of the same essential action' (Latour 1991: 129). Put another way, the presumed separation between technology and organization is a sense-making device, one of the means by which we orient ourselves in the world (Bloomfield and Vurdubakis 1994*b*). These two issues are now explored in turn.

6.2.1 Power

The perspectives on power which have been used in the PICT work at UMIST have been discussed more fully in Chapters 3 and 5 of this volume. For the purposes of this chapter it is useful to consider the differences between conventional or mainstream conceptualizations of power and IT and the approach adopted in our own research. Within the specialist literature on management information systems one finds a variety of ways of conceptualizing the interplay between information systems and organizational power. However, the overriding tendency within these approaches is to treat power as a commodity which exists in a zero-sum framework, with information systems as simply a new resource in the struggle for increments of power within that framework (Bloomfield and Coombs 1992). These 'zero-sum' views of power which envisage IT as a means of extending and enforcing control depend in part on an emphasis on its ability to gather information on organizational phenomena in one location and report it in another in a more intimate, detailed, and timely way than non-IT systems. In other words, they use a concept of control which focuses on the surveillance potential of IT. However, the distinctive property of information systems which we place in the foreground is their capacity to create rather than merely report organizational reality (Bloomfield 1991; Bloomfield, Coombs, and Owen 1994*a*). The implication of this constructivist dimension of the development and use of IT is that the nature of management control takes on a different modality as a result of attempts to implement it though the medium of IT.

In fact we argue that a disciplinary conception of power (inspired in part by the work of Foucault) provides a more substantive way of accounting for some of these special properties of information systems (Bloomfield and Coombs 1992; Coombs, Knights, and Willmott 1992). In this context discipline is understood principally in respect of the capacity of normalizing judgements *vis-à-vis* legitimate actions to create 'self-discipline' through the internalization of these norms by individuals. Unlike the notion of the 'electronic panopticon' in which normalizing judgements are seen to be facilitated through electronic surveillance (Sewell and Wilkinson 1992), the power examined here relies less on hierarchical control and more on the self-disciplinary effects of reconceptualizations of practice and professional identity. Thus the regulation of behaviour and action through normalizing judgement is also to be apprehended in relation to the other understanding of discipline—namely, a body of instruction or knowledge (Law 1986). Judgements have to be argued for in terms of theories, reasons, and causal narratives.

Accordingly, in this alternative approach to power and IT, emphasis is placed on the categories embedded in the information system and their ability to constitute reality for users. For example, a wealth of terms, both technical and 'everyday', are carefully defined and argued over in the design of information systems. When they are used in live systems to 'explain what is happening' in the organization they have the potential to 'colonize' the understanding of members and define the terms of debate. Examples of such terms are numerous; they may be so apparently benign and neutral as to hide their carefully constructed nature and their concomitant inclusions and exclusions. For instance, claims about the need for the efficient use of resources in order to maximize patient care are difficult to counter because to do so one runs the risk of being seen to oppose the well-being of patients; or at least putting one's own interest first (see: Chapter 5). Thus to the extent that the need for efficiency comes to represent a norm of behaviour against which individuals may be held accountable, it may serve to constitute self-disciplining behaviour on the part of those individuals whose conception of their role and how it should be discharged is being redefined. This shift is signalled by one senior doctor (a clinical director—see below) interviewed during our research:

I think I would be seen by my colleagues as too pro-management. It's because I believe that things have to be managed and you can't just go squandering things, they have to be used efficiently as well as effective.

Other terms which have come to characterize management reports in private sector organizations have also entered the lexicon of the National Health Service—for example, costs, overheads, customers, quality levels, performance, portfolio, assets, cross-subsidy, and so on. All of these terms have to be *defined* within the new management information systems, and organizational phenomena reconciled with them. The internalization of such constitutive concepts, and hence the willingness of an organization's members to construct their world and their work in terms of these concepts, is an instance of the exercise of disciplinary power. This modality of management control can of course be present without information systems, but it is now frequently achieved in greater measure than previously as a result of the ubiquitous character of IT and in particular its association with the definition of the modern organization.

It is important to emphasize that though this perspective on power focuses on the compliance of individuals with procedures of (self-) discipline it is not seen as an omnipotent or totalizing form of control. On the contrary, power is always subject to resistance (Knights and Vurdubakis 1994). In the case of the NHS, the introduction and application of concepts previously associated with commercial organizations have been the object of ongoing struggles and renegotiation. Moreover, while different professional groups within the NHS have agreed that they needed more information in order to carry out their jobs more efficiently and effectively, this does not mean that there has been ready agreement on exactly what kind of information would be useful. Put another way, what counts as information has been an ongoing focus of conflict, with doctors, for example, frequently complaining that IT systems tend not to deliver that which was promised, or that particular representations of medical activity (inscriptions) are more useful that others (Bloomfield 1991). Further, power is not to be seen purely in negative terms; it may also be considered as empowering—that is, power is productive of knowledge and thereby opens up a discursive space (by definition constrained) for action.

6.2.2 Artefacts and Organizational Arrangements

We now turn to the second theoretical topic mentioned at the beginning of this section—namely, the relationship between technology 'and' organization. The perspective adopted on this topic takes as a point of departure the actor-network approach. The idea of an actor-network centres on the notion that the development of technology involves the building of networks of alliances between various actors—including individuals and groups, as well as 'natural entities', forces, and machines. Of particular interest here are the related concepts of stability, irreversibility, and obligatory passage point. In a sense, network building is a search for stability which is enabled to the extent that changes set in train during network construction become irreversible (Callon 1990); either because it would be too costly to reverse them or, more subtly, because to do so becomes unthinkable. Further, if we imagine the construction of a network in terms of a journey, then is to be expected that there will be certain critical points that must be traversed: obligatory passage points. For example, in the nineteenth century ships wishing to sail from Great Britain to Australia had to round either the Cape of Good Hope or Cape Horn. Thus by analogy, each network will have certain necessary points or features that must be negotiated. For instance, in some cases these may centre on actors whose enrolment is a necessity. A successful negotiation—'translation' in Latour's (1987) terms—of obligatory passage points is therefore a condition of network stabilization.[3]

For our purposes then, we can regard organizational IT systems as heterogeneous combinations of artefacts (the hardware and software), inscriptions (including representations of organizational phenomena), and expectations about groups of users—all of these being political in nature. That is to say, the development and implementation of an IT system mediates, and is in turn mediated by, the political relationships and exercises of power within organizations. Thus, organizational politics is the medium of IT generation and use. Moreover, just as management may be regarded as a political process which actually strives to conceal its political nature, one of the (possibly intended) effects of the introduction of information systems in organizations is the displacement of politics (Bloomfield and Vurdubakis 1994a; Knights and Murray 1994). In terms of information systems this can be considered from two related angles: first, the way in which systems development is accompanied by a discourse which envisages particular pathways for the integrated development of IT and organizations—for example, representing new organizational arrangements (the political) as the inevitable outcome of the logic of technology, and so on; and secondly, in the very specificities of the 'techniques' which help constitute its practice.

Typically the fabrication of an information system involves information requirements analysis, operational requirements specifications (ORs), project management tools, and methods for benefits realization, and so on. However, these are not implemented in some purely technical way devoid of political (i.e. social) considerations.[4] Though frequently presented as techniques they are part and parcel of the exercise of power within the context of information systems development (Bloomfield 1992; Bloomfield and Vurdubakis 1997). In particular, the deployment of these techniques occurs against a background of contested understandings of 'the organization'. Even if no apparent conflict exists over the understanding of the organization—its mission and objectives—this does not signal the absence of politics but, rather, is evidence that power has already been exercised in the formation of the apparent consensus.

As suggested earlier, the power being exercised is relational and disciplinary; it does not derive from, much less map onto, the interests of the various groups within the organization. Indeed, interests are not stable variables which shape the IT: different actors invoke the notion of interests in order to argue and persuade each other about what should and should not be done, and in the process the interpretations about what is and is not in an actor's interest become renegotiated as the system is fabricated (see Callon and Latour 1982). This implies that interests should not be seen as the cause or explanation of systems development, but rather they should be read as the outcome!

As information systems are developed, it is frequently the case that users of such systems (including managers) must reconceptualize themselves and the nature of their work. For instance, information requirements analysis does not simply find out what information individuals really 'need' as if this was, as it were, already given and awaiting discovery or articulation: it constitutes them as *users* of information (Bloomfield 1992; Bloomfield and Vurdubakis 1994*b*; Bloomfield and Vurdubakis, this volume). Calling forth people with information 'needs', it serves to mediate changing conceptions of work and organization—the tasks and functions of organizational practice—and therefore of the subjects who are the focus of this disciplinary power.

Of course it is true to say that organizations often embark upon the development of IT with the deliberate aim of changing the nature of the organization. Change often goes hand in hand with moves to introduce new forms of management and organizational practice—together with the discourses through which they are articulated—such as management by objectives and quality. However, the changes envisaged, as well as those which eventually transpire, are not necessarily, if ever, equivalent. In particular, three arguments can be proposed to support this view. First, planned change—which we might regard as management control pursued at a more strategic level—is invariably supported by a calculative logic or rationality which cannot deliver that which it promises. For a good example of this point one need look no further than the vogue for treating organizational 'culture' as something to be managed and 'got right' (Willmott 1993). In adopting an instrumental view of culture as a key organizational 'variable' to be manipulated, such approaches do not reveal a sensitization towards issues of culture so much as its reification and appropriation within the business logic to which it is counterpoised. Secondly, there is the importance of the unintended consequences which flow both from the limitations of the logic of change and the 'forces' or possibilities unleashed by the development and implementation of information systems. Thirdly, and in terms of the argument here, most importantly, there is the fact that information and representations in general are always in principle contestable: they are deployed by different groups in attempts to persuade and coerce, but one cannot force someone to either agree or not disagree as to their meaning or significance. For instance, those groups who perceive themselves as likely to be the most affected by a new information system—for example, the users—and who are caught up in the processes of reconceptualization of themselves and the organization discussed earlier, can be expected to exhibit tension between compliance and resistance. Such tension will be mediated (amongst other things) by personal and professional identities.

In terms of actor-network approach, for a specific piece of technology to become 'stabilized' or 'black-boxed', it is necessary for a network to be constructed in which users are successfully enrolled. Conversely, the technology represents a *sine qua non* which stabilizes or buttresses the organizational structures and user self-images which are the other elements in the stabilized network. Translating this into the realm of information system development projects, it becomes clear that the final achievement of a functioning system with a given specification is not simply a 'technical' matter. It is only possible given the simultaneous achievement of the corresponding organizational forms and user enrolments which are part of its network. If these depart significantly from that which was expected, then the technology—both in terms of meaning (that is, its purpose for different actors) and content (the specific functional capacities of hardware/software)—will be different also. In the example we discuss next, taken from the NHS, a sustained attempt was made to build a particular piece of information technology, and to put in place specific images of the user which corresponded to that system. For some time, it seemed that this project would be successful, but eventually, the network did not stabilize in the form expected, and different outcomes emerged with respect to the understanding of the relationships between technology, organization, and users.

6.3   INFORMATION SYSTEMS AND THE 'CONVERSION' OF DOCTORS INTO MANAGERS

Our example is the long-standing political project of successive generations of politicians and NHS senior managers to persuade some hospital doctors to take on direct managerial responsibility for groups of doctors in particular specialisms, and for the financial and clinical aspects of their work.[5] We will call this endeavour the 'doctors as managers project'. This project began with the Griffiths Report of 1983 which asserted that the doctors should become regarded as the 'natural managers' (DHSS 1983: 19).[6] Thereafter, first through the Management Budgeting initiative and later through the Resource Management Initiative (RMI) (DHSS 1986), nationally organized projects were pursued in several hospitals to create the information systems which would, it was believed, enable some doctors to take on managerial responsibility for some aspects of the work of other doctors, and also for the financial outcomes of their clinical practice.[7] We will first present an outline of how this political project unfolded, up to the point at which it encountered serious obstacles which prevented a network from stabilizing and therefore compromised the final achievement of the original technical target for the information systems. We will then outline how a new configuration for a different network emerged and became (relatively) stabilized. In this second case, several of the elements in the network are similar, but the information systems are significantly different, and the doctors do not actually 'become' managers in the sense originally anticipated. Instead they become involved in some aspects of a management process, but alongside other actors, and with a different focus of attention than originally envisaged.

6.3.1 The 'Doctors as Managers' Project

During the life of the Resource Management Initiative in the NHS (from 1986 onwards), a great deal of effort was put into the development of information systems known as case-mix-management systems.[8] In brief, systems with this title are designed to generate cost-per-case information for every patient treated by attaching standard costs to each clinical procedure, drug, diagnostic test, bed-day, and so on, associated with their stay in hospital and aggregating them. Such a system is therefore essentially a large database and calculating engine, fed by many other systems in the hospital which capture data on patient events in departments such as radiology, pathology, or the operating theatre. In the original conception of case-mix systems, the purpose of collecting such data was not, in general, to charge a third party for the 'real' cost for an individual patient. Rather, the purpose was to construct average costs for particular groups of patients with particular diagnoses. This could then enable individual doctors, for example, to be the object of a 'case-mix' analysis. In such an exercise the 'mix' of patients treated by a doctor could be analysed for a particular period. Various factors could be considered. For example, the first thing might be to split the doctor's patient load into a number of diagnostic categories which have different average costs. This might reveal that two apparently similar general surgeons treat rather different proportions of patients with particular conditions. This could be the result of their preference, or of GP referral patterns, or some other factor. The next step might then be to take a particular diagnostic category and look within it at the variance in cost per case, length of stay, drug regime, and so on. Here, when looking at several doctors, different degrees of variance might be revealed. Such differences are often simple to explain. For example, one doctor may treat more severe patients because of seniority, a specific research interest, or for some other reason. On other occasions the different variances may not be easy to explain and so a further investigation may ensue which will eventually get beneath averages and look at specific (individual) clinical judgements about how to practice medicine on a particular patient with particular presenting symptoms.

It is crucial to stress that what we are witnessing here is not some mechanical exercise of power over doctors on the part of managers: for doctors too are significant players within the construction of the new systems. What is important in such a scenario can be usefully illuminated by the notion of disciplinary power which we employ in this volume. Imagine that the data from a case-mix system were to reveal that there were persistent differences in average costs between two consultants for the treatment of a particular condition. Imagine also that all 'justifiable' sources of difference were allowed for, and that what remained was a clear difference in clinical preference between the two doctors, such as an extra day of pre-operative admission, or a more complex drug regime. If the 'more expensive' doctor could not justify in *clinical* terms to his/ her professional peers that such extra costs were unavoidable, then he/she would experience a pressure to modify his/her treatment pattern to reflect the 'norm'. This pressure, though mediated through the peer group pressure of the medical profession, actually has a self-disciplining modality. The notion of proper medical practice is being reshaped in recognition of the norm of efficiency (value for money) which has become a pervasive notion in discourse in and about the NHS.

It is therefore clear that the development of the new case-mix information systems was accompanied by powerful processes of standardization; first in the area of coding medical procedures (in order that comparisons could be carried out, to ensure that comparable cases were brought into the analyses),[9] and secondly in the area of quality. But this had the potential to interact in an interesting way with the new institutional changes in the NHS which were introduced *after* the RMI initiative had already started 'rolling out' the purchase of case-mix systems to hospitals. These institutional changes involved a fundamental shift centred on the introduction of the internal market in the NHS. One of the features of this market is the emergence of contracting procedures in which purchasers (e.g. local health authorities) strike contracts with providers (e.g. a general hospital) for services (Department of Health 1989). These contracts not only define a particular target population but also stipulate details of care with a view to ensuring that quality as well as value for money is obtained. Thus in this new context case-mix systems (as well as other new systems which are emerging in the market for medical audit) could in principle be used both to monitor compliance with quality protocols and to highlight areas where modification is required. For example, a comparison of treatment outcomes across different surgeons might reveal that certain details of procedures should be changed and a new norm be agreed and adopted. On the one hand this could indicate an improvement in medical practice; on the other it implies a shift in the understanding of that practice and is thus another instance of disciplinary power.

However, there is a subtle difference between the two cases of disciplinary power discussed here. In the first case, the revelation of differences in resource usage between two doctors is the result of an internal process within the hospital, which is driven by generic efficiency imperatives. In the second case just discussed, the source of the pressure is more focused and immediate, because it derives from a specific external pressure in the form of the purchaser and the contract. Though the effects of such changes have yet to reverberate through the institutions of medical training, it would seem that the potential for a significant reconceptualization of doctors and of medical practice has been set in train. Commenting on the spread of business-oriented language and methods in the NHS, one business manager at a Trust hospital remarked:

It's actually increased, I was very reassured in a meeting yesterday when one of the consultants, who's not renowned for his grace and favour to the system, actually mentioned putting something in a business plan . . . business plans, business managers, contracting, ECRs [Extra Contractual Referrals], GP fund-holders. All those things have suddenly become regular and accepted rhetoric and the consultants are certainly using it, the nurse-managers are using it and even the ward staff.

In fact evidence of increased acceptance of at least some management-based resource allocation criteria amongst clinicians is particularly noticeable amongst the younger clinicians who may have the added advantage of being more computer literate and therefore amenable to using the information systems underpinning some of the recent reforms. As another business manager observed:

A lot of the older clinicians can't accept the charter standards and just say that they're not achievable. Whereas a lot of the younger ones can actually see that, like it or not, that is what is going to drive the health service in the future and they either play the game or else there's a chance that they'll go out of business basically.

Case-mix systems are clearly very complex in their operation and in their potential significance. The aspect of them we have emphasized is their ability to compare physician practice in new and more detailed ways than hitherto. That they are technologies which are socially constructed can hardly be doubted. But, what is equally interesting is that the construction of the systems has taken place in a process which is intertwined with, though still distinct from, the construction of a new organizational structure in hospitals, and without which the information system would lose much of its perceived significance. We now examine this phenomenon in more detail.

The new organizational form is the clinical directorate. Directorates are based on areas of medical specialty such as general surgery, orthopaedic surgery, geriatrics, obstetrics and gynaecology, and so on. Such areas have existed as professional peer bodies in hospitals for many years but have had little formal management function and no formal financial responsibilities in respect of the monies allocated to hospital units. However, in recent years, they have been established as formal elements in the structure of many hospitals.[10] They have clinical directors who are (usually) senior doctors, who hold budgets for their directorate and are responsible to the hospital for the performance of the directorate against planned workload and budget targets. The directors have time off from clinical work to engage in management, and are usually supported by a full-time 'business' or 'service' manager, and by a nurse-manager. Increasingly, directorates are seen as the 'natural' layer of management to receive the comparative information which comes from many of the hospital information systems, including the case-mix system. Furthermore, they are seen as the appropriate layer to act upon the information. It is this layer where issues of contracting, quality of treatment (protocols and standards), outcomes, and business planning are beginning to be devolved.

Interestingly, at the outset no one knew exactly what these people should do; the roles of director, business manager, and nurse manager were created and filled by people who then had to work out the respective job description which went with them.

We very quickly realized that nobody knew what they wanted of us, nobody at all. What we wanted from it we could dictate, because there was no one who had any more information about being a business manager than we had. (Business Manager)

One of the important upshots of this settling-in period has been in the sorts of information and reports which business and nurse-managers have begun to request from the case-mix systems. The specificities of the requests from directorates depend on a complex series of issues including the relationships between them and the corporate centre of hospitals, the historical role and strength of the information department, the presence or absence of independent moves to medical audit through the adoption of other information systems, and so on. In other words, variations in the development of directorates within particular sites have had important implications for the creation and ongoing operation and maintenance (i.e. in the sense of enhancement and upgrade) of case-mix systems. Thus the information demands placed on case-mix systems have been evolving and changing rapidly as a result of the evolving character of clinical directorates, the emerging job roles of the members of the management team, and the divergent ways in which the machinations of the internal market and contracting have exerted pressures on those seeking to provide services to purchasers.

It is important for our argument in this chapter to note that the case-mix information system and the clinical directorate are ideas with quite separate origins, but in practice have been progressively brought into very close engagement with each other by various groups and individuals involved in the reform of the NHS.[11] Over a period of six years we have documented the ebb and flow of arguments within the NHS concerning how these concepts should be understood; how they relate to each other; whether one should be in place before the other; how they reinforce or frustrate each other, and so on (Bloomfield, Coombs, Cooper, and Rea 1992). The point is not to say which arguments prevailed at which time, but to point out that each concept can be usefully understood as the object of an attempt to establish a network around it and to stabilize that network. One concept is construed as a technical system, the other an organizational arrangement; yet the two networks overlap to a considerable extent, and, during most of the period of the Resource Management Initiative, the stabilization of each was seen to be dependent on the other. Hence we can say that the social construction of the information systems and the organization in which it was to be used were concurrent activities. The development of the information system was seen to depend on organization—including the reconceptualization which began to take place amongst the intended users (of the system), the formation and management of a project team, and so on. Similarly the construction and operation of the new organizational structure was seen to depend on information and the specific systems which would make it available. In other words, hospitals sought an integration of IT and organization.

6.3.2 An Unstable Network: The Emergence of a New Configuration[12]

We have seen in the previous section that the RMI had a number of key elements mixed up in a rather imprecise recipe. These included: the idea of making the doctors take responsibility for managing resources; the notion of the clinical directorate as one organizational structure to facilitate that; and the idea of a case-mix information system (or something like it) as the information tool which would be the 'lens' through which a 'doctor-manager' could make visible those areas where clinical practice and resource utilization overlap, and then use that visibility as the point of entry for management interventions to improve resource utilization.

Consequently, for some time, Resource Management implementation sites (such as those we have studied) proceeded through Resource Management (RM) on two fronts: purchasing or building case-mix information systems, and setting up clinical directorates. The precise phasing and interpretation of these two tasks varied significantly between sites, but there was broad agreement that these were key ingredients, and indeed Regional Health Authorities could 'police' some degree of compliance by virtue of holding the purse strings for the RM project monies and the purchase of IT systems.

However, for a variety of reasons, in most sites clinical directorates usually became established as functioning entities at some level of day-to-day practice well before the case-mix information systems got to the point of being a functioning reality (if indeed they ever did). The main reason for this is that the re-designation of organizational responsibilities is something which can be put in place fairly quickly provided that the individuals concerned are compliant. This was not always straightforward, but on the whole was achieved fairly quickly. By contrast, the designing and building of hospital-wide information systems, and then their installation, commissioning, testing, and bringing up to operational levels of readiness, was a demanding technical and management task plagued by a number of persistent problems. Development and implementation was typically planned to take around two years but usually took much longer than that.

This dislocation in time between the stabilization of the organizational structure and the stabilization of the information systems was a phenomenon with contradictory effects. On the positive side, it was perceived by some RM sites as an opportunity for the directorates to establish a *modus operandi* and clarify the information requirements which they wished to place on the case-mix systems. Indeed, the lack of clarity surrounding the detailed information requirements of doctors was a common source of problems within Resource Management project teams. On the negative side, others found directorates to be fundamentally unable to discharge their functions if they were not provided with the information regarded as necessary to underpin management decisions. Frequently then, as the clinical directorates began to function, they experienced a lot of difficulty working out just what they were supposed to achieve and how they were to function. As indicated earlier, rather than having a blueprint available, clinical directors, business managers, nurse-managers, and senior Trust or unit managers, struggled to define their roles, their responsibilities, their reporting lines, their information needs, their targets for performance, and so on.

However, as time passed, some issues began to clarify in the collective awareness of just 'what a clinical directorate is' and 'what it is for'. In order to present this emerging consensus about clinical directorates it is useful to look in a little more detail at their features. Clinical directorates are, in a sense, 'natural' groupings of clinical activity which have a specificity with respect to the other 'natural' groups in the hospital.[13] This specificity can be seen with respect to (at least) the following items:

the processes used   (diagnostic and therapeutic)
the resources used   (specialized staff, equipment, drugs)
the 'products'   (specific treatments)
the 'markets'   (patient types, and (latterly) purchasers)

If the RMI had proceeded according to the original expectations, much of the use made of case-mix IS, and the consequent activity of clinical directors, would have been expected to have focused on the resources and the processes from the above four items. For example, comparisons of doctor's clinical activities and resource utilization were expected to be easily available. However, things did not turn out like that. We have already hinted that the locus of influence on doctors' self-disciplining behaviour began to shift from purely internal pressures to pressures arising from external contracts. We have also noted that the technical construction of case-mix information systems (which were required for detailed internal doctor comparisons to be possible) proved to take longer than anticipated, and in some cases failed altogether. These two factors combined fundamentally to destabilize the emerging network which was associated with the 'doctors-as-managers' project.

This destabilization then, has been caused by two major phenomena. The first of these was the sheer 'technical' inadequacy of many of the attempts to implement the objective of a case-mix management system in a functioning IT form.[14] An example of this failure at one site is captured in the comments of a clinical director:

I personally found case-mix to be completely inappropriate to the information gathering I wanted. I was trained in case-mix, I've got the book on case-mix, and I've got the personal number, and I've never used it and my manager's got out of it as well. I'm not even sure what it's achieved.

The second factor was the arrival of the far-reaching NHS reforms and in particular the market mechanisms. This second factor has meant that the dominant issue on the agenda of the clinical directorates has been contracting with Health Authorities and with GP fund holders, contract-monitoring, and the issue of scope and 'product-mix' which clinical directorates face as a result of the new environment. Consequently, instead of worrying about processes and resources, clinical directors began to spend rather more time worrying about products and markets. As another clinical director expressed the matter: 'The complexity of the purchaser-provider split soaks up so much energy'. This shift had dramatic implications for the perceived information system requirements. Case-mix *per se* became less of a priority, and contract monitoring became the IT need of the hour (Bloomfield 1995). In some cases case-mix systems were adapted to contract-monitoring with little or no direct involvement on the part of doctors. Of course, to some extent, this meant that some case-mix systems were hastily respecified by the firms which designed them and were re-marketed as being capable of contract monitoring. But it has also meant that in some cases case-mix systems have been effectively shelved, and contract-monitoring data has been generated by alternative information systems strategies: for example, by using upgraded Patient Administration Systems to transfer data into various types of packaged database management tools.

In fact the revision of ideas about IT platforms and their suitability to provide the various types of information-systems functionality which hospitals might need has been even more radical than is suggested by this analysis. This is true both at individual hospital level and at national level. At local level some hospitals have backed away from purchasing top-down information system solutions (such as case-mix) and then back-filling with the necessary departmental feeder systems to provide required data for the management information systems to process. Instead they are strengthening operational systems such as ward-ordering and results-reporting systems, replacing or upgrading PAS systems, and then using relatively cheap and flexible software packages for data analysis and report-writing. At the national level we have seen a similar trend with the launch in 1992 of the *NHS Information Management & Technology Strategy* (NHS Information Management Group 1993). This places a heavy emphasis on such 'bottom-up' approaches, and hardly mentions the Resource Management Initiative, despite the fact that it was the *de facto* leading edge of NHS IT strategy for several years (Bloomfield *et al.* 1994*b*).

Summarizing the 'story-line' so far then, we have a picture in which the key organizational change which was envisaged at the start of the story—the clinical directorate—has in fact begun to take root and establish itself, although still with many uncertainties and ambiguities. Furthermore, it is clear that this has had real consequences for the perceptions and values of some of the doctors who have become more involved in management. But these changes have *not* been the result of case-mix information system providing information for senior doctors to conduct intra-directorate examinations of relative performance with respect to care patterns and resource usage. Rather it has been the result of an external threat to the actual volumes of available work, and sometimes even the viability, of any given directorate. This external threat is, of course, the possibility that purchasers will change their contract requirements and go elsewhere for some of their case-load. This explains why the information spotlight has shifted to, in the language used above, the 'products' and 'markets' of the directorates rather than the processes and resources. This puts many hospitals in the position of having to re-examine information needs. A common result has been that hospitals have stopped letting their information systems agenda be written for them by the succession of national initiatives which create opportunities to get ear-marked money for this or that information system. Instead they have typically taken more direct ownership of the information systems problem, and strengthened the managerial and financial resources they allocate to it. They have also frequently adopted a more incremental approach of developing systems to enhance operational clinical activities on the wards, rather than emphasizing management information and control systems.

6.3.3   A New Network

From the start of RMI until around mid-1994 there was a sustained attempt to stabilize a network along the lines described above. That is to say, there were significant actors trying to stabilize case-mix information systems and seeing clinical directorates as an important integrating lever with which to do that. In order for the network to stabilize, the case-mix systems had to work, the clinical directorate had to exist as a unit of management control, and the doctors had to construe one of their primary tasks as using case-mix information to tighten the standardization of resource consumption patterns in their directorate. This was the doctor-as-managers project.

However, this network failed to stabilize owing to the protracted, and sometimes insurmountable, difficulties of developing and implementing working case-mix information systems and because of the intervention of other actors concerned with the market reforms. This resulted in the newly emerging clinical directorates shifting their attention to different information systems needs associated with contract monitoring. Thus we can say that a sustained attempt was made to stabilize the particular technical artefact of case-mix information systems, but that it failed, and that a rival set of IT artefacts (which in fact deliver some of the same functionality) are now in the process of being stabilized in their stead. These rival artefacts are the ones identified above, which draw data from enhanced PAS systems and produce contract-monitoring reports. These artefacts, it seems, are proving more effective in helping to stabilize clinical directorates!

Furthermore, the new network which is in the process of being stabilized now puts the doctors in a slightly different role than originally envisaged in the doctors-as-managers project. Their managerial activity is now less directed at the standardization of the practice of their peers, and more directed at the securing of an adequate and sustainable work-flow through management of the contractual position. This is a task they do not do alone, but rather in collaboration with the business manager serving their directorate, and with the 'corporate' layer of management at the hospital Trust level, which acts as the main point of nego-tiation with purchasers. It is therefore much more accurate to say that we have arrived at a situation of doctors *involved* in management, but not as full-blown managers. The new network therefore has very similar elements to the original one (doctors, IT systems, management roles, and clinical directorates), but their configuration, meaning, and interpretation are significantly different. In the case of the IT, the actual technical hardware and software are quite different, and often supplied by different companies. Indeed, as one senior information man-ager at a Trust hospital remarked, case-mix systems were now regarded as 'old technology'. As such, the intended use and users of these systems are different and so we can say that the doctors are now being configured in a different way according to a different script. These differences are represented in Figures 6.1 and 6.2, each bearing the key elements of IT, clinical directorates, doctors, and management; with the second including the additional role of business manager. In the first, IT is understood as case-mix; clinical directorates are organizations of peer groups; doctors are portrayed as managers; and management is envis-aged as management of other doctors (standardization) and the promotion of self-discipline aimed at efficiency. While in the second, IT enables the machina-tions and monitoring of contracts in the internal market; directorates are centres of accountability somewhat analogous to business units; doctors are *involved* in management; and management is seen as stewardship of the directorate, includ-ing the protection of its boundaries and resources.

It is still possible that in the much longer term, some evolution may take place which moves back towards the direction of the earlier doctors-as-managers project. The information systems being developed within the 'new network' situation do not provide data solely on contract-related issues and zero data on efficiency/ care pattern/resource consumption aspects of individual doctors. On the con-trary, some data of the latter type is available and is beginning to be used, but only in a small-scale manner. It is important not to erect too sharp a boundary line between the functionality of the case-mix systems that are now in various stages of use/disuse in NHS hospitals, and the functionality of the looser assem-blies of systems which other hospitals are using to generate various types of in-formation in a more *ad hoc* manner. In principle therefore, important elements of the organizational vision originally embedded in early case-mix systems, are still latent in the management reports generated by other means in information-systems departments. It follows then, that the disciplining potential of these visions may still be potent in the clinical practice of those doctors who are engaged with management issues in clinical directorates.

An interesting aspect of the 'new network' concerns the theoretical inter-pretation of the role of the business managers. These individuals occupy a new job position which was created along with clinical directorates. They tend to be

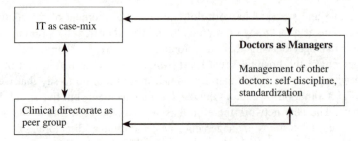

Fig. 6.1. The 'intended' network: 'doctors as managers'

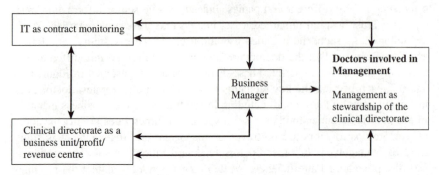

Fig. 6.2. The 'realized' network: 'doctors in management'

individuals who have come from other occupational backgrounds in the NHS (such as nursing, radiography, accounting, general management, and so on), but they are not doctors. They typically take on more of the day-to-day management activity than the actual doctor who bears the title clinical director. In particular they are the 'gatekeepers' for most of the information and reports which come out of the IT systems, and the first point of contact between the directorate and the corporate hospital management. How do these individuals fit in the new picture?

We have analysed the intersection of two related but distinct projects. One was concerned with clinical directorates and their stabilization; the other was concerned with case-mix, and subsequently with successors to case-mix, as information-systems artefacts which create informational visions of organizational reality with specific disciplining properties. The argument has been about how these projects, and the overlapping networks through which they have developed, have been mutually dependent on each other for their success. We can now see that the role of the business manager can be interpreted as an obligatory passage point between the two. These individuals occupy a position in which their interests have been constituted in such a way that they seek to stabilize both the clinical directorate and the information-systems artefacts which provide information on all the key management parameters of 'products', 'markets', processes, and resources. Business managers' use of IT reinforces the disciplinary power of the reforms in the NHS and this marks a degree of irreversibility in the changes taking place to the extent that alternative modes of behaviour become increasingly difficult to countenance. However, such constraints do not just apply to the clinicians, for business managers too are also subject to this power:

When I first started it was just a big blob of a block contract, whereas now I have to deliver contracts by purchaser, by consultant, by specialty within a twelve-month wait and there are all those patient charter issues that really cram in the role of everybody in here, the clinicians right the way through. They make everybody much more focused on what we're doing. *It's no longer good enough to do your best, unless your best is conforming to all the standards that you've been set.* (emphasis added)

Moreover, the double-edged nature of the constraints business managers facilitate also applies to the strategies they employ to enact them. In particular business managers feel bound by the information with which they seek to influence clinicians' behaviour—to the extent that it becomes difficult to imagine life without it:

People said to me, 'Why do you want that information?', but now we have it, it's very good, but it was stressful trying to get it, and *now we've got it, no one can imagine that we didn't have it in the first place.* (Business manager, emphasis added)

Thus there has been a fundamental shift within the NHS of attitudes towards information and its availability; this is indicative of what promises to be an irreversible trend.

Business managers' occupancy of their role is a key reason why it has not been possible, or even necessary, for doctors to become fully engaged as *the* managers, as was envisaged in the original project. It is to some extent the presence of the business manager role which permits the doctor's role to be reinterpreted as merely *involved* in management.

Whatever else you say, business managers, or managers and doctors can only get so close, because they each have different priorities. A doctor's priorities are a good health outcome, patient satisfaction, not hang the expense, because a good manager will worry about the money. The manager's particular motivation is the balancing of the books at the end of the day and as long as each understands that, they'll work well together. (Clinical Director)

Another clinical director described the situation in the following terms: 'the analogy that we draw is that I'm like the chairman of the board and the business manager is very much like the managing director'. The division being made here is between the clinical director's role as a strategic planner and the business manager's concentration upon detailed operational issues (see also Mole and Dawson 1993). However, business managers see themselves as having a wider strategy-producing role.

I actually spend quite a lot of time doing the strategy for general medical service because nobody else was doing it. There's delegation of operational responsibility, I usually get the Nurse Manager to do that . . . We had a conversation on contracting issues and the Clinical Director was in the room and there was some information that could only be made available to Clinical Directors and yet the appropriate Directors from the management team spent all the time looking at the Service Managers. They were the sort of real person who would actually get things done if we wanted anything doing. (Business Manager)

Thus the business managers are often keen to demarcate between senior clinicians involved in management and professional managers who get things done.

6.4 DISCUSSION

We have shown how a highly resourced and carefully planned attempt to build a very specific piece of information technology became the subject of a very unplanned process of re-targeting. This 'deviation' in the process of innovation cannot be explained solely by recourse to mere 'technical' factors. Nor can it be explained by reference to the supposed effects of some powerful social forces which were 'always there' but somehow mysteriously overlooked. Instead, we must consider the processes inherent in the building of heterogeneous networks, and in particular the question of stabilization (or the failure of stabilization). Networks do not magically self-stabilize. Moreover, any degree of stabilization that occurs is always open (in principle) to some later destabilization. Thus the broad endeavour of trying to manoeuvre doctors into accepting managerial responsibility for the resource implications of clinical practice was, at one time, expressed as an attempt to build case-mix IT systems. However, for a variety of reasons (as discussed earlier) that network did not stabilize. For the moment, a new network appears to be stabilizing around the machinations of contracting within the operation of the internal market, and this involves different information technology, and quite different arrangements for the conduct of management activity.[15] The original doctors-as-managers project presupposed a certain level of 'shop-floor' IT which doctors could use to change their clinical practice and from which inter-doctor comparisons could be derived. Suitable information systems proved to be highly elusive, but as the role of business manager developed—in conjunction with the greater emphasis being placed upon contracting and targeting information—IT systems came to be used predominantly in the activities of the managers filling this role. In turn this mediated the emergence of the doctors-involved-in-management project.

In terms of the overall theme of this volume, this analysis of the shift from the original project of doctors as managers, to the revised and more limited one of doctors involved in management, emphasizes the importance of adopting a theoretical approach that recognizes the lack of ontological separation that exists between technology and organization. In the mutation of one project into the other, and the constitutive changes in the emerging heterogeneous network of alliances and artefacts, the NHS organizational form of the clinical directorate itself can be viewed as a technology—one which mediates between clinical practices and contractual obligations. For just as case-mix systems and, latterly, contracting information systems, are inscribed with particular assumptions regarding users (and the organizations of which they are members), so too clinical directorates presuppose and enact particular technology-dependent practices of decision-making and information management. Thus in Latour's (1993) terms, clinical directorates, and organizations more generally, can be regarded as examples of 'hybrids' or 'quasi-objects', simultaneously 'technical' and 'social'.

For the personnel involved in the developments described in this chapter, the assumed relationship between IT and organization has been both a means of making sense of the developments around them, and a symbolic and discursive resource by which those changes have been prosecuted. In some situations actors would argue IT as merely a means to organizational goals and certainly not an end in itself. In others IT and organization would be regarded as interdependent in so far as the successful implementation and proper use of IT required organization (for example, in the form of training). These formulations of the relationship would often be used as rhetorical devices to assure both themselves and others that the changes under way in the NHS were not being dictated by technology; that in the end everything was being done in order to improve patient care (see Chapter 5). However, on other occasions they would argue for particular organizational or technical goals as if the terms were in fact quite separate. In other words, in practice the actors involved manifested a range of ontological positions as regards IT and organization. It would thus seem useful and appropriate for academics in the areas of organization theory, management, or information systems to display the same flexibility.

NOTES

1. Moreover, users' failure to live up to the expectations inscribed in systems design provides a useful resource in the context of failed implementation. That is, project failure can be explained (away) through the shortcomings of, for example, recalcitrant users.
2. For a variety of other academic and practitioner perspectives on IT in the NHS see Keen (1994).
3. In fact there is a diverse array of strategems through which such negotiation can take place. A realist interpretation of obligatory passage points may be taken to imply the subordination of an objective to the materiality of the world; in contrast, a constructivist reading highlights the ways in which actors may seek to translate such points, to displace or redefine them.
4. Indeed there can be nothing which is 'purely' technical, or for that matter 'purely' social'. Notions of 'the' technical or 'the' social must be considered as tied to conventional dualistic narratives.

5. For an overview of the variety of interpretations of doctors' managerial role see Fitzgerald (1992), Dopson (1994).
6. Griffiths called for doctors' managerial role to be recognized both in training—in medical school and in-service practice—and in the setting up of management budgets.
7. We have documented these experiments both nationally and in independent initiatives in a number of publications. See, for example, Bloomfield (1991); Bloomfield, Coombs, Cooper, and Rea (1992).
8. In the six national pilot hospitals, the lion's share of the project budget was devoted to contracts given to commercial software developers to write these systems. The writing was embedded in a system development process which involved pulling together doctors, nurses, managers, and other hospital staff into project teams to develop the specifications, to test the systems, and to commission them and train other clinical staff in their use. Later, when the initiative was rolled out to all the other hospitals in the UK the standard financial package to each hospital included a large sum (approx. £350,000) for the purchase and installation of case-mix software.
9. More specifically, all the diagnoses made and treatments carried out were to be given a unique code which could then be entered into the information system.
10. The concept of clinical directorates has been operationalized in a variety of ways. This has been observed in our own research in the North West Region of the NHS and in work conducted elsewhere (Fitzgerald 1992).
11. For instance, the introduction of clinical directorates at Leicester Royal Infirmary dated from 1985 (Barker 1990).
12. The material in this section is based on the longitudinal fieldwork of the PICT team in several hospitals in the north of England between 1991 and 1995.
13. Of course, these are not 'essential' differences between clinical groups, their specific clinical activities, and their reformulation as clinical directorates, but are socially constructed through complex professional discourses.
14. The reports, both official and unofficial, of these difficulties are legion.
15. In this regard it is worth noting that as the forces set in train by the internal market bring about greater and greater disparities—between local demands for health-care and the levels of provision, between purchasers and providers—there is currently talk of a potential 'meltdown' in the system.

REFERENCES

Akrich, M. (1992) 'The De-Scription of Technical Objects', in W. Bijker, and J. Law (eds.), *Shaping Technology/Building Society* (Cambridge, Mass.: MIT Press), 205–24.

Barker, P. (1990) 'The Leicester Experience', *The Health Service Journal*, 100(5220): 1428–9.

Bloomfield, B. P. (1991) 'The Role of Information Systems in the UK National Health Service: Action at a Distance and the Fetish of Calculation', *Social Studies of Science*, 21(4): 701–34.

—— (1992) 'Understanding the Social Practices of Systems Developers', *Journal of Information Systems*, 2(3): 189–202.

—— (1995) 'Power, Machines, and Social Relations: Delegating to Information Technology in the UK National Health Service', *Organization*, 2(3): 489–518.

—— and Coombs, R. (1992) 'Information Technology, Control and Power: The Centralisation and Decentralisation Debate Revisited', *Journal of Management Studies*, 29(4): 459–84.

—— —— Cooper, D. J. and Rea, D. (1992) 'Machines and Manœuvres: Responsibility Accounting and the Construction of Hospital Information Systems', *Accounting, Management and Information Technology*, 2(4): 197–219.

—— —— and Owen, J. (1994*a*) 'The Social Construction of Information Systems: Implications for Management Control', in R. Mansell (ed.), *Information, Control and Technical Change* (London: A), 143–57.

—— —— —— (1994*b*) 'The Information and Management Strategy of the NHS: A Triumph of Optimism Over Practicality?' *Parliamentary Brief*, 3(1) (Oct.), 67–70.

—— and Vurdubakis, T. (1994*a*) 'Boundary Disputes: Negotiating the Boundary between the Technical and the Social in the Development of IT Systems', *Information Technology and People*, 7(1): 9–24.

—— —— (1994*b*) 'Re-Presenting Technology: IT Consultancy Reports as Textual Reality Constructions', *Sociology*, 28(2): 455–77.

—— and Vurdubakis, T. (1997) 'Visions of Organization and Organizations of Vision: The Representational Practices of Information Systems Development', *Accounting, Organizations and Society*, 22, in press.

Callon, M. (1990) 'Techno-Economic Networks and Irreversibility', Conference on Firm Strategy and Technical Change: Microeconomics or Microsociology, Manchester School of Management, UMIST, 27–8 Sept.

—— and Latour, B. (1982) 'Unscrewing the Big Leviathan: How Actors Macro-Structure Reality and How Sociologists Help Them Do So', in K. Knorr-Cetina, and A. Cicourel (eds.), *Advances in Social Theory and Methodology: Toward an Integration of Micro- and Macro-Sociologies* (London: Routledge), 277–303.

Coombs, R., Knights, D., and Willmott, H. (1992) 'Culture, Control and Competition; Towards a Conceptual Framework for the Study of Information Technology in Organizations', *Organization Studies*, 13(1): 51–72.

Department of Health and Social Security (1983) *Report of the NHS Management Inquiry* (London: HMSO).

Department of Health and Social Security (1986) *Health Services Management: Resource Management (Management Budgeting) in Health Authorities*, Health Notice (86)34 (DHSS: London).

Department of Health (1989) *Working for Patients*, Cmd. 555 (London: HMSO).

Dopson, S. (1994) 'Management: The One Disease Consultants Did not Think Existed', Management Research Paper 9412 (Oxford: Templeton College).

Fitzgerald, L. (1992) 'Clinicians into Management: On the Agenda or not?' *Health Services Management Research*, 5(2): 137–46.

Hirschheim, R., and Newman, M. (1988) 'Information Systems and User Resistance: Theory and Practice', *The Computer Journal*, 31(5): 398–408.

Keen, J. (ed.) (1994) *Information Management in Health Services* (Buckingham: Open University Press).

Knights, D., and Murray, F. (1994) *Managers Divided: Organisational Politics and Information Technology Management* (London: Wiley).

—— and Vurdubakis, T. (1994) 'Foucault, Power, Resistance and All That', in J. M.

Jermier, D. Knights and W. R. Nord (eds.) *Resistance and Power in Organizations* (London: Routledge), 167–98.

Latour, B. (1987) *Science in Action* (Milton Keynes: Open University Press).

—— (1991) 'Technology is Society Made Durable', in J. Law (ed.), *A Sociology of Monsters: Essays on Power, Technology and Domination* (London: Routledge), 103–31.

—— (1993) *We Have Never Been Modern* (London: Harvester Wheatsheaf).

Law, J. (1986) 'On The Methods of Long-Distance Control: Vessels, Navigation and the Portuguese Route to India', in J. Law (ed.), *Power, Action and Belief: A New Sociology of Knowledge?* (London: Routledge), 234–63.

Mole, V., and Dawson, S. (1993) 'Pole to Pole', *Health Service Journal* (11 Mar.), 33–4.

NHS Information Management Group (1992) *IM&T Strategy Overview* (IMG/NHS Management Executive).

Sewell, G., and Wilkinson, B. (1992) '"Someone to Watch over Me": Surveillance Discipline and the JIT Labour Process', *Sociology*, 26(2): 271–89.

Willmott, H. (1993) 'Strength is Ignorance; Slavery is Freedom: Managing Culture in Modern Organizations', *Journal of Management Studies*, 30(4): 515–52.

Woolgar, S. (1991) 'Configuring the User: The Case of Usability Trials', in J. Law (ed.) *A Sociology of Monsters: Essays on Power, Technology and Domination* (London: Routledge), 57–99.

PART 3

Networks

7

Networking as Knowledge Work: A Study of Strategic Inter-Organizational Development in the Financial Services Industry

DAVID KNIGHTS, FERGUS MURRAY, AND HUGH WILLMOTT

In 1990, an ambitious plan to introduce electronic trading into the UK life insurance industry was formulated by twenty of the UK's large and medium-sized insurance companies. As a means of promoting and developing this innovation a company to which we give the pseudonym Switchco was established. Its purpose was to act as a focal point and facilitator of the new electronically mediated inter-organizational network designed to displace paper-based methods of trading between insurance companies and their distributors.[1]

In this paper, we examine the process of establishing and building the Switchco network as a form of knowledge work. In doing so, we draw links between two areas of study: networking and knowledge work. 'Knowledge work', we argue, is less viable as an occupational classification than as a catch phrase for signalling current changes in the organization of work in the direction of knowledge intensification. It is also associated with a post-Fordist 'information economy' in which information systems are understood to facilitate processes of 'delaying' and 'multi-skilling' within organizations (Zuboff 1988). As hierarchies are flattened, those at the lower levels are being trained to take greater responsibility for decisions, often on a teamwork or networking basis: in this limited sense, they are becoming 'more knowledgeable', self-disciplined workers. The study of networks has been undertaken, in the main, by champions of 'networking' and 'network research' as a distinctive activity or field of study (e.g. Eccles and Crane 1987).[2] The absence of more critical work on inter-organizational networks—a field that while present in some organizational study texts (e.g. Clegg 1990; Morgan 1990) is conspicuous by its absence from others (e.g. Reed 1985; 1992; Thompson and McHugh 1990)—is associated with a continuing fixation on intra-organizational work processes. This has tended to deflect attention from

This chapter was originally published in the *Journal of Management Studies* (Blackwell: Oxford), Vol. 30, No. 6, 1993, pp. 975–95.

the development and significance of *inter*-organizational networks between nomin-
ally autonomous organizations. In our case, this process has involved establishing and building a strategic network (Jarillo 1988) designed to support electronic
trading between a number of insurance companies who rely upon independent
financial advisers (IFAs) to supply them with business.[3]

Our study, then, is focused upon those knowledge workers who have been
engaged in establishing and developing this inter-organizational electronic trading network. In conducting the research, we draw upon the conceptual framework developed by Michel Callon. Prior to presenting our fieldwork, therefore,
we provide a limited account of his 'sociology of translation' arguing that it
yields certain valuable insights into the process whereby techno-economic networks, such as the one organized by Switchco are established and developed.
Our case material on Switchco is then located in the historical and institutional
context of its development where we apply Callon's concepts of 'problematization', 'interessement', 'enrolment', and 'mobilization' to interpret its formation
and progression. In our account of Switchco, we refrain from presenting an overly
rational or linear model of organizational behaviour, preferring instead to pay
attention to the conditions of its formation and the dynamics of its development.
This approach allows us to indicate how the knowledge work involved in building the network has accommodated the divergent demands of companies and
their intermediaries; and to show how, as networks develop, knowledge workers
are continuously engaged in a reworking and reconstitution of their position,
commitments, and involvement. In a discussion section, we indicate the relevance of our research for constructing a theory of networks as a distinctive form
of organizing that complements and integrates insights derived from Callon and
Foucault's diverse but complementary use of the concept of normalization.

Typically, knowledge work is associated with the activity of those who occupy a privileged position within the division of labour. 'Knowledge workers'
are understood to be highly qualified individuals who belong to, or form a
distinct component of, an élite group of professional and managerial employees.
The monopoly of expertise possessed by this élite of highly qualified, exceptionally intelligent and/or hard-working individuals is associated with the power to
design and/or control their own work, and to conceive of, and delegate to others,
tasks that are deemed to require comparatively little or no expertise.

By accepting the authority of such conceptions of 'knowledge work' there is
a danger that academic knowledge workers simply reproduce and legitimize this
social division of labour in a way that simultaneously overlooks their common positioning as wage labour within a capitalist mode of production. Without denying
that the political economy of capitalism promotes a division of labour in which
expertise traditionally invested in a craft labour is systematically appropriated
and controlled by professional and managerial strata, we argue that there is a
danger of using the concept of 'knowledge work(er)' in ways that lose sight of
the presence of knowledge in all forms of activity. As Giddens (1979, 1984) has
argued, all types of human activity involve a 'reflexive monitoring of conduct',

even though some work processes may become so habitual and devalued as to render workers unaware or ignorant of the 'tacit knowledge' upon which they routinely and skilfully draw (Manwaring and Wood 1985; Davies and Rosser 1986). A challenge for critical analysis is to study the changing organization of work without needlessly assuming or reinforcing social divisions of labour.

An alternative to engaging in forms of discourse that uncritically differentiates knowledge work(ers) from other kinds of work(er) is to understand it, genealogically, as a 'truth claim' that is currently being invoked (i) to suggest the changing profile of work in post-industrial societies (from manual/industrial to knowledge/service) or (ii) to classify a type of work, often related to the use of computer-based communication and information technologies and/or associated with the core activities of so-called knowledge industries or knowledge-intensive firms.[4] A genealogy, as Foucault (1980) characterizes it, addresses the social formation of what are routinely taken or known to be 'objects' such as the practices and discourse work which are deemed to reside within the boundaries of 'knowledge work'. When understood genealogically, Foucault argues, a phenomenon such as 'knowledge work' is no more than a diverse set of dispersed events and multiplicity of unconnected discourses and practices whose fragile, fragmented, and contingent relationships are confounded by a reconstitution of their history in terms of a coherent and unbroken continuity (Bouchard 1977: 146). In short, while the production of any phenomenon is often an accidental and intended conjuncture of discrete discourses, once they are constituted (socially constructed) as 'objects' their precarious and discontinuous formation is reinterpreted to coincide with an apparent current solidity and unity.

One benefit of conceptualizing 'knowledge work' genealogically is that it draws attention to the way in which 'reality' is an unendingly interpreted phenomenon not independent of relations of power and knowledge.

By avoiding extended debates about whether concepts, such as knowledge work, correspond to events in the world, it is possible to concentrate on the question of how interpretations or representations are produced and applied as knowledge interventions and exercises of power. For us, the term 'knowledge work' is currently being deployed in support of the 'progressive' claim that current technological developments involve the growth of new working practices that facilitate greater worker discretion and teamwork interdependence. But this is to obscure the way in which such claims represent a knowledge intervention or exercise of power to constitute reality in accordance with a desired image or belief.

Having said this, we accept that the availability of new information technologies opens up opportunities for restructuring and innovation in the organization of work; and that 'knowledge workers' are in the vanguard of this development. They are key workers within the so-called post-industrial sectors of advanced capitalist economies, including the financial services industry that is the focus of our case study. Indeed, our case study illustrates a form of trading that is virtually unimaginable in the absence of these technologies whose relevance and mobilization is identified and pursued by an élite of 'knowledge workers'. However, we are reluctant to use the term 'knowledge work' uncritically to study these developments and we are conscious of previous exaggerated claims to have discovered a new political vanguard (e.g. Burnham 1945; Mannheim 1949) destined to replace the progressive role attributed to the proletariat in theory. Instead, we use the sloganizing of knowledge work as an invitation to engage in some critical reflections upon what such work—as practised by members of the Switchco network and as a discursive field developed by consultants and academics.

For us, 'knowledge work', as a discourse and normalizing practice has a specific genealogy that is very much in process. What counts as 'knowledge work' is not simply imposed by management gurus or by organizational fiat. Nor is it determined or reflected through a process of academic idealization. With this proviso, we can agree with Reed (1992) who makes a direct connection between the emergence of a new stratum of knowledge workers and the growth of network forms of organization:

Knowledge workers provide intangible assets and resources which become vital to sustained competitive success and growth . . . The more reliant that organisation becomes on such intangible assets or resources . . . the more likely that the structural forms (of organisations) . . . will push towards . . . configurations in which the 'network', rather than hierarchy, emerges as the predominant mode of organising. Such a shift towards network forms . . . implies the need for much more deeply-set environmental inter-connectedness— as a precondition for anticipating and successfully managing environmental threat and opportunity. (Reed 1992: 11)

7.1 KNOWLEDGE WORK AND NETWORKS

Those involved in building the Switchco network fit both usages of the 'knowledge work' slogan identified above. First, they are operating in an industry that has expanded dramatically within post-industrial capitalism; they are involved in the design, marketing, and distribution of highly complex, abstract products —products that are increasingly sold as forms of investment rather than insurance (Knights 1988; Knights and Willmott 1990). The insurance industry and financial services more generally are predominantly involved in seeking, exchanging, and using information,[5] with considerable potential for further development, as our case study indicates. Secondly, within this industry, builders of interorganizational networks are very much involved in the development of information technology and software that is designed to deliver electronic trading between companies and their intermediaries. As networkers, these knowledge workers are indeed in the vanguard of the development of what Poster has called 'a mode of information' in which 'new forms of social interaction based on electronic communications devices are replacing older types of social relations' (Poster 1984: 168).

7.1.1   A Conceptual Framework

The increased use of the term network to characterize the 'new forms of social interaction' signals the understanding that they differ markedly from established contractual and hierarchial patterns of corporate governance (Thorelli 1986; Thompson *et al.* 1991). As one author puts it:

In network modes of resource allocation, transactions occur neither through discrete exchanges nor by administrative fiat, but through networks of individuals engaged in reciprocal, preferential, mutually supportive actions . . . (Reed (1992) 'Experts, Professions and Organisations in Late Modernity', *Proceedings of the Employment Research Unit Annual Conference*, Cardiff Business School, Sept.)

In general, studies of networks as new organizational forms (Coulson-Thomas and Brown 1990; Johanson and Mattson 1991; Powell 1991) have tended to be 'heavy' on notions of negotiation and trust between members of the network, and exceptionally 'light' on domination and power-relations-interdependent relationships based upon reciprocity and mutual trust, where self-interest is sacrificed for the communal good. Our case study suggests that this view of networks is superficial since it neglects their embeddedness in institutional power relations that are hierarchial, competitive, and instrumental. Participants in the Switchco network were positioned hierarchically within their employing organization as well as, and indeed before they were, network members; and this reminds us that their actions were part of the wider structure of economic relations in which network-building activity is a medium and an outcome. Despite a plea from Aldrich and Whetten (1981: 401) that researchers develop a fuller understanding of the dynamics of inter-organizational systems by studying 'the forces of conflict and coercion and the use of power and exploitation', networks continue to be portrayed as interdependent relationships based upon reciprocity and mutual trust, where self-interest is sacrificed for the communal good. Network researchers have indeed been slow or reluctant to follow the early lead of Benson (1975) who stressed the importance of theorizing inter-organizational networks as a political economy.

Associated with the decontextualization of networks is a tendency to exaggerate their rational design and to account for their development in terms of universal considerations such as uncertainty reduction or environmental stabilization (Allen 1974; Pfeffer and Salincik 1978; Pennings 1981; Dasmalchian 1984; Miles and Snow 1986; Hagg and Johanson 1988). Without denying that the establishment of networks is informed by definite intentions, the findings of our case study suggest that the often *ad hoc* and contingent development of networks takes place in conditions of considerable uncertainty, contestation, and constraint. If our case is typical, this suggests that the process of network evolution may be far less coherent, controlled, and rational than conventional wisdom in this field contends.

A convenient way of conceptualizing the process of building networks has been developed by Michel Callon (Callon 1986; Callon *et al.* 1983). Very briefly, his 'sociology of translation' addresses the question of how resources are made available for the construction and reproduction of techno-economic networks. The term 'translation' is adopted to characterize how an idea (e.g. the development of a network) is translated, through the identification of a problem or opportunity, from an idea into reality. Callon formulates this process as a series of moves in which agencies are enrolled and locked into a project by making the new organization (e.g. Switchco) an 'obligatory passage point' for agencies operating in the field.

Problematization is the first moment in Callon's theory of translation. At this stage, one or more agencies is engaged in defining and exploring a problem which, in our case, was perceived as the problem of an uneven playing field in the market for insurance services. Under the terms of the Financial Services Act 1986 (FSA), companies that relied heavily upon the independent financial adviser sector were deemed to have become disadvantaged *vis-à-vis* those that operated through direct sales or tied agents. As a consequence of the Act, they had been burdened with direct liability for regulatory and compensatory costs. The Act also required full commission disclosure under the rules of the FSA, as later interpreted by the Office of Fair Trading (OFT). Despite these shared circumstances of disadvantage, the stage of *problematization* was far from a smooth, continuous, and uninterrupted process. Initial efforts to identify and agree on common areas of concern were found wanting and, under competitive pressure, collapsed as we discuss below. The second of Callon's moments is that of *interessement* in which those who profess to have a relevant solution persuade others to accept their definitions of the situation, and to collaborate in pursuing their favoured solution. In our study, a number of those who were to become members of Switchco had been working on individual 'solutions'. They shared an understanding of the potential of computer technology for facilitating trading by improving service and reducing cost. But they were also 'keeping their options open' in case support for Switchco collapsed or pressures to accommodate the diverse demands of its members produced the organizational equivalent of the camel in a wet climate. The moment of *enrolment* occurred with the development of arrangements for tying agencies into the means of producing solutions. These were the various coordinating mechanisms developed to establish and maintain the operation of the network. Finally, the concept of *mobilization* describes methods deployed by agencies to sustain commitment to the organization. For example, accommodations were made to the demands of its members. Switchco also introduced features that increased the material or symbolic costs of withdrawal.

For heuristic purposes, it can be helpful to present these elements of 'translation' as sequential moments in a serial process. However, it is perhaps more satisfactory to conceptualize them as parallel dimensions of the social practice of organizing. As we have already indicated, the stage of 'problematization' had no clear cut-off point but remained throughout the development of the network:

new ways of defining and interpreting 'the problem' continued to arise despite involvement and mobilization around solutions to previous definitions. The alliance between the insurance companies and their efforts to enrol the intermediaries was far more precarious than, say, Callon's (1986) account of the relationship between the scientists and the scallop fishermen of St Brieuc's Bay. Furthermore, as we argue later, an understanding of the dynamics of knowledge work in processes of network building can benefit from an appreciation of the broader context as well as the specificities of inter-organizational work. In this we include an understanding of the genealogy of cooperation (e.g. between founding members of Switchco), an account of the recent history of the industry including the impact of legislation upon 'the playing field' of insurance business, and, not least, an awareness of moral as well as politico-economic structures of a capitalist mode of production in which efforts to build the Switchco network are embedded (Knights and Willmott 1990).

Before moving on to apply Callon's sociology of translation to our study of Switchco, it is relevant to explore in more detail Callon's understanding of how communication between actors (e.g. members of a network) is mediated. Or, as Callon (1991: 13) puts it, how network members define each other 'by way of the intermediaries they put into circulation'. According to Callon (1991: 6), communications are intermediated through four categories of intermediary:

- texts or what he prefers to call literary inscriptions including anything that is written, such as advertisements, reports, or software and the media (e.g. paper, disks, tapes, and so on) through which it is circulated;
- technical artefacts which include all non-human entities (e.g. machines, computers, commodities, and so on) that facilitate performing functions and tasks;
- human beings and the skills or knowledge they generate and reproduce;
- money in its multiplicity of forms.

In so far as they are brought into circulation by actors, whom they also define in their relations with one another, each of the four media may be seen as forming and giving order to particular networks. In practice, however, most networks are combinations of different categories of intermediary or 'hybrids', as Callon (1991: 11) prefers to call them. Taking our own case as an example, the electronic data interchange was a hybrid of technical artefacts (computers), literary inscriptions (software), the purchase of software companies (money), and knowledge workers (skills). From this perspective, knowledge work is one form of intermediary that is put into circulation with other intermediaries (i.e. electronic hardware and software, money) by the network (i.e. Switchco). Thus, Switchco is conceptualized as a medium and outcome of the developing relations between these intermediaries: a process that, as we noted earlier, Callon (1991: 19) describes through the term 'translation'. The value of this conceptualization is that it allows us to highlight analytically what our observations of an inter-organizational network in insurance indicate empirically—namely, that knowledge work needs to be studied not with a focus upon the actors *per se* but in their relations as intermediaries with others in the network, as well as those potential users of the network (e.g. IFAs) not yet involved.

Two additional concepts developed by Callon are of direct relevance for analysing our empirical material: convergence and irreversibility. A highly convergent network is one in which mutual definitions (translation) of actors and intermediaries are so compatible and integrated that any actor 'can at any time identify and mobilise all the network's skills without having to get involved in costly adaptations, translations or decoding' (Callon 1991: 27). In these circumstances members of the network can work together in pursuit of common objectives and do not feel their identities and activities under constant threat from one another or in continuous need of justification. As will be seen, Switchco did not display high levels of convergence which may account, at least initially, for a partial success in securing IFA support and a limited adoption of the network's informatic systems. Irreversibility characterizes a situation in which translations (i.e. definitional relations between actors and intermediaries) other than those currently in existence are blocked or are improbable. This may occur, for example, when the heterogeneity of the interrelationships comprising the network are highly complex and difficult to unravel. While convergent networks are likely to exhibit low levels of reversibility, the two are not a necessary condition of one another. Indeed, despite low levels of convergence, the heterogeneous and complex nature of relations in our insurance network has made reversibility highly unlikely even though, as we will show, some earlier translations were reversed as Switchco emerged out of aborted efforts to establish similar kinds of networks.

In sum, Callon's sociology of translation provides us with a framework for analysing processes of network formation and development that avoids a voluntaristic approach to understanding knowledge workers and their participation in networks. What is missing in his analysis, however, is a recognition of the role of power and its relationship to networks and knowledge. For this reason, it is useful to complement Callon's analysis with a Foucauldian appreciation of how power and knowledge circulate in a 'capillary-like' fashion throughout every corner and crevice of the social body of organizations and society. We return to, and elaborate upon, this suggestion in the discussion section that follows the presentation of the Switchco case.

7.2 NETWORKING AS KNOWLEDGE WORK: THE CASE OF SWITCHCO

In this section of the paper we examine the process of translation concerning the establishment of an innovative inter-organizational network aimed at redressing certain competitive disadvantages in the post-FSA independent sector of financial services distribution.[6]

The impetus behind this development, we argue, was commercial, not technological. The twenty insurance companies that formed the network hoped to improve their trading position by (i) controlling the technology rather than being controlled by technology suppliers; (ii) be leading, and in command of, what they trust will become the industry standard; and, perhaps most importantly, (iii) using the technology to raise the profile and trading position of independent advisers whose very commercial survival has been put in question *vis-à-vis* direct sales and tied agents. However, despite the importance to the insurance companies of improving customer service and reducing (transaction) costs within the independent adviser sector, the formation and development of Switchco has been dogged by the difficulty of persuading and reassuring companies that Switchco will (i) retain the support of these companies' competitors; (ii) provide a more effective, usable system than rival systems under development; *and*, (iii) be used by the independent advisers if and when the Switchco system became fully operational.

Established to support the organization, design, and implementation of electronic trading between a number of companies and their intermediaries (cf., Cash and Konsynski 1985), the espoused mission of Switchco was to introduce and manage the technology infrastructure and services necessary to make possible the electronic transfer of insurance quotations, proposals, and claims between the participating insurance companies and their intermediaries. In many 'strategic networks', such as those examined by Sydow (1992), their operation is overseen and managed by one dominant company. In contrast, Switchco is overseen by a large, and some would say cumbersome, consultative structure whose purpose is to bring together insurer and IFA interests.

The emergence of Switchco is a considerable novelty in the insurance industry, which is renowned for its staid and conservative culture.[7] The novelty lies in the extent and anticipated lengthy duration of explicit inter-company collaboration between competing organizations. Our initial focus is upon the changing conditions that have made the emergence of Switchco possible and the forms of knowledge work developed and mobilized in this process.

7.2.1   *The Industrial Context*

The insurance industry has a long history in which its constituent companies have enjoyed a considerable degree of government support and protection from potential competitors within what, only recently, has become known as the 'financial services industry' (Knights and Tinker 1997). The industry has developed a tight community of interest which it has been adept at protecting. However, in the last twenty years, the comparatively cosy world of insurance has been disrupted by a series of developments (Knights and Willmott 1993): new, aggressive entrants selling unit-linked policies have forced their way into the market; a new regulatory regime has been imposed on the industry; the banks have launched a full-scale assault on the highly profitable life insurance business and the building societies, as agents, have creamed off much of the mortgage-linked endowment business once available to independent financial advisers.

The emergence of Switchco can be seen as a response by a number of insurance companies to changes that have been undermining their established position in the market-place, a threat that has been represented by the promoters of Switchco as an opportunity to lead and dominate a new machinery of transactions. The idea of creating the Switchco network has been heralded as a (strategic) move to re-establish control of ICT initiatives that had previously been led by 'technology', rather than 'insurance', interests. Switchco is represented as being of strategic importance to these companies because, if successful, it would enable them to reassert control over the market and manage their relationships with the independent advisers. To gain a clearer picture of the dimensions of this struggle and the knowledge work employed within it we here briefly outline the processes that gave rise to Switchco.

7.2.2   *Videotext as an Accidental Mother of Switchco*

In the early 1980s a new technological artefact emerged: the viewdata service, such as Prestel, which allowed the transmission and display of data over an electronic network. At the same time, various insurance companies were pursuing collaborative projects with software and telecommunications companies to make possible computer-to-computer communications between insurance companies and their intermediaries. Most of these initiatives were technologically complicated and failed. One, however, achieved a remarkable success. This was a videotext system, developed by technology companies, that provided computerized insurance quotations. Although initially regarded with suspicion by the insurance industry, videotext soon became an industry standard.[8]

Stimulated by the widespread use of videotext, a network of actors with an interest in developing some form of electronic, computer-to-computer insurance information service between insurance companies and their distribution channels began to emerge and coalesce. This consisted of an ill-defined and heterogeneous group of players who possessed insurance skills/knowledge, an appreciation of the impact of videotext technologies, and a grasp of the significant implications of new government legislation on mortgage interest tax relief. This network was given a decisive push by the building societies who had most directly administrative responsibilities to process mortgage tax relief.

As a consequence of this new development building societies began switching the bulk of their customers from repayment to endowment-linked mortgages. The value of this policy was that the fee or commission income deriving from the life insurance component of each mortgage more than compensated for the extra costs of administering mortgage interest tax relief at source (MIRAS). The result was a dramatic increase in the sale of endowment mortgages from an average of around 20 per cent to more than 50 per cent of all mortgages (Knights *et al.* 1993: 24). As the largest distributor of these life-insurance-based products, the building societies found themselves in a powerful position *vis-à-vis* the producers of these policies. The building societies also found videotext an important 'selling aid' because they provided real-time mortgage estimates at point of sale. It therefore came to pass that the *de facto* standard demanded by videotext was imposed on insurance companies wishing to do business with the building societies.

So, partly as a consequence of the change in administering mortgage tax relief, the insurance industry lost control of the inter-organizational use of IT as an important part of its relationship with independent[9] distribution outlets. Instead, this became mediated by 'technology' companies. For insurance companies, this loss of control had two drawbacks. Most obviously, there was the problem of the duplication of costs and the insurance companies' dependence on outside providers for core business functions. But there was also dissatisfaction amongst many companies about the adequacy of the videotext service. It was widely viewed as a 'Mickey Mouse' technology that was incapable of delivering the cost savings that were potentially achievable, in their judgement, through a 'full blown' system of electronic trading.

Here, then, we can see an exemplification of 'problematization', 'interessement', and 'enrolment' in an embryonic value-added network service largely organized around the building society's commercial 'clout', and satisfaction with videotext as a solution to their 'electronic trading' needs. The insurance companies, who at this point were divided amongst themselves, did not develop a convergent problematization of their electronic trading needs that could organize the translation process in the emerging actor-network. However, the intensity of dissatisfaction with videotext did lead a number of separate groups of insurers to pursue their own inter-organizational technology initiatives. To this end, they developed special 'gateway' services over the existing videotext networks; they also acquired equity stakes in electronic trading software companies; and in some cases they even developed electronic trading software amongst themselves. However, most of these initiatives were costly failures.

At this point, the development of an electronic trading network was still in a stage of 'reversibility': it could be pushed in many different directions and lacked the codified practices of a stable and normalized network. Prior to the establishment of a state of irreversibility, Callon (1991: 38) argues, 'the more the actors composing the network can be understood in terms of concepts like strategies, variable and negotiated aims, revisable projects and changing coalitions'. Callon's (1986: 83) assertion that 'engineers must be sociologists' if their inventions are to become successful held true for the knowledge workers engaged in developing and managing the diverse range of networks seeking to enrol a variety of insurance interests. In cases where services and software were developed, very few other companies or independent advisers could be persuaded/enrolled in support of their use. Technology solutions proliferated but none could attract a critical mass sufficient to ensure adoption as an industry standard. According to Switchco's Managing Director, this period was marked by the loss of 'millions and millions and millions' of pounds as individual companies pursued discrete and ultimately futile inter-organizational technology initiatives. Help, though, was soon to come from an unexpected quarter.

7.2.3   *Tilting the Playing Field*

In 1988 the Financial Services Act radically changed the regulatory structure of the life insurance industry. A polarized distinction between independent and single company or tied financial advice was created. This change was supposed to ensure a level playing field between the different distribution channels: independent financial advisers (IFAs), tied agents, and internal sales forces. However, the effect of the Act was perceived by the insurance companies (principally, the mutuals), who depended most heavily upon the IFA distribution channel, to be highly disadvantageous to them. Many of these companies joined forces to campaign for the importance of independent financial advice, and for the recognition of the key role of the IFAs charged with the provision of this advice under the FSA. Although this campaign eventually collapsed, it focused the collective attention of these companies on ways of promoting the survival of a strong IFA distribution channel.

Partly as a consequence of the collapse of the campaign to promote the IFAs, two of the bigger players initiated a major survey of IFA IT use as a basis for collecting data with which to persuade other companies of the value of developing better IT support. The results of this survey effected a 'problematization' that drew in and forged a growing consensus of interest amongst insurance players. Initially, the problematization stimulated a major initiative to support IT use by IFAs. This resulted in the establishment of ITPUSH (another pseudonym) funded by twenty insurance companies, to provide advice and consultancy to the IFA market. Instrumental in this process were three companies who had made heavy investments in the development of workable, but virtually unused, electronic trading technology. However, dissatisfaction with the effectiveness and scope of ITPUSH's activities resulted in a rethink (or re-problematization) and a more ambitious project, Switchco, was born.

7.2.4   *The Marketing of Switchco*

The creation of Switchco was indicative of a growing belief in the IFA-dependent segment of the industry that its long-term survival rested upon asserting its leadership in the field of electronic trading. Reflecting this belief, Switchco had as its strategic mission the task of establishing 'a widely used, quality, electronic trading environment for the Principals and Agents of insurance and other associated products by the development and distribution of new technologies'. Since its inception, Switchco has attempted to establish itself as the 'obligatory passage point' (Callon 1986) through which all parties involved in the development of insurance electronic trading must proceed. This has been pursued by enrolling insurance company support, rigorous marketing to IFAs, and attempts to marginalize and exclude competitors.

However, progress has been less speedy than desired and anticipated. Major difficulties were encountered in cajoling IFAs into using new technology. Many remained unconvinced of its merits for *their* particular business needs. Amongst leading advocates of Switchco the view was held that the industry had yet to realize the scale and cost of the cooperative effort (or translation) needed to bring about the benefits deliverable by electronic trading. The Managing Director of Switchco directly admonished the industry for its tendency to get into 'Mexican stand offs' (*sic*) involving 'small, petty rivalries and silly arguments'.

Getting resources for a network is clearly a precondition of its creation and survival. But there is also a broader and recurrent battle to win hearts and minds to the idea and viability of a network. Creating and sustaining the credible impression of a 'winners all' situation is crucial to extending the network and getting commitment from its members. Formal commitment can quickly dissolve—note the reference to 'Mexican stand-offs' when 'corporate interests' are seen to be at risk or inadequately served. A key actor in Switchco said 'getting clear corporate views' was difficult. This was so not only due to the problem of involving the right level (chief executives) in Switchco decisions but also because of the 'mix' of insurance company representation within Switchco. This consisted of marketing people and IT people, 'senior' and 'junior' people, and 'positive' and 'negative' people. Such a mix placed constraints on establishing a 'clear corporate view' or precise problematization within Switchco. This led to problems. In particular, apparently random trouble and disagreements have arisen when 'somebody at a high level has *perceived the thing in the wrong way*'. Such troubles, of course, occur in all organizations. However, in a network forum it may be more disruptive and take greater effort to cajole and shepherd 'wrong perceptions' into the 'appropriate' arena of problematization.

7.2.5 Participating in the Switchco Networks

Difficulties in winning and maintaining support for Switchco have arisen as a consequence of the numbers of organizations and individuals involved in the network, a problem that is compounded by the lack of a common organizational culture and set of normalized rules. But the problems have also been associated with the considerable ambiguity and suspicion felt by managers in participating companies when committing themselves to collaborative agreements in a climate of increasing competition. At a conference on electronic trading in insurance, different managers repeatedly asked the question: where do you draw the line between competition and collaboration in these areas?—a problem that has continually beset the banks in their 'arms length' dealings with the clearer APACS (see also note 5).

The knowledge work mobilized during the construction and management of Switchco has involved learning from past inter-organizational processes and practices and scanning the relevant horizons for exemplars to guide future developments. In turn, this has required contacts, travel, curiosity resources, considerable autonomy and an ability to appreciate the context-specificity of its members' experience. A combination of the political skills necessary to build the network and the technical know-how to understand its proposed operation and defend its credibility has been necessary. For IT networks have been rapidly changing, they have been open to multiple problematization, and they have been inhabited by a vast array of providers of different networks, software packages, standards, and interface technologies, all angling to become obligatory passage points on the road to electronic trading.

Notably, there has been the challenge of gaining senior management commitment from the member insurance companies. This has proved a time-demanding process that depends upon the ability of internal actors and external agents to convert senior managerial nervousness and scepticism into active support. Managers charged with the responsibility of managing the boundaries between their company, Switchco and other insurance companies have been striving to bring 'their' company along with them while reassuring their senior managers that the company's interests are being looked after. They have also needed to reassure other network members that the company remained committed to the network. This has led to considerable role ambiguity as key actors have had to negotiate conflicting commitments. Whilst protecting their uncertain career interests, they have sought to hold a network and organizational perspective simultaneously.

Set against this, but creating additional difficulties for the management of the network, those staff employed in network-intensive activities have had the opportunity to use their boundary-spanning roles to change existing, or create new, career ambitions and trajectories. Controlling and channelling these forces of fragmentation and building trust and commitment amongst staff who are not under the day-to-day control of any particular network partner has been, to say the least, a delicate, risky, and time-consuming type of knowledge work.

7.2.6 Discussion: Power and Knowledge in Network Analysis

In our all too brief analysis of networking as a form of knowledge work we have sought to give a flavour of the practical dynamics of network building. But, as Powell (1990: 328) rightly observes, there is much work to be done in exploring what might be termed the shifting subjectivity of networking: a shift that might transform 'organization men' (*sic*) into 'network persons'. In particular, it is relevant to examine the normalization of networkers and the means by which the relative autonomy bestowed upon them is monitored and controlled, in often ill-defined boundary spanning activities; and how those carrying out these activities may seek to define and represent their tasks in ways that maximize their opportunities for career advancement within, or beyond, the network.

In common with supporters of institutional analysis (e.g. Granovetter 1985), we accept that networking, as a species of knowledge work, must be understood in terms of the distinctive qualities of the normative order and sectoral recipes—'the concrete arrangements', as Biggart (1991: 225) has put it—that 'direct investment and trade in particular ways'. In our case study, we sought to indicate the embeddedness of Switchco in the institutional context of the insurance industry and the genealogy of its adoption as a plausible move, or recipe, for regaining control from the suppliers of the technology involved in electronic trading. However, we also believe that the exclusive focus upon 'the middle range of social life', which Biggart (1991) acknowledges to be a limitation of institutional analysis, courts the danger of marginalizing the significance of wider, historical forces that underpin and condition the dynamics of normative development and sectoral change. It can lead to an excessively voluntaristic account of knowledge work and network building in which its architects are depicted as autonomous agents who possess sufficient resources to make the network a reality.

For these reasons, we believe that an adequate analysis of the dynamics of network building must be located in an appreciation of the political economy of (knowledge) work through which actors strive to secure/advance their position, materially as well as symbolically. We have shown how Callon's (1986) sociology of translation is useful for exploring the processes through which support for Switchco has developed, been sustained, and was rendered virtually irreversible. However, in common with institutional theory, Callon's conceptual framework endorses a preoccupation with the 'middle range', that marginalizes consideration of the wider structures of inequality that are a condition and consequence of the reproduction of power/knowledge relations. It is therefore necessary to complement analysis of the dynamics of network building with an appreciation of power/knowledge as a principal medium of network construction and reproduction.

Conventional, or what Foucault (1980: 92) has termed juridical, conceptions of society treat power as a property of agents, organizations, networks, or institutions that is possessed or allocated according to some criterion of market or distributive justice. An alternative formulation is to identify power as that which animates the practices making social life possible: it is productive of whatever discourses and practices mediate the social and organizational relations within and through which subjects are constituted. Examples include the material and disciplinary technologies—such as strategic inter-organizational networks—whereby subjects are constituted and positioned in relation to other subjects through a process of mutual definition, or what Callon (1991) terms, translation.

We believe that the contemporary popularity of networking, as a practice and as a topic of research, may be understood as an example of the innovative ways in which capitalist economies revolutionize their means of production. This revolution of recent time has been much facilitated by information technology whose impact has coincided with, and been compounded by, the lessons drawn from Japanese-style management practices in which a form of commitment and trust, aped in the West by a very widespread espousal and use of Total Quality

Management (Wheatley 1992; Ezzamel *et al.* 1992; Kerfoot and Knights 1992), has demonstrated its effectiveness in avoiding or minimizing major sources of cost and wastage.

A combination of Callon's sociology of translation and Foucault's (1980) analysis of power/knowledge relations seems fruitful when we examine the way in which they both consider the concept of 'normalization'. For this shows how accidentally random as well as purposeful interactions can combine to install particular forms of knowledge work, in this case networking, and the discourses that support and shape these activities and their associated shifting subjectivities. By employing the concept of 'normalization' we seek to illustrate the problematic, partial, and particularistic genesis of new practices of work and organization.

As we noted earlier, for Callon the normalization of a techno-economic network occurs as it becomes convergent and relatively irreversible. At this point, relations between actors and intermediaries are made stable: they are routinized and embedded in codifiable norms and procedures: infinite possibility is converted into normalized practice. But as Callon argues, and our case study of Switchco shows, the achievement of normality can be a slow, painful process in which original goals and problematizations undergo multiple translations as actor relations are reworked and as the cast of intermediaries shifts and changes.

Thus we sought to trace the development of Switchco including its series of 'false starts' when shared objectives between network members seemed insufficiently convergent to prevent projects being completely reversed. Having now narrowed its horizons by concentrating on the single goal of creating, promoting, and distributing electronic trading systems to IFAs, and buying in the science (literary inscriptions), technology (technical artefacts), and knowledge workers (skills), the network is currently becoming more convergent and less reversible.

Callon's sociology of translation also alerts us to the different potential forms of knowledge work in network-building activities. In an unstable network the processes of problematization, interessement, enrolment, and mobilization require considerable reflective and political activity on the part of knowledge workers in order to assess and mobilize winning network strategies. However, our case study of the insurance industry has also indicated that even the most astute and 'powerful' Machiavellian can be blown off course by unpredictable events and the emergence of new actors on the network stage. It has taken managerial actors from the insurance industry many attempts at problematization and interessement in rapidly changing sectoral conditions before some degree of network convergence emerged. Indeed, at the time of writing, the network is still far from attaining a normalized and codified condition and, though unlikely to suffer a complete reversal, is continually open to the threat of more minor disruptions.

Foucault's concept of normalization bears some similarity to Callon's in its sense of routinizing and stabilizing social relations. But in Foucault there is a greater emphasis on normalization as the establishment of a set of comprehensive disciplinary mechanisms: rules of inclusion and exclusion, hierarchical surveil-lance, and continuous normalizing judgements (Foucault 1979: 170–94). This system of normalization establishes what is to be a 'good' subject. Thus, in the case of networking the normalization of this particular practice depends upon a knowledge of how subjects are (productively) disciplined to work within such networks. This, in turn, requires that (through training programmes, and so on) subjects be constituted to understand themselves not just as members of net-works but as visible 'experts' in the use and development of knowledge and skill relevant for networking.

When considered in this way, conventional analysis of 'knowledge work' and 'networking' can itself be interpreted as an expression of power/knowledge re-lations. That is to say, it takes the form of a disciplinary technology that objec-tifies/confirms/reinforces the identity (or, better, identities) of (selected) subjects as members of networks. Actors—particularly senior and middle managers—are being encouraged to acquire a knowledge of themselves as network builders, and to understand their visibility and success in this activity as critical both for their personal advancement and for the strategic development of their industry/firm/department, and so on. The principal effect is to disseminate, legitimize, and further solidify existing 'truths'—such as the 'truth' that

in every network there is a power structure where different firms have different power to act and influence the action of other firms. This power structure in combination with the interest structure of the network affects the development of the network. (Hagg and Johanson 1988)

One of the strengths of Foucault's genealogical and archaeological investiga-tions of power/knowledge regimes is the emphasis he places on the non-linear, complex, and coincidental processes that give birth to and extend raw disciplin-ary technologies. In the case of networking as knowledge work, this approach counsels against voluntaristic analyses which assume that certain conditions and choices will necessarily be combined by different actors to create new condi-tions of normality. Rather, it is suggested that new regimes of truth, and the knowledge objects that underpin them, undergo a process of multiple translation and accident as their champions rethink, and are challenged, subverted, and blown off course by recalcitrant actors and unexpected intermediations.

7.3 CONCLUSION

In this paper we have examined the emergence of a contested, but increasingly stable, problematization of electronic trading in the insurance industry through an analysis of the short and troubled history of Switchco. We argued that the emergence of this novel network provides an instructive example of knowledge work as networking. Informed by Callon's sociology of translation, the genesis of networking as knowledge work has been shown to be a complex, non-linear process consisting of a broad range of actors and intermediaries. Processes of multiple translation, accident, and contingent circumstance were seen to combine to shift the emergence and development of Switchco and to call into question the adequacy of conventional conceptions of networking and knowledge work.

Our study of Switchco has also demonstrated that networking as knowledge work is far from normalized in a Foucauldian sense. By adopting a Foucauldian conception of normalization, it becomes more evident that proponents of knowledge-work discourse are important actors in a contemporary sociology of translation that is proposing a new problematization of work.

Rather than seeking simply to describe, elaborate, or refine common-sense knowledge of networks,[10] a challenge for critical organizational analysis is to study networks as a vehicle for understanding power–knowledge relations in particular instances of their genesis, reproduction, or transformation: to show, that is, how networks, as practices and discourses, are sustained by power relations that are themselves supported by particular regimes of truth.

NOTES

1. The research reported in this paper follows a long line of research in the field of financial services both on the role of information technology (e.g. Knights and Murray 1990; 1991; 1992; Knights and Sturdy 1990; Murray and Knights 1990*a*; Murray 1991) and more general issues such as regulation, strategy, human resource management, gender, and the Single European Market (e.g. Knights 1988; Knights and Willmott 1987*a*; 1987*b*; 1990; Kerfoot and Knights 1992; Murray and Knights 1990*b*; Morgan and Knights 1991).
2. It is also the case that much of the research on networks has been undertaken by researchers from either an institutional economics background or by marketing specialists who have been heavily influenced by economics. Moreover, much of the research undertaken by sociologists or political scientists has been in non-profit organizations.
3. In this respect, our network organization Switchco exemplifies both types of inter-organizational network identified by Fombrun (1982). That is to say, it is simultaneously an 'attribute network' that links organizations by virtue of their shared membership of the insurance industry; and it is a 'transaction network' that is concerned with the development of exchange processes between these organizations.
4. In a similar vein, Aldrich and Whetten (1981: 401) have suggested that inter-organizational 'networks are essentially constructs created by researchers to aid the process of conducting inter-organizational research'. We would argue that they are mistaken about this. In contrast to 'knowledge workers', which we view as principally a construction of academics and associated pundits, the term 'network' has a longer currency outside of academia, especially amongst IT specialists. Indeed, we would

argue that part of the appeal and acceptability of networks as a concept has been its positive association with new technology.

5. Hence they have been both one of the earliest and most vociferous users of information technology.

6. The disadvantage relates to the fact that independent financial advisers pay the costs of regulation themselves and, under the FSA, cannot be compensated by the insurance companies. By contrast regulation of their competitor-tied agents and company representatives (including the large banks and building societies) is the responsibility of the insurance companies with whom they are contracted. But perhaps more importantly, serving large numbers of IFAS whose volumes of business are out of their control is becoming a luxury that the insurance companies are seeking to rationalize through such cost-saving initiatives as electronic trading.

7. There is a parallel in another part of the financial services for in 1986 the banks were persuaded by government to establish a quasi-autonomous collaborative network—APACS (The Association for Payment Clearing Services)—to support the clearing house for money transmission settlements.

8. This was largely an unintended consequence of a series of changes sparked off by the shifting of administrative responsibilities for administering tax relief on mortgages from the government to the building societies.

9. At this time the building societies had all registered as independent financial advisers (IFAs) although later they mostly opted for tied agent status as a result of the commission disclosure directive leading to a competitive disadvantage for the former.

10. The basic difficulty with accepting the authority of common-sense reasoning is that this procedure disregards the way in which what counts as knowledge is an effect of power. The connectedness of knowledge and power (that is power/knowledge) is naturalized as common-sense notions of networks are uncritically adopted as a conceptual basis for network analysis.

REFERENCES

Aldrich, H., and Whetten, D. A. (1981) 'Organization-Sets, Action-Sets, and Networks: Making the Most of Simplicity', in P. C. Nystrom and W. H. Starbuck (eds.), *Handbook of Organizational Design*, (Oxford: Oxford University Press).

Allen, N. P. (1974) 'The Structure of Interorganizational Elite Cooptation', *American Sociological Review*, 39.

Astley, W. G., and Fombrun, C. J. (1983) 'Collective Strategy: Social Ecology of Organizational Environments', *Academy of Management Review*, 8(4).

Atkinson, J., and Meager, N. (1986) *Changing Working Patterns: How Companies Achieve Flexibility to Meet New Needs* (London: NEDO).

Benjamin, R. I., de Long, D. W., and Scott Morton, M. S. (1990) 'Electronic Data Interchange: How Much Competitive Advantage?' *Long Range Planning*, 23(1): 29–40.

Benson, K. (1975) 'The Interorganizational Network as a Political Economy', *Administrative Science Quarterly*, 20: 229–49.

Biggart, N. W. (1991) 'Explaining Asian Economic Organization: Towards a Weberian Institutional Perspective', *Theory and Society*, 20: 199–232.

Bouchard, D. F. (ed.) (1977) *Language, Counter-Memory and Practice: Selected Essays and Interviews by Michel Foucault* (Oxford: Blackwell).

Bresser, R. K., and Harl, J. E. (1986) 'Collective Strategy: Vice or Virtue?' *Academy of Management Review*, 11(2): 408–27.

Burnham, J. (1945) *The Managerial Revolution* (Harmondsworth: Penguin).

Callon, M. (1986) 'Some Elements of a Sociology of Translation: Domestication of the Scallops and the Fishermen of St. Brieuc's Bay', in J. Law (ed.), *Power, Action and Belief: A New Sociology of Knowledge?* Sociological Review Monograph No. 32 (London: Routledge & Kegan Paul).

—— (1991) 'Techno-Economic Networks and Irreversibility', paper delivered at the International Conference on the Economics and Sociology of Technology, UMIST.

—— Courtial, J. P., Turner, W. A., and Bauin, S. (1983) 'From Translations to Problematic Networks: An Introduction to Co-Word Analysis', *Social Science Information*, 22: 199–235.

Cash, J. I., and Konsynski, B. R. (1985) 'IS Redraws Competitive Boundaries', *Harvard Business Review*, Mar.–Apr., 134–42.

Clegg, S. R (1990) *Modern Organizations* (London: Sage).

Cooke, P. (1988) 'Flexible Integration, Scope Economies and Strategic Alliances: Social and Spatial Mediations', *Environment and Planning D: Society and Space*, 6: 281–300.

—— (1990) *Back to the Future: Modernity, Postmodernity and Locality* (London: Unwin Hyman).

Coulson-Thomas, C. (1991) 'IT and New Forms of Organisation for Knowledge Workers: Opportunity and Implementation', *Employee Relations*, 13(4): 22–32.

—— and Brown, R. (1990) *Beyond Quality: Managing the Relationship with the Customer* (Corby: British Institute of Management).

Dasmalchian, A. (1984) 'Environmental Dependencies and Company Structures in Britain', *Organization Studies*, 5(3).

Davies, C., and Rosser, J. (1986) 'Gendered Jobs in the Health Service: A Problem for Labour Process Analysis', in D. Knights and H. Willmott (ed.), *Gendered the Labour Process* (Aldershot: Gower), 102–16.

Eccles, R. G., and Crane, D. (1987) 'Managing Through Networks in Investment Banking', *California Management Review*, 30(1): 176–95.

Ezzamel, M., Lilley, S., and Willmott, H. C. (1992) 'How has Management Changed? Perceptions of Organisational Transformation in UK Companies', Employment Research Unit Annual Conference, Cardiff Univ.

Fombrun, C. J. (1982) 'Strategies for Network Research in Organizations', *Academy of Management Review*, 7(2): 280–91.

—— and Astley, W. G. (1983) 'Strategies of Collective Action: The Case of the Financial Services Industry', in R. Lamb (ed.), *Advances in Strategic Management*, 2: 125–39 (Greenwich, Conn: Jai Press).

Foucault, M. (1979) *Discipline and Punish* (Harmondsworth: Penguin).

—— (1980) *Power/Knowledge: Selected Interviews and Other Writings 1972–1977*, ed. by Colin Gordon (Brighton: The Harvester Press).

Giddens, A. (1979) *Central Problems in Social Theory* (London: Macmillan).

—— (1982) 'Power, the Dialectic of Control and Class Structuration', in A. Giddens and

G. Mackenzie (1982), *Social Class and the Division of Labour* (Cambridge: Cambridge University Press).

——— (1984) *The Constitution of Society* (Cambridge: Polity Press).

Granovetter, M. (1985) 'Economic Action and Social Structure: The Problem of Embeddedness', *American Journal of Sociology*, 91: 481–510.

Hagg, I., and Johanson, J. (1988) 'Firms in Networks: New Perspecive on Competitive Power', mimeo, Centre for Business and Policy Studies, University of Uppsala.

Jarillo, J. C. (1988) 'On Strategic Networks', *Strategic Management Journal*, 9: 31–49.

Johanson, J., and Mattson, L. G. (1991) 'Interorganizational Relations in Industrial Systems: A Network Approach compared with the Transaction-Cost Approach', in G. Thompson, K. Frances, R. Levacic, and J. Mitchell (eds.), *Markets, Hierarchies and Networks: The Coordination of Social Life* (London: Sage).

Kerfoot, D., and Knights, D. (1992) 'Managerial Evangelism?—Planning for Quality in Financial Services', delivered at the European Institute for Advanced Studies in Management (EIASM) Workshop, on Quality Management in Services, Maastricht, The Netherlands, 21–2 May.

Knights, D. (1988) 'Risk, Financial Self-Discipline and Commodity Relations', *Public Interest in Accounting*, 2 (New York: Jai Press), 47–69.

——— and Morgan, G. (1991) 'Corporate Strategy, Organizations and Subjectivity: A Critique', *Organization Studies*, 12(9): 251–73.

——— ——— and Sturdy, A. (1993) *Bancassurance and Consumer Protection in the UK: Problems and Prospects*, Report prepared for the Centre de Recherche sur L'Epargne, Paris as a contribution to the EC Project 'Inter-Penetration of Financial Services and Consumer Protection', Manchester School of Management, UMIST.

——— and Murray, F. (1990) 'Information Technology and the Marketing-Driven Firm: Problems and Prospects', *PICT Policy Paper* (Oxford: ESRC).

——— ——— (1991) 'Competition and Control: The Strategic Use of IT in a Life Insurance Company', in K. Legge, C. W. Clegg, and N. J. Kemp (eds.) *Case Studies in Information Technology* (Oxford: Blackwell), 165–74.

——— ——— (1992) 'Politics and Pain in Managing Information Technology', *Organization Studies*, 13(2): 211–28.

——— and Sturdy, A. (1990) 'New Technology and the Self-Disciplined Worker in Insurance', in M. McNeil, I. Varcoe, and S. Yearly (eds.) *Deciphering Science and Technology* (London: Macmillan), 126–54.

——— and Tinker, T. (eds.) (1997) *Financial Service Institutions and Social Transformations: International Studies of an Industry in Transition* (London: Macmillan).

——— and Willmott, H. C. (1987*a*) 'Organizational Culture as Management Strategy; A Critique and Illustration from the Financial Services Industry', *International Studies of Management and Organisation*, 17(3): 40–63.

——— ——— (1987*b*) 'The Executive Fix: A Teaching Case Study', in J. McGoldrick (ed.), *Behavioural Case Studies in Management* (London: Van Nostrand), 1–17.

——— ——— (1990) 'Exploring the Class and Organizational Implications of the UK Financial Services Industry', in S. Clegg (ed.), *Organization Theory and Class Analysis: New Approaches and New Issues*, (Berlin: de Gruyter).

——— ——— (1993) 'Its a Very Foreign Discipline: The Genesis of Expenses Control in a Mutual Life Insurance Company', *British Journal of Management*, 4: 1–18.

Lockett, C., and Holland, C. (forthcoming) 'Planning For EDI: Some Case Comparisons', *Strategic Management Journal*.

Manheim, K. (1949) *Ideology and Utopia* (London: Routledge & Kegan Paul).

Manwaring, T., and Wood, S. (1985) 'The Ghost in the Labour Process', in D. Knights, H. C. Willmott, and D. Collinson (eds.), *Job Redesign* (London: Heinemann).

Miles, R., and Snow, C. (1986) 'Organizations: New Concepts for New Forms', *California Management Review*, 28: 62–73.

Mintzberg, H., and Quinn, J. B. (eds.) (1987) *The Strategy Process* (Englewood Cliffs, NJ: Prentice Hall).

Morgan, Glenn (1990) *Organizations in Society* (London: Macmillan).

—— and Knights, D. (1991) 'Gendering Jobs: Corporate Strategy, Managerial Control and the Dynamics of Job Segregation', *Work, Employment and Society*, 5(2): 181–200.

Murray, F. (1991) 'Technical Rationality and the IS Specialist: Power, Discourse and Identity', *Critical Perspectives on Accounting*, 1(3).

—— and Knights, D. (1990*a*) 'Inter-Managerial Competition and Capital Accumulation: IT Specialists, Accountants and Executive Control', *Critical Perspectives on Accounting*, 1(2): 167–89.

—— —— (1990*b*) 'The Uncommon Market in Life Insurance and the Use of IT Post-1992', in G. Locksley (ed.) *ICTs and the Single European Market* (London: Wiley).

O'Reilly, J. (1992) 'Banking on Flexibility: A Comparison of the Use of Flexible Employment Strategies in the Retail Banking Sector in Britain and France', *The International Journal of Human Resource Management*, 3(1): 35–58.

Pennings, J. (1981) 'Strategically Interdependent Organizations', in P. Nystrom and W. Starbuck (eds.) *Handbook of Organizational Design* (Oxford: Oxford University Press).

Peters, T. (1989) *Thriving on Chaos* (London: Fontana).

Pettigrew, A. (1985) *The Awakening Giant* (Oxford: Blackwell).

Pfeffer, J., and Salincik, G. (1978) *The External Control of Organizations* (New York: Harper & Row).

Poster, M. (1984) *Foucault, Marxism and History: Mode of Production v. Mode of Information* (Cambridge: Polity).

Powell, W. W. (1987) 'Hybrid Organizational Arrangements: New Form or transitional Development', *California Management Review*, 30(1): 67–87.

—— (1990) 'Neither Market nor Hierarchy: Network Forms of Organisation', *Research in Organisational Behaviour*, 12: 295–336.

—— (1991) 'Neither Market nor Hierarchy: Network Forms of Organization', in G. Thompson *et al.* (1991).

Reed, M. (1985) *Redirections in Organizational Analysis* (London: Tavistock).

—— (1992) *The Sociology of Organizations* (London: Wheatsheaf/Harvester).

Sydow, J. (1992) 'On the Management of Strategic Networks', in H. Ernste and V. Meier (eds.), *Regional Development and Contemporary Industrial Response: Extending Flexible Specialization* (London: Belhaven Press).

Thompson, G., Frances, K., Levacic, R., and Mitchell, J. (eds.) (1991) *Markets, Hierarchies and Networks: The Coordination of Social Life* (London: Sage).

Thompson, P., and McHugh, D. (1990) *Work Organizations: A Critical Introduction* (London: Macmillan).

Thorelli, H. B. (1986) 'Networks: Between Markets and Hierarchies', *Strategic Management Journal*, 7: 37–51.

Weber, M. (1949) *The Methodology of the Social Sciences* (Glencoe, Ill.: Free Press).

Wheatley, M. (1992) *The Future of Middle Management* (Corby: British Institute of Management).

Whittaker, A. (1992) 'The Transformation in Work: Post-Fordism Revisited', in M. Reed and M. Hughes (eds.) *Rethinking Organization* (London: Sage).

Williamson, O. E. (1975) *Markets and Hierarchies* (New York: Free Press).

Zuboff, S. (1988) *In the Age of the Smart Machine: The Future of Work and Power* (New York: Basic Books).

8

Putting Information Technology in its Place: Towards Flexible Integration in the Network Age?

FERGUS MURRAY AND HUGH WILLMOTT

> Information technology is altering everything. It's causing the most significant change in the way we organize, live, make war, and do politics in a thousand years. The world has been turned upside down, and the computer, along with telecommunications networks, is the engine of the revolution.
>
> (Peters 1992: 108)[1]

Open up a leading US or UK business magazine or guru handbook these days, and one is immediately struck by the prophecy and celebration of a changing world—unless, of course, you have become inured to novelty to the point at which its power is 'merely' normalizing. Article after article trumpets the demise of the modern organization, the culling of middle management, the decay of old occupational and career certainties.[2] In place of a world destined to become the subject of the TV 'disappearing world' series, the pundits, business chiefs, and consultants are either willing the creation of a new world or assuming its inevitability.

The flags flying in this brisk wind of change proclaim a new business language: empowerment, total quality management, process re-engineering, and so on. Each is represented as a 'must have' for executives seeking a way through the uncertainty and turbulence of rapidly changing markets and business practices. When making their pitches, most pundits assume and commend the vital contribution and transformative power of information and communication technologies (ICTs). In combination with the new recipes for business success, ICTs promise to revolutionize the old ways of managing business organizations.

How are such claims and promises interpreted? Broadly, there seem to be

The chapter is based upon an earlier draft written jointly by Fergus Murray and Hugh Willmott. This version was prepared by Hugh Willmott after Fergus Murray's departure from academia. It should not be assumed that Fergus Murray accepts, or bears responsibility for this chapter. We would like to acknowledge comments and suggestions made by Brian Bloomfield on an earlier version of this chapter.

three possibilities: celebratory, dismissive, and sceptical. The celebratory interpretation accepts and applauds such claims, and assumes that their realization
is comparatively unproblematical—practically and ethically. In contrast, there
are those who emphasize 'the "reality gap" between the claims of the powerful
and the realities of power'[3] where, for example, the prospect of 'empowerment'
is viewed unequivocally as a mystification that heralds increased intensification
and control. Finally, a sceptical view accepts that new business ideas amount to
more than mere rhetoric; but it questions how readily these ideas can be translated into realities. In this chapter, we suspend disbelief sufficiently to develop
a way of discussing these changes. But we do this not in order to celebrate their
existence or to promote their arrival. Instead, our intent is to develop an overview that may serve to stimulate further reflection and debate upon the nature
and significance of this thinking and the changes that it identifies or anticipates.

We begin by setting our analysis within broader discussions of the development of an 'information society' and sound some notes of caution about such
claims. We then consider each of the elements of organizational change represented in diagrammatical form in Figure 8.1: the context of change, the forms
of change within organizations, and the structural, technological, and cultural
aspects of networking. Our account of each element is necessarily sketchy and
unqualified. However, our purpose here is not to focus narrowly upon any individual component but, rather, to offer a broad picture of actual or expected
developments. It is worth noting that our discussion concentrates upon developments that we deem to be of most immediate relevance for the analysis of work
organizations. Minimal attention is paid to national and international politico-
economic and cultural conditions that operate to support or impede particular
forms of organizational change.

8.1 THE RISE OF NETWORKING

Prophecies of organizational transformations are hardly new. In Drucker's 'The
Coming of the New Organization',[4] IT is identified as central to a process of
accelerating, even radical, change. But so had it been in Drucker's *Landmarks
of Tomorrow* published in 1959.[5] In short, we have been here before—several
times. Remember the 'microchip revolution', the 'paperless office', and those
visions and promises of factories without people? Back in the late 1970s, predictions were being made, accompanied by great hopes or dark fears, that the
'mighty micro' would force fundamental change on organizations and working
lives. In the event, paperwork frequently mounted; it did not disappear. The
lights in the remaining factories continued to burn. Changes there have been.
But the revolutionary vision of change has not materialized. Or, at least, not yet.
There are, then, grounds for scepticism about the predictions and prescriptions
of the most recent wave of prophets and gurus.[6] But there is also a danger of

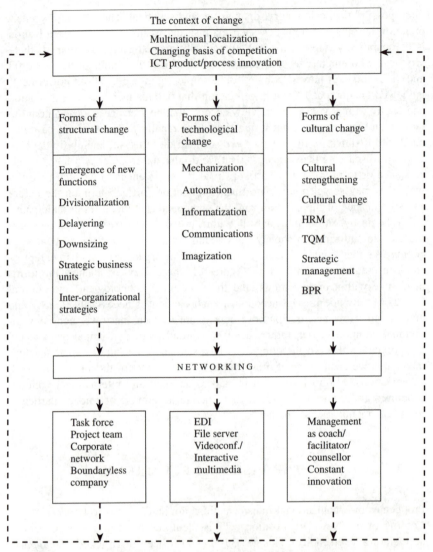

Fig. 8.1. The rise of networking: from piecemeal to holistic change strategies in new competitive conditions

dismissing the work of these prophets and 'shakers' as mere hype and rhetoric, turning away with an easy shrug of the shoulders equivalent to the nonchalant 'Wolf, what wolf?'

When contemplating the changes that are vaunted, one is struck by the fragmentation of theory and practice. Competing theories and prescriptions jostle for attention and application. Specific pressures for change are identified and seemingly unique techniques for managing change are promoted. But these are generally prescribed and considered *in isolation*, with a very strong tendency for problems and opportunities to be diagnosed in terms of the particular remedies that are prescribed. Lacking has been a framework—dare we say a metanarrative? —for appreciating the diversity and dynamics of change—structural, technological, and cultural—and the relationships and linkages between different aspects of change. Figure 8.1 presents one way of modelling the context and forms of change in a way that is suggestive of a dynamic process of development which is moving in the direction of increased technological and intra/inter-organizational networking.

Comprising three major dimensions of change which we examine in some detail shortly, this Figure provides the framework for the rest of the chapter. The box at the top of the diagram identifies elements of the 'new competitive conditions' in which business operates in the 1990s. The middle section of the diagram represents different partial organizational responses to the context of change in terms of structural, technological, and cultural transformation. The bottom third of the diagram identifies the coalescence and radicalization of the above responses into the idea, and nascent practices, of networking. Of note, here, is the manner in which network theories and strategies aspire to span and integrate the hitherto largely separate spheres of structural, technological, and cultural change. Central to the argument of this chapter, then, is that there is a degree of convergence between changes occurring in the three dimensions—a convergence that is supportive of various manifestations of networking that we identify in the bottom three boxes in Figure 8.1.

Central to the 'new' images and ideals of work and organization, we suggest, is the notion of networks, social and electronic, as media of corporate transformation and a potent source of competitive advantage.[7] These images and ideals are appealing and seductive precisely because they mesh so well with the repeatedly promised advent of 'the information society'—a representation of reality that derives its plausibility from the more or less evident use of ICTs in so many areas of everyday life.[8] The new networking literatures are directly linked to the rapid pace of innovation in ICTs.[9] Much is also currently being made of the coming communications superhighways and the integration of voice, image, and information technologies in interactive, multimedia technologies[10] that herald the development of radically different 'virtual' organizations: loose, flexible, and composed of physically dispersed symbolic analysts engaged in nationwide or worldwide conversation over voice and image networks.[11] ICTs, Quinn has argued, will be particularly important as a medium of logistical coordination of complete product development, manufacturing, marketing, and distribution chains. He cites the example of the Japanese group, Mitsubishi, which is planning to spend a vast sum (some estimate over $10 bn) to build a worldwide finance and logistics system to support its broad portfolio of manufacturers.[12] Such examples certainly provide some empirical confirmation of Masuda's prediction, made in 1985, that in the information society, 'the information utility . . . consisting of information networks and data banks' will replace the factory as the premier symbol of productive activity.[13] Whether networking can achieve conceptual coherence and translation into detailed strategy and implementation remains an open question. However, given the forces ranged behind this innovation, there is little doubt it is having a major impact on managerial thinking and business practice in the 1990s and beyond.

In principle, the integration of piecemeal change strategies represents a major innovation which, if effective, acts to further accelerate and transform the new competitive conditions (as indicated by the dotted lines in Figure 8.1). However, before proceeding further, it is worth sounding two or three notes of caution. First, it is one thing to acknowledge the presence of ICTs. It is quite another to argue that they are radically transforming the structure of organizations and societies. It is pointless to deny the ways in which ICTs have made inroads into everyday life in advanced capitalist societies (and elsewhere). The computer chip has become ubiquitous, replacing all kinds of mechanical means of information production and control in homes as well as at work. But it is perhaps more plausible to argue that they are increasing the speed and compressing the operation of established practices rather than changing their direction. Their power resides primarily in providing tighter integration of more diverse and distributed activities, and not in revolutionizing the nature of those activities. In the context of work organizations, forms of change facilitated by the widespread use of ICTs, such as business process re-engineering, are more plausibly interpreted as an extension of the ambitions of scientific management rather than a departure from them. Secondly, it is worth recalling that most R&D in ICTs is funded by the state and by big business—the military-information complex.[14] Big business, especially companies that derive growth and profits from an expansion in the use of ICTs have a vested interest in promoting their development and encouraging consumers to believe in the reality of the information society. There is a process of heterogeneous engineering through which consumers/users are constituted whose sense of self-identity is invested in the consumption of ever more powerful and sophisticated ICTs. Clearly, 'the information society' must be sold to consumers in order to make the demand for such products a reality, not least when many consumer goods markets are mature. It is implausible simply to dismiss talk about the impacts of ICTs and the development of networking and other related notions as pure 'hype'; or, relatedly, to dismiss such notions on the grounds that none of them is true, albeit that 'none' is quickly acknowledged to be a slightly exaggerated claim. It is also relevant to note how the routine development and use of ICTs can have unintended consequences— consequences that may problematize and corrode established values and institutions. Comparatively inexpensive and instantaneous communications can enable oppositional groups to keep in touch with their members, mobilize support rapidly, and respond effectively to emergent challenges. More generally, when reviewing the literature that examines the impact of ICTs upon diverse social institutions, Kumar[15] observes how

The compression of space and time made possible by the new communication technology alters the speed and scope of decisions, enhancing the capacity of the system to respond rapidly to changes but by the same token rendering it more vulnerable through a tendency to amplify relatively minor disturbances into major crises (for example, the global stock market crash of 'Black Monday').

Those who champion the use of ICTs to monitor, control, and 'enhance' every conceivable activity, including virtual sex, are inclined to argue that more of the same medicine will remedy the limitations of today's information systems. But, by the same token, the more societies and organizations depend upon ICTs, the more vulnerable they become to those who are willing and able to exploit the power of ICTs for subversive ends or who may marshall them to develop new forms of citizenship and democratic accountability. With these notes of caution firmly in mind, we now outline the elements of Figure 8.1.

8.2 THE CONTEXT OF CHANGE

Much ink continues to be spilled in extolling the virtues of networking and the value of the 'networked organization'.[16] Much less has been used to explore the context of change from which network ideas and practices have sprung. What are the conditions that make plausible, and perhaps imperative, the managerial embrace of new images and ideals of work organization? We identify three key developments: the geographical spread of competition; the shifting basis of competition; and the pace and commercialization of technological innovation.

Multinational Localization   The globalization of markets is a key concept in changing strategic thinking. Trade liberalization has allowed *inter alia* Japanese companies free access to Western markets, and particularly those of the USA and UK. In the European context, moves to create and expand a single market are expected to lead to an expansion *and* intensification of competition within the EU, both from EU and non-EU companies. Increasingly companies compete across a range of different national markets. In this sense, competition has been 'multinationalized'—as is evidenced by the continued growth of small and medium-sized multinationals.[17] A second and vitally important change in competition is the phenomenal growth of Japanese companies as competitors in key multinational markets. The so-called 'Japanese threat' has shaken complacent managements into action as industry after industry has succumbed to Japanese dominance.[18] At the same time, many national markets have maintained their distinctiveness with regard to standards, regulation, taste, and custom and indeed have been exploited precisely because they provide a powerful basis for product differentiation and securing a competitive advantage. As Harvey[19] has noted, the globalizing forces of capitalist expansion are capable of encompassing and selectively supporting differentiation and diversity:

The shrinkage of space that brings diverse communities across the globe into competition with each other implies localized competitive strategies and a heightened sense of awareness of what makes a place special and gives it a competitive advantage.

The capacity to nurture and protect distinctive local communities, including the infrastructure that supports their organization, depends upon their relevance for competing globally in markets for goods (e.g. computer chips) and services (e.g. tourism). In sum, though, we can say that a process of intensified multinational localization of competition is taking place.

Changing Basis for Competition   Competitive pressures have grown dramatically in increasingly open and interlinked national and multinational markets. New players, often supported by comparatively interventionist and illiberal states, have entered markets and succeeded in penetrating them by combining high quality with low cost. A shift in the nature of competition has occurred, captured in the jargon as the shift towards 'quality-based' and more recently 'time-based' competition. Here the argument runs that survival, let alone profitability, is conditional upon continuous product innovation where the crucial aspect is the time taken to develop and deliver new products to the market.[20] In this context, manufacturing to a certain price and quality becomes *de rigueur*. But it is not sufficient to beat the competition. Time to market and continuous innovation in product and service development, design, production, and delivery are increasingly significant keys to competitive advantage.

ICT Product/Process Innovation   Information and communication technologies are assigned a key role as both a condition and consequence of moves towards networking practices. Of particular importance here are the dramatic and continued improvement in the price-to-power ratio of mini and personal computers that has fuelled the growth of inter-computer connections and coordination through local and wide area networks file-serving technologies, electronic mail, and electronic data interchange. ICTs are also playing a key role in the process of product innovation, the pace and scale of which has unsettled established markets and created completely new markets. ICTs have also served to reinvigorate the mature markets for such goods as cars and washing machines in addition to creating vast new areas of consumer goods ranging from the video camera to the computer games console. By deploying ICTs, companies have been able to pursue strategies of mass customization in which increased product variety and speed of response to changing patterns of consumer demand are accomplished at little or no additional cost.[21] Having sketched some ingredients of the context of change, we now turn to consider transformations within organizations.

8.3   FORMS OF ORGANIZATIONAL CHANGE

Organizations are at once the targets and champions of the changes that we sketched in the previous section. For this reason, the distinction between 'the context' of change and its 'forms' within organizations is heuristic. It is also potentially misleading. For, clearly, those working in organizations enact the world that they conceptualize as a context of their action. Managers and other employees wrestle with the changes that they monitor and measure in terms of the health of their order books, calculations about market share, return on investment, levels of customer satisfaction, and so on. It may be said that the initial response by many organizations to the gathering pace and strength of the forces of multinational localization, the changing basis of competition, and ICT product/process innovation during the 1980s was to experiment with reforms of a comparatively small-scale, *ad hoc*, and uncoordinated nature.[22] But it is important to appreciate how these reforms themselves contributed to a climate and process of change to which they are generally understood as a response. These reforms were many and varied in character and primarily located in the spheres of what we have called structural, cultural, and technological initiatives.

With the benefit of hindsight, we suggest that it is possible to detect a gradual shift in each of our three dimensions of organizational change that is indicative of a more holistic, strategic orientation to organizational transformation in which the dimensions are increasingly understood to be interlocking and independent. There is an emergent view that only a more totalizing approach can maximize the synergies to be gained from a closer integration of the three dimensions. As Boynton *et al.* have expressed this view,

Management must decide exactly how their firms will compete in the face of their firms' particular changing environments . . . all elements of the (organizational) design, including process capabilities, control systems, information systems, culture and personnel, must be strategically aligned with each other.[23]

Where we depart from such claims is in their assumption that managers are currently in a position to make informed decisions, and that they can mobilize the resources, without resistance or perverse consequences, necessary to realize their designs. Managers rarely have the luxury of being able to predict accurately how 'environments' will move and therefore are unable to ensure that the various elements of organizational design identified by Boynton *et al.* are aligned. Indeed, from a managerial perspective, the expenditure of resources and effort in attaining this ideal could well prove disastrous as changing environmental conditions render a meticulously planned design inappropriate for the demands that are placed upon it. In any event, in our view, it is hopelessly romantic to believe that rational planning, rather than struggles between managers over the distribution of material and symbolic resources often dressed up in the garb of rationality to secure authority and legitimacy for sectional interests, will be the principal driver of management decision-making.[24] To the extent that 'strategic alignment' is possible or actually occurs, it may be accomplished despite the decision-making of managers rather than as a consequence of their seemingly omniscient, rational calculations.

We now discuss the shift from *ad hoc* to more integrated organization change strategies in three interlinked dimensions of organizational functioning: structure, culture, and ICT use. It is perhaps worth stressing once more that the separation implied by these divisions is a heuristic device for discussing the complexity of organizational change. We acknowledge that the contents ascribed to these elements are interconnected and, indeed, that their closer, planned integration is increasingly prescribed as a key means of securing competitive advantage. This particularly applies to the technology arena, which has so often threatened to impose its own logic and priorities on organizations. In Figure 8.1, we identify major initiatives that have occurred in each of these dimensions, listing them more or less chronologically. This ranking, we will suggest, also indicates a gradual shift from piecemeal to more holistic approaches to organizational change that take greater account of the interdependent nature of the dimensions.

8.3.1 Structural Changes

Structural change comes in many shapes and sizes. Its effect is to alter the configuration of relationships, the distribution of resources and the operation of command and control procedures. One largely unplanned and incremental structural change is the emergence of *new functions*. The numerical growth and rising proportion of resources controlled by IT and marketing functions is particularly noteworthy. One unintended consequence of the growth of the IT function has been the increased dependence of other functions upon IT and the associated exacerbation of the centrifugal forces of management. In the 1970s and 1980s IT and IS divisions controlled huge resources and tended to pursue 'technology-driven' agendas. In the late 1980s and 1990s, finding a workable balance between technological and business-driven innovation has proved a central concern for many organizations.[25]

Divisionalization has been one manifestation of attempts to bring smaller departments under centralized control and thereby moderate centrifugal managerial forces, increase accountability, and subordinate specialist labour to strategic direction. Indeed, divisional reorganization often went hand-in-hand with the introduction of strategic management. Divisionalization may have increased central control over diverse specialisms. But it also had the largely unintended consequence of reinforcing boundaries and thus tended to work against the development of informal cross-divisional networks.[26] The rise of the IT specialism and the broader process of divisionalization can be interpreted as expressive of different efforts to deal with problems of control in the face of growth, complexity, and intensifying competition. In contrast, *delayering* attacks extended hierarchical structures. The stripping out of layers of, often middle, management has been justified in terms of the capacity of ICTs to render much middle managerial work redundant.[27] However, in their zeal to cut costs, shorten chains of command, and flatten hierarchies, the champions of delayering have risked creating unmanageable spans of control and losing employees with invaluable local knowledge of processes whilst placing enormous workloads on remaining managers.

Downsizing refers to corporate size reduction through, often large-scale, redundancies. It differs from delayering in that it is often associated with the refocusing of strategic business objectives around so-called core competencies. It is often linked to programmes that make recourse to the subcontracting of non-core activities formerly carried out in-house. Downsizing is closely associated with the programmes that are intended to improve the 'leanness' of organization by streamlining procedures and the removal of activities that produce little value-added. The creation of *strategic business units* (SBUs) is a further instance of structural change. SBUs are intended to take businesses closer to the market, to inject entrepreneurialism, and give business managers greater autonomy. The downside of such initiatives lies in their tendency to increase parochialism along with focus. Horizontal links between SBUs may be minimal, opportunities for synergy and new business may be missed, and vital infrastructural standardization and coordination, for example, with regard to organization-wide information systems and databases, may be ignored or subverted by SBUs pursuing their own narrow, sometimes idiosyncratic, information and technology strategies.

A more recent development is the increasing attention to *inter-organizational strategies*. These range from increasingly collaborative links with suppliers and subcontractors around issues such as R&D and Just-in-Time delivery, through the use of EDI and electronic trading to reduce order processing and accounts costs and personnel, to informal and formal strategic alliances realized through such mechanisms as cross-shareholdings. In its wilder moments, the new organization literature predicts the emergence of boundary-less or virtual organizations where once separate inter-organizational domains are increasingly integrated.[28]

To summarize, we have suggested that the emergence of new functions and divisionalization involves an expansion of existing functions and a rationalization of established activities. In contrast, the establishment of quasi-autonomous profit centres and strategic business units within organizations involves more extensive changes that are underpinned by a totalizing approach to redesign, even though such moves may have the unintended effect of fragmenting and unbalancing established structures. Even when delayering, downsizing, and the development of inter-organizational strategies are pursued as *ad hoc*, panic measures to deal with deteriorating performance, they contribute to wider-ranging forms of change in the structuring of organizations.

8.3.2 Technological Changes

The history of organizational IT use is a story about the gradual harnessing and refocusing of IT for business ends, sometimes sloganistically represented as a change from a technology-driven use of IT to a market- or user-driven use of IT. It also concerns the gradual shift from incremental, partial uses of IT to the creation of integrated organization-wide and inter-organizational systems.[29] This 'wiring up' of the organization creates the possibility of a more transformative use of ICTs.[30]

Initial IT use focused on *mechanization* and *automation*. In particular, IT was used to provide support for, or was intended to expel labour from, existing work processes. In this phase, IT specialists were hired to automate work processes, such as back-office applications in areas like accounting and clerical processing. In this process, a chasm developed between the mind-sets of IT specialists and business managers which eventually stimulated an awareness of the importance of user relations in systems development and IT strategy.[31] It also became clear that when information is collected or stored within one function or organization, it can easily reinforce a tendency towards parochial information hoarding and thereby intensify information-based organization politics.[32] As ICTs were adopted and applied in most areas of organizational activity, previously neglected knowledge-creating and communication-facilitating aspects of ICTs have been recognized and more intensively exploited.

Informatization, a rather clumsy concept, has been coined to represent the diffusion of ICTs into virtually every aspect of organizational functioning. It heralds the fully wired organization, with its ICT-based control and coordination systems and its masses of accumulated data that can be systematically exploited to render more visible and communicable activities and processes that previously were inaccessible or opaque. This development implies a progressive intellectualization and abstraction of work processes that promises greater control and coordination of all organizational activity. In its more optimistic formulations, informatization prefigures a democratic transformation of organizational structures and power relations.[33] At the very least, informatization reflects and promotes the growing importance of information and knowledge as a strategic resource comparable, or even superior to, financial and material resources. The possession of information, and the ability to analyse it and broker deals with it, is seen as a vital organizational competence.

Communications technologies, such as fax, electronic mail, and local and wide-area network technologies, and so on, have accelerated and opened new paths and types of communication. In principle, e-mail, for example, makes possible rapid communication across geographic space and vertical and horizontal organizational boundaries. Such communications technologies, it has been argued by some, are productive of a disembodied and (more) egalitarian 'cyberspace' free from the constraints of established styles and paths of intra- and inter-organizational communication.[34]

A further development in ICTs opens up new organizational and communicative possibilities: the convergence of information and communications technologies in telematic and multimedia applications. Telematics refers to the fusion of telecommunications and computer technologies—the most celebrated and controversial example being the Internet. The increasing use and virtually limitless potential of fibre optics allows the rapid transfer of masses of data between cities, countries, and continents. Telematics clearly presents enormous opportunities for real-time intra-and especially inter-organizational communications by greatly facilitating the surveillance and control of spatially dispersed activities.

Multimedia is the combination of data, moving, and still image, and voice technologies. It is greatly enhanced by new storage technologies, such as CD Rom and more sophisticated and flexible network management technologies. We have coined the phase electronic *imagization*[35] to describe this development because it makes possible the greater use of still and moving images. It is a development in its early stages at the time of writing, and is in a process of intense experimentation in areas as diverse as artistic practice, video games, and training programmes. Its potential for interactive usage, and the manipulation and transformation of imagery and reality have been widely commented on. Multimedia and virtual reality technologies open up the spectre of the creation of technology-based realities that appear as real, if not more real, than non-ICT-based realities.[36]

8.3.3   Cultural Changes

During the 1980s organization and management theory rediscovered and celebrated the importance of culture as a vital factor in the revitalization and redirection of organizations. This focus gave rise to a number of organizational initiatives. Where culture was identified as a key variable for achieving an 'excellent' performance, programmes of *cultural strengthening* were introduced. Where culture was weak, disjointed, and unfocused, wholesale programmes of *cultural change* were undertaken. In principle, such programmes drew together and energized often fragmented and conflicting organizational forces around core values that would guide the work of all organization members from Chief Executive to clerical staff. Such programmes were often developed as an integral part of a process of *strategic management* that sought to redesign organizational culture in a way that rendered employees more capable of responding effectively to the challenges posed by the changes outlined earlier in this chapter.

The growing importance of strategic focus, planning, and cultural change, has been reflected in a rethinking of how to tap the creativity and adaptability of human beings. The rise of *human resource management* has signalled a concern to link the management of employee skills and careers more directly to the pursuit of business strategy.[37] Perhaps the most visible sign of increasing attention being given to a more holistic, strategic approach to management has been the rise and pervasiveness of the total quality movement.[38] *TQM* views the organization as a totality of interrelated activities that are amenable to continuous improvement, albeit in an incremental and localized manner. Its emphasis is on managing internal as well as external customer relations where various measures of quality can be improved *inter alia* by eliminating bottlenecks and costs associated with a failure to 'get it right first time'. Closely associated with TQM has been the use of IT to record and monitor progress in improving quality both within and between manufacturing plants and offices.

The most recent and far-reaching technique for accomplishing corporate transformation is *business process re-engineering* (BPR).[39] This technique, which seeks to exploit the networking power of ICTs, proposes a wholesale rethinking of organizational process, predicated on a shift from sequential scheduling to parallel and iterative processes. It is argued that organizational practice can and should be changed to develop new ICT-mediated processes rather than mirroring obsolete and obstructive organizational divisions and dysfunctions. BPR can be applied to any area of organizational activity but its main claim is to reduce cost and time-to-market for existing or new products and services without any loss of quality. It is argued that, to date, ICTs have been used rather unimaginatively to automate and, to a lesser extent, to integrate established functions and procedures. They have not been applied to achieve a transformation that demands an 'obliteration' of existing practices—such as sequential scheduling of activities, parochial (e.g. functional or SBU) perspectives, fragmented skills and specialisms, and the dominance of top-down vertical communication and authority structures. BPR calls for the full exploitation of ICT to unveil horizontal, multidisciplinary, and parallel approaches to product and service innovation and delivery.[40]

8.4 FLEXIBLE INTEGRATION IN THE NETWORK AGE

So far we have sought to chart broad shifts within the dimensions of organization structure, technology, and culture from partial, often *ad hoc* incremental change, towards more integrated strategies of change. We now elaborate our argument that these developments are tending, individually and in combination, towards flexible integration through increased networking. First, we consider the networking vision before turning to address its enactment.

8.4.1 *Networking: The Vision*

At its most simple, networking means communication between people.[41] Those who subscribe to the idea of a 'network revolution' are inclined to associate networks with an increase in horizontal, informal, and spontaneous communication within and between organizations. This has been accompanied by more detailed discussion of different forms of network—personal, task, functional, corporate, and inter-organizational—the management of such networks, reporting, performance structures and measures, and skill and career requirements.

Linked ICT systems in production, distribution, finance, product development, and strategic management have the potential to bring together previously fragmented flows of data into one continuous and integrated cycle. This promises to provide feedback loops that allow the real-time monitoring of markets, product performance, and competition. Such feedback loops themselves can then be fed into multidisciplinary design/production/finance/marketing teams working in particular product/market/core activity areas. Networked computers using real-time rapid communication systems, such as those envisaged in the fibre-optic superhighway, thus make possible a quantum leap in the detail, timeliness, and integration of corporate and inter-corporate control systems. At a mundane level, this suggests scope for further gains in areas such as just-in-time delivery and product performance and modification. Within organizations, computer networks promise to forge vertical links between strategic and operations management while lubricating horizontal linkages between discrete and geographically dispersed functions.

The sponsors of networking see it as a means of releasing the potential for synergy and collaborative entrepreneurialism through the destruction or erosion of barriers to communication and cooperation. As a condition and consequence of increased networking, its advocates envisage a weakening of hierarchy; a decline in control and command functions; and a revised formulation of the skills, labour, and experience upon which the modern organization is based.[42] Evidence of increased networking can be found in each of our dimensions of change: structural, technological, and cultural.

Within *structure*, networking challenges existing organizational boundaries, divisions, and hierarchy itself. At its most radical edge, it commends a shift towards an amorphous, amoeba-like structuring of organization that is comparatively fluid, flexible, and responsive. Within it, network activity is expected to dissolve functional, divisional, and SBU boundaries as self-directed networkers search out synergy and dynamic complementarities. Inter-organizationally, the networked organization has weak and shifting boundaries: it functions with other organizations through osmosis, grafting, and mutation. As a 'virtual organization', it is seen as a temporary network of suppliers and customers that develops around specific opportunities in fast-changing markets, with information technology being used to link teams of people working in different companies in real time.[43] More prosaically, the networked organization is manifest in the creation of temporary task forces and project teams that form and reform to address particular issues but which lack any stable or enduring structure. Recurrent reorganization is normal and a valued expression of agility and flexibility rather than regarded as exceptional or symptomatic of a deep pathology.

With regard to *technology*, commentators identify ICT developments as crucial for much networking. These range from the use of file servers and shared data over local area networks to the use of multinational corporate R&D networks that bring together far-flung engineers, production managers and market experts to collaborate over product innovation. Fax, e-mail, Electronic Data Interchange, video-conferencing, and the use of multimedia are ascribed key roles[44] as a major shift occurs in the use of ICTs to provide essential coordinating and controlling links to geographically dispersed sites of production and distribution. Commentators suggest that organizations will be able increasingly to divest themselves of all but their core intellectual activities.[45] IT and communications systems, it is anticipated, will be used to identify and work with best suppliers as leading-edge firms plug into what Webber calls 'the global conversation of the new economy'.[46]

Finally, changes in *culture* are critical in so far as the development and effective operation of networking practices is predicated on a shift in the character and style of management, and the identity and activities of managers. As 'symbolic analysts',[47] managers are expected to analyse and broker information-based deals within fast-moving global markets. Networking also requires managers to act as coaches and counsellors, negotiators and facilitators in order that employees have the space and support to become self-learning and self-disciplining agents, thereby reducing managerial overheads as well as enabling greater flexibility and responsiveness to customers. In principle, the manager-cum-facilitator and coach becomes a broker where trust, cooperation, and sharing are crucial if networking's optimistic vision is to be realized. In such 'learning organizations', employees are understood to become empowered and self-organizing as they 'network' with others to shape as well as fulfil corporate goals and the means of their attainment.

8.4.2   Networking: The Enactment

In principle, networking challenges traditional organization structures, but, in practice, may well reinforce hierarchical principles of control and exploitation. Take the case of Cypress Semiconductor, a US-based microchip maker. This company has been widely identified as the epitome of the networked organization that operates effectively in fast-moving, intensely competitive mass and niche markets. Many of the features of change identified in Figure 8.1 can be found within this company and have been celebrated as its public face. However, ICTs are also extensively and intensively used to support a system of micro management control that monitors the performance of each employee on an array of measures. This system enables senior executives to render transparent each individual employee's day-to-day performance.[48]

By removing forms of direct surveillance by supervisors and middle managers, networking demands greater self-discipline (policed by peer-group pressures) and encourages increased cooperation and communication. For precisely this reason, networking may be perceived and even embraced as a new and exciting possibility. But in the context of an employment relationship that treats employees as disposable commodities whilst expecting them to act responsibly as dependable resources, moves towards networking may well be interpreted less positively or at least equivocally as a threat to job security, careers, and identities, and not simply as a welcome release from close supervision and repetitive work. The networking literature is full of politically correct feel-good words like 'cooperation', 'empowerment', and 'teamwork'. Yet, it can also unveil changes that may be of a not-so-feel-good nature for many employees. At the giant firm, GE, a continuing programme of aggressive delayering and 'hollowing out' aims to reduce management positions by a third by the end of the decade. Embracing the new culture of cooperation is not so much about empowerment as intimidation and enforcement. One GE executive told Business International,[49] 'People better be co-operative. No one gets ahead by being unco-operative—it'd kill you. The word gets round through informal and formal channels, and you're out'. Organizational controls may therefore become tighter and more intensive with the use of networked real-time systems.

An awareness of this difficulty is beginning to dawn upon the strongest advocates of networking. In an article that reviews much of the recent networking literature, Webber[50] persuasively identifies the issue of trust as central to the achievement of any sustained shift towards networked forms of organization. He acknowledges that the fostering of trust in such a potentially threatening context remains problematic. He also notes that this inconvenient observation is ignored by most writers in the area. Instead, a messianic technological determinism leads them to assume that the pace and possibilities of market and technological change will simply force networking willy-nilly upon organizations, and that cooperative, trusting employees will somehow be manufactured in this process.[51] We accept that moves in the direction of networking are well under way. But we have also stressed the 'cultural' dimension of this change. In the networked organization, the full commitment and involvement of employees becomes even more critical, but this cannot be taken for granted or realized through endless exhortation or the mantric repetition of feel-good words.

There is a paradox here. While the rhetoric of empowerment is used liberally by commentators and practitioners, there is also a good deal of coercion in companies experimenting with networking. This may be of the 'cooperate or else' form of coercion; or it may be more subtle and insidious but no less coercive. At the heart of the matter is the employment relationship. To illustrate this argument, we will focus upon business process re-engineering[52] as an example of a widely adopted, far-reaching technique for advancing organizational transformation.

Advocates of BPR identify the need to make organizational and human resource changes in order to secure the effective operation of re-engineered processes. They also are inclined to assume that the conversion of employees to the 'new values and beliefs' depends principally upon the rhetorical skills and persuasive powers of senior managers and 'coaches'. Any resistance to change is interpreted as an irrational response that can be overcome by strong leadership. However, the lived reality of employment relations is invariably more complex and unruly than managerialist representations of this world can admit without undermining the basis of managerial legitimacy. Managerial efforts to secure more dedicated employee commitment to corporate values and objectives repeatedly run up against the difficulty that, when push comes to shove, employees are not only hired and 'developed' as 'valued human resources' but also fired as disposable commodities.

Employees' knowledge of their disposability means that, for many, commitment to the organization is likely to remain partial and conditional, if not narrowly instrumental. As Conti and Warner observe, 'Workforce reductions caused by Reengineering can dramatically reduce costs but raise questions about their effect on the commitment of the survivors and their willingness to cooperate in process improvement'.[53] Undaunted by such concerns, the champions of BPR continue to perpetuate and embellish the managerial fantasy that there exists a technical fix for these recurrent problems. As Davenport articulates the BPR creed, making direct links between the structural, technological, and cultural dimensions of change:

Human and organizational development approaches such as greater employee empowerment, reliance on autonomous teams, and flattened organizational structures are as key to enabling process change as any technical tool. In fact, information technology is rarely effective without simultaneous human innovations.[54]

However, far from heralding a radical shift towards a world in which there is more room for 'creativity and worker autonomy',[55] BPR contrives to make work even more tightly prescribed by urging or requiring employees to dedicate their hearts and minds, and not just their bodies, to tasks that have been designed by others. These tasks may be performed by teams in which members are required to coordinate their activities, exercise their discretion, and monitor their own performance. But, crucially, they are tasks that have been (re-)engineered *by others*, and which in principle require employees to be more self-disciplined as they monitor each other, as team members, to ensure that processes are effectively managed. In effect, BPR involves an ICT-mediated updating of Taylor's crusade against custom and practice in which the silicon chip plays an equivalent role in BPR to that performed by the stopwatch in Scientific Management. BPR identifies ICTs as providing the technological means of obliterating the custom and practice that has grown up around extended hierarchies that have been divided into fiefdoms (or 'chimneys', as Hammer terms them) controlled by functional specialists. Moreover, and in contrast to Taylor's linking of performance with monetary reward, the transformations envisaged by the champions of the network organization are comparatively costless as the inducements of piecework are replaced by the largely symbolic and psychological rewards attributed to teamwork and empowerment. Such moves rarely articulate a benevolent concern to develop more caring, trusting, or open relationships at work. Rather, as we have argued, they are primarily a response to conditions of intensified competition and technological innovation. These conditions seem unlikely to decelerate. Despite a rising tide of structural, technological, and cultural change, there are reasons for being sceptical about the transformative potential of BPR, and not least the suggestion that it presages a progressive dissolving of hierarchy and centralized command and control.[56]

8.5   CONCLUDING REMARKS

Our purpose in this chapter has been to provide a framework for appreciating the links between different forms of organizational change that are often discussed independently of each other. In constructing this framework, we have made a series of heuristic distinctions—for example, between 'context' and 'organiza-tional change' and between 'technological' and 'cultural' dimensions of organizational change. Our hope is that our framework may stimulate and support informed discussion and debate about the nature and direction of change. In addition, we have argued that insufficient attention has been given to the social relations of production—the employment relationship—upon which the flexible integration promised by the network age is inescapably dependent. At the heart of this vision, we have suggested, is a contradiction between requiring a form of work organization that relies upon trust and involvement and retaining a structure of ownership and control that, when push comes to shove, treats employees as disposable commodities.

In principle, changes in the structure, technology and culture of organizations might yet usher in an era of networking characterized by dynamic cooperation, open and trusting relations, and the empowerment of both managers and employees. However, it is difficult to reconcile this vision with the reality of employment relationships in which, beyond the hype of empowerment and self-management, employees continue to be treated as commodities whose work is continuously intensified and whose labour is laid off, casualized, or discarded without ceremony. Even if the fundamental issue of ownership and the limited capacity of employees to moderate the treatment of their labour as a commodity is set aside, moves towards networking pose a threat to established positions, careers, identities, and practices that is likely to render its realization partial and precarious. The task of transforming the vision of networking into a reality is a political one. Its realization requires not just a change of style or even a change of heart but, more fundamentally, a radical change of politico-economic system.

NOTES

1. Peters, T. (1992) *Liberation Management* (New York: Macmillan), 108.
2. See, for example, Byrne, J. A. (1993) 'The Virtual Corporation', *Business Week* (8 Feb.), 98–102; Stewart, T. A. (1992) 'The Search for the Organisation of Tomorrow', *Fortune* (18 May), 92–8; Fortune International (1993) 'How we will work in the Year 2000', *Fortune International* (17 May), 31–7; Oliver, J. (1993) 'Shocking to the Core', *Management Today* (Aug.), 18–23.
3. Thompson, P., and O'Connell Davidson, J. (1955) 'The Continuity of Discontinuity: Managerial Rhetoric in Turbulent Times', *Personnel Review*, 24(6): 24.
4. Drucker, P. (1988) 'The Coming of the New Organization', *Harvard Business Review*, (Jan.–Feb.), 45–53. See also Quinn, M. D. (1993) *Rebirth of the Corporation* (New York: Wiley).
5. Cited by Thompson and O'Connell Davidson (1955).
6. For a listing of key US consultants driving the new managerial thinking see Byrne, J. A. (1992) 'Management's New Gurus', *Business Week* (Aug.), 44–52.

7. See e.g. Business International (1993) *The Management Network Revolution: How Innovative Firms are getting Results From Flatter Organizations* (London: Business International); Charan, R. (1991) 'How Networks Reshape Organisations—For Results', *Harvard Business Review* (Sept.–Oct., 1991), 104–15; Sproull, L., and Kiester, S. (1991) *Connections: New Ways of Working In the Networked Organisation* (Cambridge, Mass.: MIT Press); Quinn, J. B. (1993) *The Intelligent Enterprise* (London: Free Press); Davidow, W. H., and Malone, M. S. (1992) *The Virtual Corporation: Structuring and Revitalising the Corporations of the 21st Century* (York: Burlingham/ Harper).

8. There is an increasing normalization of ICTs so that they become a mundane, unremarkable feature of the goods and services that are routinely purchased and used.

9. See e.g. Taylor, W. C. (1994) 'Control in the Age of Chaos', *Harvard Business Review* (Nov.–Dec.), 64–76.

10. See e.g. the influential vision of the potential of fibre optics in the realm of inter- and intra-organizational change. Gilder, G. (1991) 'Inside the Microcosm', *Harvard Business Review* (Mar.–Apr.), 150–61.

11. See, in particular, Reich, R. B. (1991) *The Work of Nations: Preparing Ourselves for the 21st Century* (London, Simon and Schuster).

12. Quinn (1993: 224).

13. Masuda, Y. (1985) 'Computopia', in J. Forrester (ed.), *The Information Technology Revolution* (Oxford: Blackwell), cited in K. Kumar (1995) *From Post-Industrial to Post-Modern Society* (Oxford: Blackwell), 12.

14. See Webster, F., and Robins, K. (1985) *Information Technology: A Luddite Analysis* (Norwood, NJ: Ablex).

15. Kumar (1995: 155).

16. See n. 6.

17. See United Nations, (1993) *Transnational Corporations and Integrated International Production*, World Investment Report 1993 (New York: UN).

18. See e.g. Forester's account of emerging Japanese dominance in high technology industries: Forester, T. (1993) *Silicon Samurai: How Japan Conquered the World's IT Industry* (Oxford: Blackwell).

19. Harvey, D. (1989) *The Condition of Postmodernity* (Oxford: Blackwell), 271.

20. See Stalk, G., and Hout, T. (1990) *Competing Against Time: How Timebased Competition is Reshaping Global Markets* (New York: Free Press).

21. Boynton, A. C., Victor, B., and Price, B. J. (1993) 'New Competitive Strategies: Challenges To Organisations and Information Technology', *IBM Systems Journal*, 32(1): 40–64.

22. Ezzamel, M., Lilley, S., and Willmott, H. (1993) 'Reflections on Recent Changes in UK Management Practice and the Implications for Management Accounting', Working Paper, Manchester School of Management, UMIST.

23. Boynton *et al.*, (1993: 40–1).

24. See Knights, D., and Murray, F. (1994) *Managers Divided* (London: Wiley).

25. See Friedman and Cornford's historical analysis of successful IT use: Friedman, A., and Cornford, D. (1989) *Computer Systems Development: History, Organisation and Implementation* (London: Wiley).

26. For a recent study of crystallization of organization politics around divisional boundaries see Murray and Knights (1994).

27. e.g. a recent *Industrial Society* (1993) showed that the combined effects of recession

and delayering resulted in British managers working on average a 55-hour week. Charles Handy reacted to the survey with the following comment: 'We have half the number of managers as before, paid twice as much, and expected to be three times as productive'. See Kelloway, L. (1993) 'Macho Managers Under Fire', *Financial Times*, 3 July.

28. See e.g. ch. 12 in Sculley, J. (1987) *Odyssey: Pepsi to Apple* (London: Fontana/Collins).
29. See The *Financial Times* (1993) 'Special Report on Computer Networking', 29 June.
30. See Quinn, J. B., and Paquette, P. C. (1990) 'Technology in Services: Creating Organizational Revolutions', *Sloan Management Review*, 31(2), 67–78.
31. Friedman and Cornford (1989).
32. Davenport, T. H., Eccles, R. G., and Prusak, L. (1992) 'Information Politics', *Sloan Management Review*, 34(1), 53–66.
33. See Zuboff, S. (1988) *In the Age of the Smart Machine* (New York: Basic Books).
34. See Pruitt, S., and Barrett, T. (1990) 'Corporate Virtual Workspace', in M. Benedikt (ed), *Cyberspace: First Steps* (Cambridge, Mass.: MIT).
35. A similar concept is also used by Morgan. His concept concerns the power of visual image and metaphor as a means of exploring and changing organizations. Like many writers discussing novel approaches to organizations he has little to say regarding the new potentials being opened up by communications and multimedia technology. See G. Morgan (1990) *Imaginisation: The Art of Creative Management* (London: Sage).
36. Imagization includes more than using image technologies such as video and still pictures. At its more futuristic end, it is the idea that computer graphics and virtual reality technologies will provide three-dimensional visual images and imagescapes of data and organizations. For example, corporate databases could be imagined and represented as cities or bookshops through which managers could walk and browse. Turning vast stores of data into virtual worlds might enable managers to develop a more global view of their organization and its inter-organizational links, while simultaneously simplifying the identification of key interfaces, resources, and skills. Underlying the notion of imagization is the transformation of spoken and written representations of organizations into visual representations. Visualization has a tremendous ability to simplify and order complexity but, of course, the way in which this is achieved is not an innocent process but often a redefinition of a particular reality. The use of visualization might have three particular advantages. First, the necessarily interpretive character of pictures as representations can be a powerful stimulus to rethinking the organizations (see Morgan 1990: 214–34). Secondly, virtual reality representations could allow rapid movement through complex arrays of 3D images where everyday navigational skills, curiosities, and accident are invoked. And thirdly, visual representations, their clustering, and juxtaposition, make possible rapid idea associations and connections that may be vital for discovering organizational synergies and opportunities.
37. It is also relevant to note the elective affinity between government-led attacks on trade union rights in the USA and UK enabled by policies which created mass unemployment.
38. See e.g. Hammer, M., and Champy, J. (1993) *Re-engineering the Corporation* (New York: Nicholas Brealey); Morris, D., and Brandon, J. (1993) *Re-engineering Your Business* (New York: McGraw-Hill).
39. Hammer and Champy (1993).

40. See particularly Hammer and Champy (1993).
41. The concept of networking has a rich linguistic past. In economics and sociology networks denote socio-political, inter-firm, and familial structures of acquaintance and loose interdependence. Key texts on networking are Business International (1993), Quinn (1993), and Reich (1991). In feminist discourse 'networking' is understood as a conscious and 'alternative' or 'oppositional' strategy of contact making and mutual support in the face of entrenched career and power structures dominated by men. As such it is closely linked to a critique of the established order and its profound inequalities. In this guise networking is closely associated with notions of empowerment, egalitarianism, and progressive politics.
42. Thompson, G., Frances, J., Levacic, R., and Mitchell, J. (eds.) (1991) *Markets, Hierarchies and Networks: The Coordination of Social Life* (London, Sage).
43. Byrne (1992).
44. See Davidow and Malone (1992: chs. 3 and 4).
45. Quinn (1993: ch. 2).
46. Webber, A. M. (1993) 'What's so New about the New Economy?' *Harvard Business Review*, 71(1), 25.
47. Reich (1991: 220).
48. See Rodgers, T. J. (1990) 'No Excuses Management', *Harvard Business Review* (July–Aug.), 95.
49. Business International (1993: 13).
50. Webber (1993: 30–2).
51. See e.g. Michael Hammer's technologically driven vision of business process re-engineering in Hammer and Champy (1993).
52. The following paragraphs draw upon the following articles where BPR is discussed in greater detail: Willmott, H. C. (1994) 'Business Process Reengineering and Human Resource Management', *Personnel Review*, 23(3): 34–46; Willmott, H. C. (1995) 'The Odd Couple: Reengineering Business Processes, Managing Human Resources', *New Technology, Work and Employment*, 10(2): 89–98.
53. Conti, R. F., and Warner, M. (1994) 'Taylorism, Teams and Technology in "Reengineering" Work Organization', *New Technology, Work and Employment*, 9(2): 93–102; 97.
54. Davenport, T. H. (1993) *Process Innovation: Reengineering Work Through Information Technology* (Cambridge, Mass.: Harvard Business School Press), 13.
55. Davenport (1993: 316).
56. Business International (1993: ch. 4).

Index